Edwardsville P.

0 00 08 033...

MW00784045

Withdrawn

Edwardsville Public Library
112 South Kansas Street
Edwardsville, IL 62025

3372907
ITEM # 11895932

B
NEIHARDT

LONESOME DREAMER

The Life of John G. Neihardt

Timothy G. Anderson

266660

UNIVERSITY OF NEBRASKA PRESS | LINCOLN AND LONDON

© 2016 by the Board of Regents of
the University of Nebraska

All photographs in this volume are courtesy
of the John G. Neihardt Papers, Western
Historical Manuscripts Collection, State
Historical Society of Missouri, Columbia MO
or the John G. Neihardt Center, Bancroft NE.
Used by permission of the Neihardt Trust.

All rights reserved
Manufactured in the United States of America

Publication of this volume was assisted by a grant
from the Friends of the University of Nebraska Press.

Library of Congress Cataloging-in-Publication Data
Names: Anderson, Timothy G., 1952– author.
Title: Lonesome dreamer: the life of John
G. Neihardt / Timothy G. Anderson.
Description: Lincoln: University of Nebraska Press,
2016. | Includes bibliographical references and index.
Identifiers: LCCN 2015035010
ISBN 978-0-8032-9025-9 (cloth: alk. paper)
ISBN 978-0-8032-9037-2 (epub)
ISBN 978-0-8032-9038-9 (mobi)
ISBN 978-0-8032-9039-6 (pdf)
Subjects: LCSH: Neihardt, John G., 1881–1973.
Poets, American—20th century—Biography.
Classification: LCC PS3527.E35 Z55 2016
DDC 811/.52—dc23 LC record available
at http://lccn.loc.gov/2015035010

Set in Fanwood by Rachel Gould.
Designed by N. Putens.

For Ben and Lucy

Then what of the lonesome dreamer
With the lean blue flame in his breast?
And who was your clown for a day, O Town,
The strange, unbidden guest?

JOHN G. NEIHARDT, "The Poet's Town"

CONTENTS

ILLUSTRATIONS

10. Mona Neihardt with a bust of her husband

11. Mona and John Neihardt, ca. 1956

12. Neihardt at bust unveiling, Nebraska State Capitol, 1961

13. Neihardt teaching, University of Missouri, 1963

14. Neihardt with Mari Sandoz

INTRODUCTION

Each year on the last Saturday of April the John G. Neihardt Center in Bancroft, Nebraska, hosts its annual spring conference. Some sixty to seventy attendees—among them people old enough to have met John Neihardt, who died in 1973, or at least heard him speak or recite his poetry—spend the day listening to historians and musicians and other writers and artists present a program on Neihardt and the issues he cared about.

Many of the attendees are repeat customers at this outpost of the Nebraska State Historical Society, and they are likely to know more about Neihardt than the average person. They are likely to know, first of all, that Neihardt moved to Bancroft in 1900, living there for two decades, and that he spent the last part of his long life teaching at the University of Missouri. They know the book for which he is best known, an as-told-to biography of a Lakota holy man titled *Black Elk Speaks*. Perhaps most important, they are likely to know that he also wrote a great many other books, works of fiction and nonfiction and books of poems, both short and epic.

Most people in the twenty-first century, if they have heard of John Neihardt at all, know of him because of *Black Elk Speaks*, first published in 1932, then reissued to wide acclaim in the 1960s. For two decades after Neihardt's death, a considerable body of scholarship arose around *Black Elk Speaks*, much of it an attempt to discern how much of it was Black Elk speaking and how much of it was John Neihardt. Questions were raised about Neihardt's appropriation of Lakota culture, about the influence of Christianity on Black Elk and on Neihardt, about what Black Elk had told Neihardt that had not made it into the book, and about passages Neihardt had added on his own. The situation was clarified substantially in the mid-1980s, when Raymond DeMallie published the transcripts of Neihardt's interviews with Black Elk, originally recorded in shorthand by his daughter Enid after being translated from Lakota by Black Elk's son Ben. Throughout the years, people continued to read and admire the book.

What many people outside this circle of Neihardt devotees may not know is that *Black Elk Speaks* was a byproduct of what Neihardt considered his life's work, five volumes of long narrative poems he hoped would preserve the history of white exploration and settlement of the Great Plains and of the wars between the U.S. Army and the Indian population that resulted from Euro-American intrusion.

Like many others, I came to Neihardt through *Black Elk Speaks*. I had read the book in college in the early 1970s, and after stumbling onto it again nearly twenty-five years later, I began to wonder about the man who wrote it. About a year before Neihardt died, I had met him briefly at a book signing for his memoir *All Is But a Beginning*, and I tried to imagine how this little white-haired man shakily autographing books had managed to interview a Lakota man who remembered the Battle of the Little Bighorn and the Wounded Knee Massacre. How had he found Black Elk, and why had Black Elk spoken to him? What had prepared Neihardt for that meeting? In the front of Neihardt's memoir was a long list of other books he had written, none familiar to me, and I wondered what was behind them. Before long, I had so many questions I knew I was going to have to find answers.

This book is what I found.

Timothy G. Anderson
Lincoln, Nebraska

LONESOME DREAMER

PROLOGUE

January 8, 1881

Winter had brutalized the open flatlands surrounding Sharpsburg, Illinois, the small town whose original name, Horseshoe Prairie, suggested the vast, open flatness that stretched in every direction. Frigid temperatures had accompanied punishing north winds and snow, and on the afternoon of Saturday, January 8, 1881, the day John Neihardt was born, temperatures had dropped to single digits. Neihardt later pieced together a picture of his entry into this world from stories told by his mother and other relatives. "It is almost as though I had seen it all with my own eyes," he wrote near the end of his life, "the picture is so definitely drawn."[1]

Neihardt's parents, Nicholas and Alice, and sisters, Lulu and Grace, were living in a rented farmhouse outside Sharpsburg. Their house was most likely not much more than a shack, but Alice had done all she could to make it a home, taking the cover from their prairie schooner, for example—the very thing that made it a covered wagon—staining it with the juice of green walnuts, and turning it into a carpet that rested atop a layer of straw on the floor. At the windows she had hung curtains made of newspapers cut into intricate designs.

Despite the dangers of childbirth in the nineteenth century, there was no money for a doctor, and Alice was assisted in John's birth by a neighbor woman, a German immigrant, who had trudged along the frozen, rutted country road carrying her own featherbed as protection against the chill inside the family's unplastered, uninsulated house. Lulu, by now nearly four, and Grace, just two, sat quietly in a corner. It was late in the evening when John was born, and a wood fire burned in the cook stove, upon which steamed a kettle. John's father was either not part of the moment or simply left out of the later retellings.[2]

The details of this intimate scene, though impossible to verify, are important. They represent John Neihardt's own version of his origin story, a personal preview, a dramatization of his life in microcosm, with the members of his family cast in roles they would play for the rest of his life. His mother, Alice Culler Neihart, is the heroine, a clever and resourceful provider, able always to turn nothing into something, very little into enough.[3] His sisters, though older, sit off to the side, not quite even supporting players, patiently making way for their younger brother, the first and only son, who will become the center of the family's attention. His father, Nicholas Nathan Neihart, is missing.

Yet it is Nicholas, though he remains mysterious in the opening scene of his son's life, who suggests where this story is headed. For it is Nicholas who names his son. The first name came from Nicholas's own father, an admired forebear, who in his own small way helped carve a country out of the western wilderness in the mid-1850s, the period in American history that would come to mean so much to the boy, born on what would have been his grandfather's seventy-ninth birthday. But it is the middle name that is noteworthy. For with it Nicholas chose to honor John Greenleaf Whittier, the popular American Quaker poet and abolitionist who had started writing verse as a boy after having been inspired by reading a volume of Robert Burns's poetry.

Nicholas named his son, at least in part, for a poet.

I   A HEART-BREAKING
FAREWELL

By the time John Greenleaf Neihardt was born, members of his family had been in America for nearly 130 years. Though he knew most of them only through family stories—even his paternal grandfather and namesake died before he was born—he always believed he knew what kind of men and women they had been. Generation by generation, they had followed the sunset, participating in the westward movement that forged a nation, a migration, John would offer proudly, that was "in the blood of my family."[1]

When Conrad Neuhart, a German immigrant still in his twenties, arrived in Philadelphia in the fall of 1754, he became the first recorded Neihardt ancestor in the colonies. Conrad, a carpenter by trade and John Neihardt's great-great-grandfather, was an indentured servant, arriving under charter to a Philadelphia merchant.[2] Eventually Conrad joined his fellow colonists—as well as thirteen of his relatives—in their fight for independence.

Conrad and his wife, Eva Sauerbrey, lived in eastern Pennsylvania, in an area of concentrated German immigration. As these new Americans grew restless for new opportunities, thousands ventured west, among them Conrad and Eva's youngest child, a son they named Conrad Jr. Once married, Conrad Jr. and his wife, Elizabeth, moved first to central

Pennsylvania—where their son John, John Neihardt's grandfather, was born on January 8, 1802—and later to Holmes County, Ohio.

Once grown and married, John Neihart—over the generations the family name changed from Neuhart to Neihart to Neihardt—and his wife, Teresa, continued the move west, following one of his brothers to the northwestern corner of Ohio, where they bought eighty acres in 1838, and another eighty soon after. In 1854 they sold their farm at a handsome profit and moved to Indiana, where they bought 240 acres. They reserved half an acre for a family cemetery, evidence that here, finally, was where they meant to stay. John and Teresa had seventeen children— seven girls and ten boys—and together the family gathered sap from the sugar maples for syrup, farmed, mined, and raised livestock. At least four of the children died young, and three of the boys served in the Civil War, fighting, among other battles, at Shiloh, Vicksburg, and Chattanooga. John and Teresa's youngest son, Nicholas Nathan Neihart, was born on July 16, 1853, in Sandusky, Ohio, on the shores of Lake Erie. Nicholas—John Neihardt's father—grew up in the backwoods, the sixteenth child and last boy. He had no formal education and spoke only German until he was eleven years old.[3]

Neihardt's maternal forebears—the German Cullers and the Irish Hotts—had followed much the same route and were not far behind. John's maternal grandfather, George W. Culler, born in southwestern Pennsylvania, was two years old when his parents moved the family west to the same part of Ohio where Conrad and Elizabeth Neuhart had settled. When he was twenty-five George married nineteen-year-old Catherine Hott, born to Irish immigrants, and together they raised six girls and two boys, the oldest of whom was their daughter Alice, born on December 21, 1858. In 1863 the Cullers, like John and Teresa Neihart, moved to Indiana, where they settled in an uncleared wilderness.[4] In the late 1870s they moved again, this time to northwestern Kansas, but Alice, still a teenager, did not accompany her family this time. Somewhere in the wilderness of Indiana she had met a handsome young man.

Little is known about Nicholas and Alice Neihart's initial years together, except that when they married in Coal City, Indiana, in March 1876—Nicholas was twenty-two years old, and Alice was just seventeen— they were a couple with few prospects.[5] By the next year, when daughter Lulu Dell was born, they had moved to Springfield, Illinois. A year later, when daughter Grace was born, they were living in Grinnell, Iowa. By the time their last child, John, was born three years later, they had returned to Illinois, this time to Sharpsburg. By 1883 Nicholas Neihart had taken his wife and three children twenty miles northwest, back to Springfield. There Nicholas worked, in relatively short order, as a peddler, wagon driver, and confectioner.

As a confectioner Nicholas was able to provide a stable life for his family. He had his own shop, at Fourth and Capitol, where the Neiharts also lived, and it was from this vantage point that young Johnnie watched men working on the state capitol down the street. From the front of his father's shop, Johnnie, now four years old, had a good view of the construction, and years later he could still recall the experience: "The new State House is slowly nearing completion, and many teams of horses, harnessed in a long string, are dragging one of the great stone columns down the street. It is riding on rollers that are being switched from rear to front as lathered horses squat and strain, leaning to the load, or plunge and bicker, inching forward down the avenue, whips cracking, men shouting."[6]

The time in Springfield provided the boy with his first opportunities to hear of great deeds and heroes, incidents forever tied to memories of his father. "I can remember exactly where I stood with my Father when we heard from a shouting newsboy that a great man called Grant had died."[7] And he would recall the Lincoln Memorial, the tomb of Springfield's own hero. "There for the first time I knew the spell of awe, inspired, no doubt, by what my Father must have told me."[8] Nicholas admired soldiers, and he took his son at least once to the Illinois National Guard's permanent camp and rifle range, "Camp Lincoln," where on Sundays visitors could see a dress parade as well as target practice and, most exciting for an impressionable young boy, maneuvers.[9] "They formed along the brow of a low hill—a long line of mounted men in blue, with restless horses prancing and guidons flying. And a bugle sang, and a great cry went up, and the horses surged forward in a brisk trot that grew into a wild gallop, full of flying manes and tails and naked sabers flashing in the sun, and rolling thunder in the dust beneath!" as John would remember the tableau. "It wasn't fear that made me feel like crying."[10]

Nicholas, meanwhile, was failing as a business owner. The struggle to support their family was serious enough that instead of keeping the family together as they searched for a new opportunity, Nicholas and Alice chose to split up the family. Alice took Lulu, Grace, and Johnnie to north-central Kansas, where her parents were homesteading. Nicholas moved to Kansas City, Missouri, then experiencing a real estate boom, to look for work. Whatever his parents' intentions, to John the move to his maternal grandparents would always be just a visit, a place to stay "until my Father found a better place for us to live."[11]

After the Civil War, pioneers had swept into Kansas in waves of tens of thousands. The first wave had settled, naturally, on the best farmland, in the eastern parts of the state. Each successive wave had searched farther west; by the late 1870s, when George and Catherine Culler arrived, much of the best land had been taken. The Cullers found a spot on the Solomon River, southeast of Stockton, a town with a name representing the residents' dream of someday becoming a livestock center. Like others around them, the Cullers began carving a home and a life out of the prairie. Few years would be tougher than 1886, the year Alice Neihart made the train trip west with her three small children. The summer's heat was endless, drying up streams and setting fire to the grasslands. The winter was one of the worst ever recorded.[12]

Living on the prairie forced people to have a wide view of things. Everywhere they looked, the distances were great, the landscape unchanging. A sense of immensity, of unending vastness, enveloped people, a feeling many compared to being at sea. There was no end in sight, and John later recalled it as "an endless yellow blur."[13] The terrain offered no city skyline, no mountains or ocean in the distance, nothing to stop either the winds, which blew year-round, or the imagination.

In Kansas John experienced firsthand the American West, the land of buffalo, prairie fires, and Plains Indians. He traveled across the unfenced prairie, bouncing along in a wooden farm wagon, torn between wanting to go faster to get to his grandparents' place sooner and wanting to slow down to make the ride slightly less rough. From the moment he arrived, John began accumulating unforgettable images and experiences. "There were no trees about here yet. The two-room house looked out upon a world of grass and sky, save where green corn made careless, extravagant promises on a field to southward."[14] In addition to their sod house and straw-roofed barn, his grandfather had built a blacksmith shop, in which he made and fixed not only his own tools and equipment but also those of the few scattered neighbors, men who swapped help and stories, tales of the true West.

Neihardt's heroes, throughout his life, were always larger than life. To young John his Grandpa Culler, fifty-one years old when John arrived in Kansas at the age of five, was Olympian. "Why, with his naked hand, hammer-hardened to the likeness of a hoof, he could scrape the crusted metal from a white-hot iron bar, and never feel it!"[15] His grandmother was forty-seven, and when conventional words failed to reflect her meaning adequately, she invented her own vocabulary. John recalled her "positively 'throughother' to see things all 'glakid' and 'clatty' with the dust she was forever chasing" around her sod house.[16] "It was a cozy, homey house, thick-walled against the summer heat and winter cold. The sod, laid up like slabs of stone, but lacking mortar, had come from where the corn was waving yonder," John remembered. "The floor was clay, hard-beaten and foot-polished to the semblance of smooth stone. The ceiling was a sheet of unbleached muslin stretched from wall to wall, partly 'for looks,' but more to catch the slowly sifting dust."[17] Outside the house were the garden and the cool cellar.

The Cullers' closest neighbors to the south were the Nivens family, African American homesteaders. Neihardt remembered the two families getting along well, sharing food and visiting when someone was ill. For the rest of her life Catherine Culler would tolerate no prejudice against African Americans. But it was not necessarily a lesson in tolerance for young John. This same grandmother, an Irish Protestant—"the anti-Catholic party," in John's recollection—regarded Catholics as wrong, misguided, dislikable even, and no one could convince her otherwise. Rather it was a lesson in stubbornly trusting oneself, believing what one saw with one's own eyes: when it came to knowledge, his grandmother's philosophy was that nothing was better than personal experience. Know something from your own experience, know it in your bones, and no one need ever change your mind. It was a lesson that John would remember.

For John and his sisters, the time with their grandparents was a joyful one. The family made an outing of picking sunflowers for kindling and summer cooking. For the winter stove they gathered cow chips and likely even buffalo chips. They rode Zip, their grandfather's horse, and attended box socials and square dance parties, where John's uncle played the fiddle. For the adults it was undoubtedly a life of hard work and worry—Kansas had suffered a drought the previous year, and Alice must have wondered how her husband was faring in Kansas City—but any concerns were kept from the children.

The only time John remembered being afraid was that first fall, when a prairie fire threatened the Culler homestead. "I remember the tickly feel of danger in the air, the fearful thrill of something big about to happen. I could feel that even Grandfather was afraid, at least a little."[18] Prairie fires were all too common then, caused by lightning, a careless campfire, even the discharge of a gun. They stormed through with the regularity of thunderstorms, especially in the fall when the grass was dry.

That fall, after neighbor men arrived on horseback at the Culler homestead, John's grandfather harnessed a team of horses and plowed around the buildings. Cows and calves were moved to a barbed-wire pen behind the house, the horses and wagon tied nearby. The children were ordered to stay at the house, as the grownups began setting backfires to try to stop the advancing blaze. "That night it swept past us," John later recalled. "And when it came by it was the most glorious and terrible thing you can imagine. . . . And it looked to me as though that fire was after me."[19] John broke and ran for his mother, but his grandfather grabbed him and returned him to the house, where the plowing and backfires had created "an island of safety." The fire burned past them, sparing the house, their barn, their animals. John would never forget the terror and fear of that night.

With the spring came word from Nicholas. He had found a job as the night watchman at a hotel in Kansas City and had located a home for his family. Nicholas and Kansas City had never been far from the thoughts of his children during the year they spent in Kansas. "When we were at Grandpa's out West, Kansas City was a tall beautiful town where wonderful things were always happening, and all the people there were kind and good," John recalled. "We talked and talked about it."[20]

The reality, however, did not match the children's dream. The hotel where Nicholas worked was more brothel than hotel; "disreputable," as John would describe it later in life. The home, in a brick tenement at Fourth and Oak, frightened the children after the wide open spaces in Kansas. "No grass grew there," John remembered, "and strange, unfriendly people who looked dirty lived there too. At night they made loud noises, and sometimes there was fighting."[21]

Nicholas never kept a job for long, however, and soon the hotel job and the tenement apartment were replaced by other jobs and other rundown homes. "I don't remember living long in any one place," John wrote later.[22] Nicholas tried selling horses and buggies without success before he found a job that returned some stability to the Neiharts' lives. Kansas City was the third city in the country to develop cable railways, and by this time it had nearly thirty-five miles of railway in operation.[23] Nicholas was hired as a cable car conductor and frequently worked extra night shifts repairing and replacing cable.[24] For Kansas City—and the Neiharts—it was a boom time. The family rented a house, and helped by the extra money Alice earned by taking in sewing, they could afford a series of payments to buy an ornate clock that stood two feet high.[25] There was money for Lulu to study painting, for Grace to study piano and elocution.[26] Once Nicholas took the whole family on a roundtrip steamboat ride to Leavenworth, Kansas.[27] John would remember it as their "Golden Age."[28]

John's obvious admiration for his father was evident in the games he played. America was enjoying the Age of Edison, and young boys everywhere dreamed of becoming inventors. Sometime in 1889, by now eight years old, John built a miniature cable car layout behind the house, and he managed to acquire a bright red science textbook, *Magnetism and Electricity* by Arthur Poyser, which introduced him to magnetism and frictional and voltaic electricity.[29] John also made a friend, Dick Scammon, who opened a new and wondrous world to the boy. Younger but taller than John, Dick had a dog named Plato and was deeply interested in the Trojan War. He had a special room in his father's barn plastered with posters of heroes and gods with names like Achilles and Zeus, and of far-away places like Troy, where warriors rode in splendid carts called chariots. "It was all most exciting and bewildering," John recalled.[30]

Dick's parents were no less unusual to John. Dick's father, James, was a judge, who sometimes read to the boys from books in his "great, silent library." One of the books John remembered was Samuel Johnson's *Rasselas*, which marked the first time John had heard any tales of the "exotic" east. Written in the genre of the "Oriental tale," popular in the eighteenth century, *Rasselas* is the story of an imaginative young man who leaves his Eden-like valley to wander in search of an education. The lesson in the story is that life is not about having, but desiring; not attaining, but seeking.[31] Though he was too young to understand it fully, this idea stuck with John, becoming a key part of what he would call his life's "striving." Dick's mother made no less an impression. John would remember Laura Everingham Scammon as "a sweet, gracious lady," and she was also a writer. Mornings she spent in her study, writing books and stories for the popular children's newspaper, the *Youth's Companion*. She too read to the boys, and John recalled that she made Homer's *Iliad* and the *Odyssey* come alive.[32]

As in Springfield, Kansas City offered young John time to spend with his father. The two were often together on Sundays, Nicholas's one day off, and they would walk, with little or no conversation, to where the city ended and the country started, through the woods with the requisite bees and squirrels and whippoorwills and raccoons, or on to Brush Creek to swim.[33] As always, John linked his memories of his father to memories of heroes. He remembered seeing President and Mrs. Grover Cleveland during their visit to Kansas City in October 1887, as they stood on a balcony of the Flatiron Building. And he remembered walking along the docks with his father, listening to the stories told by the men lounging there, of fur trappers and Indians, of far-away places, all reached by this muddy, mighty river from the wilderness, the Missouri. These men talked about riverboats going to somewhere called Fort Benton, Montana, about something called "the mountain trade." "You could stand on the very tallest building in Kansas City, and you could look and look and never see a mountain," John wrote later. "But the old men on the docks—they had been there and all the way back, perhaps hundreds of times. . . . What a picture I made out of their kaleidoscopic chatter."[34]

These stories, like those he had heard from his grandfather's neighbors in Kansas, reminded John of the mythical tales of courageous men who completed heroic tasks and fought ferocious battles that he heard from Dick Scammon's parents. He never forgot them, and they percolated in his memory, becoming part of his very life and his future writings. Fort Benton "filled my day-dreams with wonders—this place that seemed halfway to the moon."[35] When he played, he pretended he was a steamboat pilot on the Missouri. "Once I was captain of a trunk lid that sailed a frog-pond down in Kansas City; and at that time I thought I knew the meaning of pride."[36]

Children who grow up on the prairie learn about the power and mystery of water from rivers and streams, and John's lessons came from the Missouri. At least once, he and his father saw the river during a flood, and as John remembered, "[T]he terror I felt made me reach up to the saving forefinger of my father." But the Missouri was not after little boys that day. "Far across the yellow swirl that spread out into the wooded bottomlands, we watched the demolition of a little town."[37] The sight may have terrified the boy, but John saw only bravery in his father. Nicholas was fit though small, never quite reaching five feet, five inches, but to his son he towered over the river. "He seemed to fear it almost not at all. And I should have felt little surprise had he taken me in his arms and stepped easily over that mile or so of liquid madness."[38]

John and his father went frequently to the Missouri after that, and with time John's feelings about the river changed. "Many a lazy Sunday stroll took us back to the river; and little by little the dread became less, and the wonder grew—and a little love crept in."[39] John found himself wondering why his father would not want to engage in the fur trade: "He should have been a captain and taken me on for cub pilot."[40]

John was not alone in doubting his father. Once again Nicholas was not prospering, and this time Alice had had enough. Once, after the couple argued, Nicholas left. When he returned a few days later, Alice refused to let him in. Years later Lulu remembered simply that her father "was never a consistent money maker."[41] At the time, his leaving hit the children hard, especially John, who recalled "with a twinge of heartache, the angry, terrifying voices that hurt me deep in the middle of my breast."[42]

When much older, John remembered, or at least chose to tell, far more stories of his boyhood adventures with his father than of time spent with his mother. Perhaps this is just the way of boys: they want to be like their fathers, and their joint activities are deeply imprinted. Perhaps it was simply that his times with his father, those Sundays they spent together apart from the women in the house, were designed to be special, hours removed from the routine of scraping by, of cooking and cleaning, of washing and struggling. Perhaps, since these were memories John shared late in life, it was that by then, he had had a lifetime with his mother; the experiences with his father, so few and far removed, remained forever frozen in time. Always, though, he associated his father with powerful elements in his life: the Missouri River, soldiers, heroes, physical strength. In the final days of 1890 Nicholas left the family for good. John had known his father for scarcely ten years, and the day would soon come when he would be unable to recall his father's voice. The only physical connection he would remember would be hanging onto his father's finger while watching the Missouri River.

When the Neiharts split up, Nicholas left his wife and three children everything he had, even a red leather billfold he had carried in the inside breast pocket of his coat.[43] He had sometimes amused his son on rainy Sundays by writing fanciful verses, and in the billfold was one such poem, written three years earlier on a scrap of paper, and now serving as a father's heart-breaking farewell:

> I love Johnnie, I love Gracie, I love Lulu just as well;
> I love Johnnie for his genius, number of wheels I cannot tell.
> Pullies, ropes and cogs and fixings,
> Cars and signals, shafts and riggings
> All combined to show his greatness,
> For he's Papa's little "tootness."
> I love Gracie, oh! That curl,
> I love Lulu, kind sweet girl,
> To wash and scrub, to clean and sew,
> Be ahead of class at school you know,
> 100 percent and a smile we'd see
> When home they'd come with us at tea.[44]

Also stuffed inside the wallet were articles about subjects Nicholas held close to his heart and the men he most admired. One was about his favorite poet, and his son's namesake, John Greenleaf Whittier. Another was about Robert G. Ingersoll, the nineteenth-century orator and social reformist known as the "Great Agnostic," an iconoclast Nicholas greatly admired.

Yet another was about the killing of a band of Indians at Wounded Knee Creek in South Dakota. A Miniconjou named Big Foot and more than three hundred of his followers had surrendered to the Seventh Cavalry. On December 29, 1890, as the Indians were being disarmed, a gun discharged, and the soldiers opened fire with four small shrapnel-firing cannons that killed nearly all the men, women, and children. John Neihardt never learned why his father had kept a clipping about the Wounded Knee Massacre. He vaguely recalled his father reading to him from a newspaper account about the fight just before he disappeared, remembering that as a young boy, he was afraid Indians might attack

Kansas City at any moment.[45] The clipping was just one more way that Nicholas remained forever a mystery to his son.[46]

For now, though Nicholas wrote to his wife occasionally, he was gone from his family's life. Lulu and John both remembered their father sometimes sending money to their mother, which she always returned.[47] After he left, he was never discussed at home, his name never mentioned.[48] It was as though Nicholas was dead. Forty years later John's mother explained her attitude about life with Nicholas. "I had long ago learned that I must think of only the good," she wrote to John. "And I have in a great measure succeeded to such an extent that many instances or incidents have been blotted out."[49]

Not surprisingly, for young John, losing his father was a terrific blow. "[S]ometimes it all came back with the ache in my throat of tears too big for crying. Then I would go out into the cornfield—deep into its green, whispering solitude, where no one could see me. And there I would remember and remember."[50]

2 A VOICE ECHOING IN THE DISTANCE

Alone with three children and without even inconsistent income from her husband, Alice was once again drawn to her family. Her brother George Culler had settled on a farm in the fertile, rolling prairie of northeastern Nebraska. Alice decided it would be good to be near him and her parents, who had already joined George after years of unsuccessfully trying to carve a farm out of the Kansas grassland and an even briefer, and no more successful, battle against drought in south-central Nebraska. George's farm sat amid the tall grass and rich soil just outside Wayne, a village that came to life the year John Neihardt was born, 1881, when the railroad extended a line through the county.[1] By the time Alice arrived by train with her children ten years later, more than a thousand people called the prosperous town home. Six stores carried general merchandise, and two more sold dry goods. Two grocery stores, three drug stores, two hardware stores, and a furniture store were open for business, as were three lumberyards and two grain elevators, two livery stables, a roller mill, and a broom factory. Two banks competed for the financial accounts of the townspeople, and already brick buildings were beginning to replace the earlier wooden ones.[2]

As she had done in Kansas City, Alice turned to sewing to keep her family in "respectable poverty," essentially the standard rural or small town lifestyle for the lower classes of the late nineteenth century.[3] "My mother was a dress maker, and she worked for a dollar a day, ten hours, when she could get the work," John remembered. Somehow she managed to make a home for herself and her three children, who soon attended public school. "I do not remember feeling 'deprived,'" her son wrote years later.[4]

In 1892, their second year in Wayne, John suffered an illness, which in a short time changed his life. He had come home from school so feverish that his mother called a doctor to their house on Main Street. As his mother tried to keep him cool by placing cold washrags across his forehead, he experienced a mild delirium, slipping in and out of a nightmarish state in which he dreamed he was flying above the earth's surface. "It came upon me suddenly and with little or no warning. The world tottered and began to rotate. Then there was blackness," he wrote years later.[5] "I dreamed that I was flying through space . . . my hands in front of me like a diver and my face between my arms."[6]

John was frightened by the dream. "I was going so fast that whatever it was that was beneath me, whether it was air or ether, was like slick glass, it was hard with my speed. But it was beautiful, beautiful and terrible."[7] In his dream, John tried to stop flying, desperately wanting to rest. He had an overwhelming feeling of homesickness. "I wanted to go back to my mother, and I couldn't stop. And then I would wake, and she'd be there putting cloths on my forehead. And then I'd go back again, and I'd hang on to her because I didn't want to go back."[8] To the young boy it seemed that he could hear a voice faintly echoing in the distance, summoning him, encouraging him to take some leap of faith. Exactly to what, though, he did not know.

The next morning the fever broke. Though John soon recovered from the illness, he remained haunted by the dream. "At first it seemed only a curious nightmare," John said later. "Then it began to take on the mood of sublimity, with less of fear and more of wonder."[9] He became obsessed with trying to figure out what the dream meant, and he began to believe that its persistent "great voice" was something powerful, almost spiritual, calling to him. He lost all interest in the world of mechanics and electricity, the world, he now believed, that he was supposed to leave behind. But he was far less certain of what was ahead of him. Like Rasselas, in the story read by Dick Scammon's father back in Kansas City, John found he "was fired with the desire of doing something, though he knew not yet with distinctness, either end or means."[10]

While in school in Wayne, John was introduced to the great poets, mostly by reading from a random collection of books near the teacher's desk.[11] Sometimes it seemed the poetry spoke to him personally: a section of Alfred, Lord Tennyson's *Dreams of Fair Women*, for example, reminded him of a favorite teacher he had had in Kansas City.[12] Eventually, though, that first winter after his fever dream, he felt compelled to write poetry himself. And he came to believe that "it was the dream that changed the direction of my life."[13]

His first poem grew out of a routine but emotional event, at least in the life of a twelve-year-old: his mother scolded him for his messy hair, and though he apologized, she refused to say goodbye as he left for school. Later, after John was gone, she found a poem on her bedroom bureau. "It was a beautiful poem. The most wonderful thing I had ever read. It wasn't very long, but it was entitled, 'Your Stubble-Haired Boy,' and in it John told me how much he loved me, and he made me feel how sorry he was to have acted so that I wouldn't tell him goodbye."[14]

At first John was proud of the poem. "I went about with a glorified feeling because of it," he wrote years later. Soon, though, upon re-reading the poem, he found it silly, and it made him ashamed. When his mother was not looking, he burned it in the kitchen stove. "For days thereafter the world seemed dreadfully empty and lonely—like being homesick."[15] Before destroying the poem, John had committed at least the first stanza to memory:

> At the age of 12, in the city of Wayne,
>   I was my mother's pride and joy,
> Till not combing my hair did stain
>   The beauty of her stubble-haired boy.[16]

Though it was a simple poem, and though in the end he destroyed it, John was captivated by the experience of writing it. He had had a message to impart—his apology—and he had communicated it. He kept writing, and wanting to improve, he instinctively looked for help in the poems of the masters. Already familiar with and touched by Tennyson, John turned to him, helped in large part by his sisters.

In the late nineteenth century many products offered coupons that could be traded for premiums when collected in large enough quantities. Lulu and Grace, always supportive of their little brother, started saving soap wrappers, eventually amassing enough for a paperback copy of Tennyson's *Idylls of the King*.[17] John found Tennyson's poetic treatment of the King Arthur legend, the poet's longest and most ambitious work, a revelation: "[W]ords taught to march in such a manner that their very going was like a river of music! My poet could do that; and he could make a noble tale come forth singing out of an enchanted world where great heroes met in desperate battle and beautiful women mourned."[18] John read the words:

> The sudden trumpet sounded as in a dream
> To ears but half-awaked, then one low roll
> Of Autumn thunder, and the jousts began:
> And ever the wind blew, and yellowing leaf
> And gloom and gleam, and shower and shorn plume
> Went down it.[19]

And he was captivated by the sound, by the rhythm, by the story. Tennyson became "his father, his teacher, the one Holy One entirely to be loved, trusted and followed."[20] John was only too eager to follow, eventually coming to think of Wayne as his "Pisgah height, my hill of vision," the place where he had first glimpsed the promised land of poetic creation.[21] To John, being called to poetry was nothing less than spiritual.

He next acquired a copy of Robert Browning's *Selected Poems*. During what he called his "eager apprenticeship," wherever he went, whatever he did, John carried these two books. "I used to weed beets with a copy of Tennyson in one pocket, a copy of Browning in the other."[22] He came to believe that his cheap copies of the two poets created in him a passion that took him beyond "the fixed and duller passions of the community." Rather than be "the product of his county," he would choose the higher plane of a life of letters.[23]

By age thirteen John had made a new friend, another boy his age, John Elias Weston Chaffee, and the boys became great comrades. "We were alive from our toes up to the tops of our heads," Neihardt recalled years later. "We *invented* adventures."[24] Together they challenged themselves, running and walking long distances, by day and night. They once trekked forty-five miles, round trip, to visit Lulu at a country school where she was teaching.[25] Whenever they walked, John recited poetry.

All the while, John thought about—and wrote—poetry. The two boys once walked ten miles to the town of Lyons to hear an Italian harpist play in a saloon. Soon after, John, in fifty-six lines, compared the ebb and flow of life to a harp string.[26]

> I thought our lives are as the harp string;
>> Ever changing in their strain;
> Singing joy and love and beauty;
>> Singing grief and hate and pain.[27]

One of Wayne's weekly newspapers, the *Wayne Democrat*, published "The Harpist," and at age fourteen, John Neihardt became a published poet.

He soon moved on to a new, larger topic, and to a form he found more appropriate to a serious student of Tennyson: an epic. Specifically, he began writing a three-part narrative poem called *An Epic of the Stone Age*. More familiarly, he called it his *Cave Man Trilogy*. "I had planned 'Chalboa' as the first of three related narratives, the second to be called 'Tlingilla,' and the third to be entitled 'The Wizard of the Wind.'"[28] Chalboa was the hero, and Tlingilla was his lady. "And, boy, believe me, that hero was a cuss," Neihardt recalled years later. "And the heroine was worse yet."[29] John dedicated "Chalboa," unpublished and now lost, to "John Elias Weston Chaffee, Prince of Pals."[30]

John was bright and already bored by school, so when an opportunity for something more challenging presented itself, Alice Neihardt took it. Among her sewing customers were the wife and daughter of the head of Wayne's new normal school, James Madison Pile. Normal schools trained their graduates to be school teachers, and "Mr. Pile's College," as it was first known, had opened in November 1891, after Pile, a mathematics professor at Fremont Normal School seventy miles to the southeast, had offered summer school classes in Wayne and been impressed by the residents' desire for higher education. A group of local citizens organized the Nebraska Normal College Association and raised twenty thousand dollars to construct a one-building college that soon enrolled its first seven students, one of whom was John's uncle Charles Culler. Pile, the school's first president, also taught ten hours a day. Finding John's mother at his home one evening with her sewing, Pile asked what she was going to do with her bright young son. When she said she was unsure, Pile offered to take him on as a student.[31]

In the fall of 1894 John entered Nebraska Normal College as its youngest student. Tuition was $125 a year, a sum quite out of reach for many residents of Wayne during the hard years of the 1890s and certainly out of reach for Alice Neihardt. But Pile was inventive: some students paid their tuition in garden produce or in eggs, butter, or milk. Others were given jobs at the school to work off their tuition, and Pile found such a job for John: relying on an old key-wind watch Pile lent him, John rang the bell in the school's tower, calling the students to meals and classes.[32]

Nebraska Normal had started in a false-front wooden building on Main Street, but by the time John enrolled it had moved to a new building, a healthy walk from the Neihardts' home. The dominating square bell tower on the southwest corner was reserved for John and his new responsibility, one he took very seriously. "It was a strenuous business for me in the time of the blizzards. Often it was a blind struggle through the drifts to reach the college a mile and a half from my home in the pitch dark of 6 a.m."[33] But John loved the school. "[I]t was as though the little college had been created for me. It released me from the listless boredom I had come to feel in school and lifted me to a higher, creative level of being."[34] Since he was younger than the school's other students, in many of his classes he was the only pupil, and he advanced rapidly.

In addition to Pile, Nebraska Normal employed eight other teachers, among them Mrs. Pile and a gifted professor not yet thirty years old, Ulysses Sylvester Conn, who later became John's advanced Latin instructor.[35] "Under his tutelage I read all of the *Commentaries*, most of Cicero, and much of Tacitus before we tackled Horace on the way to *The Aeneid*."[36] For John, reading the Latin poets and later Homer, the Greek tragic poets, and Aristophanes, Plato, and Aristotle provided him the opportunity to share "the thoughts of the great men, the great spirits, that have passed through this world."[37]

At about this same time John also made the acquaintance of two eccentric and influential men of Wayne, Reuben Durrin and James Brittain. Durrin, known usually as "Professor," though no one knew of what, was a talented amateur sculptor who made his living in Wayne as a tombstone carver. Not quite fifty years old, Durrin was tall and thin and had a dark complexion.[38] He occasionally wore a top hat and a cutaway coat around town, and a local newspaper once suggested he could have been the model for Mark Twain's Pudd'nhead Wilson.[39] He claimed to have studied sculpture under Thomas Buchanan Reed, the once celebrated poet and artist, and nearly to have married Ella Wheeler Wilcox, author of the erotic *Poems of Passion*, but her family had disapproved.[40] John frequently listened to Durrin recite poetry from memory, especially Byron, as well as passages from Shakespeare.

Durrin's friend Brittain was a lawyer and later a county judge. He also owned and managed Wayne's 800-seat opera house, the center of community activities, presenting shows from back East, local plays, band concerts, and political speeches. Compared to Durrin, Brittain was ordinary, but he had "an extraordinary talent for provoking controversial discussion."[41] He was dignified and poised, something of an amateur philosopher, and John thought that in a toga, he would look just like an ancient Roman senator. Brittain loved the theater, and Shakespeare was his favorite. Like Durrin, he could recite much of it from memory, and John enjoyed listening to the two take turns doing their dramatic readings.

John had met the men one day while running an errand downtown for his mother. Passing Durrin's shop, John saw him carving an angel from stone and stopped to watch. "Leaning over his work and tapping with great care, he was unaware of my presence for some time. Finally, rising to his full height, he gazed far down upon me, his keen gray eyes slowly coming into seeing focus, as though he had been a long way off and was just getting back."[42] After a brief conversation, Durrin surprised the boy with the offer of a part-time job polishing marble. There would be, he implied, pay and plenty of talk about poetry. Years later John could never remember actually having been paid, but he never forgot the conversations.[43] Barely into his teens, John became part of what he came to call "our Tombstone Trinity."[44]

Growing up as the only male in a house with a mother and two sisters, John relished his time with the two men. "[Durrin] was a rebel in every sense of the word. He liked me, and we used to cap verses on each other."[45] Brittain, through his opera house, had been around actors and loved mimicking them as he recited, and John worked hard to do the same. "[I]t was a thrilling experience to hear his well-modulated, dark-brown voice making the pentameters come gloriously alive!"[46] The conversations ranged beyond poetry to include politics, art, and often religion. Wayne had the usual Great Plains mix of churches—Presbyterian, Methodist, Baptist, Lutheran, German Lutheran, and Catholic—but neither Durrin nor Brittain attended any of them. The members of John's family were primarily Methodists, but his mother had a distaste for "churchy" religion, something her son had grown to share.

At the tombstone shop the three often made sport of the local churchgoers, and one incident brought their sport to public notice. For fun, John and his friend John Chaffee attended a tent revival service in Wayne run by an evangelist named Reverend Cordner. It was in the fall, and during the service a cold front struck out of the northwest. Cordner had just boasted that the Lord wouldn't blow his tent down because he was one of the faithful when a gust of wind did just that. And then the tent caught fire. "There was straw on the floor to keep people's feet warm," John recalled, "and there was a great fire and it burned his tent."[47] The boys found the scene hilarious, and when John related it to Durrin and Brittain, they encouraged him to mark the occasion with an epic-style poem. Durrin gave him space in the backroom of the tombstone shop, and two days later John, seeking to imitate Homer's *Iliad*, had completed "The Tentiad." In it a prophet fights the devil, and his hell-fire speech ignites the very straw beneath the feet of the mob. The Four Winds, summoned by Jehovah, blow the fire out of control, and in the end the prophet is saved only by divine intervention.[48]

The *Wayne Democrat*, the newspaper that had published "The Harpist," was edited and published by "an angry young man," a friend of Durrin and Brittain, named W.S. Goldie.[49] Goldie, who satisfied himself that "The Tentiad" would interest "the unpoetic generality of humankind who read the *Democrat*," agreed to print it, using two columns of his front page.[50] When the paper was published, John was branded an infidel and Durrin and Brittain as bad influences. "That was the old-fashioned religion," Neihardt said years later, "and our opposition to it wasn't popular."[51]

With "The Tentiad" John had written himself into the role of outsider, egged on by two men he admired and looking down on many of the townspeople. The revival itself, and what it represented to John about mob rule, stuck with him. "[I]f you have ever found yourself in the midst of a vast revival meeting crowd when the frenzy of salvation was at its height, you will know how hard it is to keep your balance where the mob mind rules," he wrote nearly thirty years later.[52] Having felt sometimes the clown, sometimes the "strange, unbidden guest" in Wayne, he discovered that with the support of a few—in this case Durrin, Brittain, and Goldie—he truly enjoyed the role of outsider.[53] Neihardt's ambitions for his work expanded as he grew older, but he forever believed in the pattern that developed during his "Tombstone Trinity" period: having a small number of the right people in his corner was worth more than the broader support of the masses.

For John, being around the paternal Durrin and Brittain augmented the education he was receiving at school. "So I had that sort of atmosphere, when the atmosphere of the other kids was that of hogs and corn and just the everyday thing, no thought of Shakespeare."[54] Or, as he put it in a poem he later wrote about his time in Wayne:

Dull to the worldly duty,
Less to the town he grew,
And more to the God of Beauty
Than even the grocer knew!"[55]

Conversations with Durrin and Brittain, even when about religion, did not always revolve around making fun of Wayne's churchgoers. Among the topics the three discussed were Hindu philosophy and religion. "[Durrin] was acquainted with many things, and we were always discussing such matters," John told a friend years later.[56] Eastern religions, especially that of the Hindus in India, had become a popular subject for discussion after a much-publicized speech at the Chicago World's Fair in 1893 by a young swami who simplified, modernized, and popularized his religion's ancient teachings.[57] Brittain frequently loaned John books from his private library, and among them was a little volume of the *Upanishads*, the core teachings of Hinduism. Durrin, at the same time, loaned John *The Bible in India*, an English translation of a French book written thirty-eight years earlier by Louis Jacolliot, at one time the French consul in Calcutta. In the book Jacolliot outlined his theory that Jesus Christ was but a recent reconstruction of an old Indo-Aryan tradition, that of Jezeus Christna. Jacolliot believed all modern civilizations had originated from a single ancient one. The book, which basically said the Christ story was just that, a story, and one based on someone else's story at that, had been controversial when published. It was just as controversial for John: his grandmother protested, deploring "them awful Hoodoo books," and begged him to quit reading them.[58] He did not, and instead became deeply interested in Hindu religion and Vedanta philosophy. Given his own personal experience with a powerful dream, he was especially drawn to a story outlined in the Jacolliot book about the virgin Devanaguy, mother to Christna, who was to be savior of the world. Devanaguy "was made pregnant by the divine . . . the same as our story of the virgin Mary," John recalled. "And while she was carrying her child, which was to be a boy, an arrangement was made by the divine powers that she should dream a dream that would educate her in the mysteries, in all the beauties and wonders of the universe. Her dreaming of it, while she was carrying the child, would instruct the child, and he would be born far ahead of the average person in understanding."[59]

John decided to focus on Devanaguy's dream for his next long poem. Writing the new poem gave him an opportunity to explore more fully his own dream, which, though it had occurred five years earlier, was becoming key to his own spiritual awakening. John's poem, which he called *The Divine Enchantment: A Mystical Poem*, was a teenager's examination of religion, his first attempt at grasping the mystical. It also underscored what he was learning in his study of Roman and Greek poets: facts may change, stories may evolve, but truth is ancient and universal. The key to understanding the present can be found in the past.

With Tennyson still his model, John, now sixteen, wanted to write something momentous. Over the course of a year and a half—he had started it not long before "The Tentiad"—he worked on the poem, fashioning a ten-part narrative of more than a thousand lines. "Often I wakened in the night to light my little coal-lamp and work awhile in the enchanted silence of the sleeping house."[60] It was an ambitious and difficult subject, and it stretched John far beyond his gifts and experiences at the time. He used a variety of forms, among them blank verse, Spenserians, tetrameter, and heroic couplets.[61] The writing was inconsistent, often sounding exactly like what it was: a teenager trying desperately to sound like a master. At times, however, John created beautiful images: an ancient prophecy that the savior would come "like sun at dead of night."[62] He described evening as "dusky daughter of the Day."[63]

The second part of the book, "Enchantment," at 270 lines the longest section, recalls John's own enchanting dream, the fevered push that had sent him headlong into a life of poetry:

And soon from out the brilliance sprang anew
What should be voice, for it was eloquent
Beyond all speaking; yet it rather seemed

A new-born element, that steeped the soul
In profound knowledge, suited unto it
As ear and eye are formed for sound and light:
And so flowed forth the mystic, lucent words
Unto the silent question of her soul.[64]

The Divine Enchantment allowed John to explore themes that were beginning to occupy him, among them "the interrelation of all living things" and "the element of fierce strength in nature," and to serve a self-imposed apprenticeship by writing long, sustained if not entirely successful poetry.[65] "I developed the idea of a universe which might be likened to a vast brain, haunted by a dreaming mind, whose dreaming was creative—all of us and our doings being details of the Cosmic Dream."[66] He was seeking his own spiritual path, he told a reporter years later.[67]

While John worked on *The Divine Enchantment*, he finished both the professional teachers course and the scientific course at Nebraska Normal College. In that time he completed four terms of grammar and six of mathematics; two each of political science, general history, and German; and one each of geography, philosophy, rhetoric, literature, and science, receiving only three final grades below ninety. He was fascinated by grammar and was for a time the only student enrolled in German.[68] In a literature course John read Hippolyte Adolphe Taine's monumental *History of English Literature* and accepted the author's position that the works of great men stretched, in a line, back into history.[69] In Taine, John first read the stories of Sigurd and the French epic poem *The Song of Roland*, and he learned more about his idol, Tennyson. Having carried his copy of *Idylls of the King* into the sugar beet fields, John must have been delighted when he read Taine's opinion that "the favourite poet of a nation, it seems, is he whose works a man, setting out on a journey, prefers to put into his pocket."[70]

John's favorite subject in school was Latin, and he studied it in seven of the ten terms he was there.[71] Reading the Latin poets, John believed, put him "on the great highway of time at last, with all the enchanted classical world ahead of me, and mighty Virgil like a towering peak in the far offing yonder."[72] Later he described his early encounters with Virgil's *Aeneid* as "being at the gate of a splendid world, the key to which only a few might have."[73] John had hoped to continue his studies at the University of Nebraska in Lincoln, but when he graduated from Nebraska Normal in the summer of 1897, he could not afford the tuition. In fact, though his graduation photograph shows him holding a rolled diploma, it was a prop: he did not even have the four dollars to spare for the real one.[74]

The next January John turned seventeen, and soon after, he finished *The Divine Enchantment*. That summer he and John Chaffee took the train to Kansas City, partly to find work, for jobs were scarce in Wayne, and partly to have one final youthful adventure, but mostly to find a publisher for his poem.[75] It took John a week to gather up the courage to call on the one publisher he found when they got there, a firm called the Hudson Publishing Company. When John told a man at Hudson that he had written a book-length mystical poem about Hindu religion and Vedanta philosophy, he was quickly turned away. The Hudson Publishing Company did not print poems, he was told, only pamphlets, catalogues, and telephone directories.[76]

By this time the two boys had less than five dollars left between them.[77] In 1898, however, a fine dinner could be found for a dime, and their only luxury was taking the city's cable cars, at a nickel a ride, to visit scenes from John's childhood. Still, before long, their money ran out. They tried washing dishes, and they sold an extra pair of pants. They tried riding the rails as hoboes to Sumner, Missouri, where they had heard there were jobs cutting hickory timber for ax handles, but after a rain-drenched trip on an oil tank car, they discovered that the hickory timber, like them, was soaked, under water. Waiting for morning to begin making their way back to Kansas City, they were arrested and jailed for vagrancy. The next morning, released without being charged, they began their week-long walk back to Kansas City, along the way being tutored by a pair of professional hoboes in the art of begging for food. They told the boys to skip the homes of the rich. "Stick to the nice little places that maybe needed a bit of paint and had flowers blooming in the front yard," the boys were told. When talking to the lady of the house, call her "ma'am."[78]

Once back in Kansas City, John was able to find temporary work as a marble polisher in a tombstone shop. Eventually the boys earned enough money to get to Omaha, where John mailed *The Divine Enchantment* manuscript, his "most precious possession," to his mother in Wayne. Then the two walked the last hundred miles home.[79]

His last boyhood adventure now behind him, John set about finding a teaching job. Only six years earlier Nebraska had enacted a compulsory school law that guaranteed all the state's children the opportunity for a common school education, and by now most of them were attending a one-room school with a single teacher.[80] In December 1898 John Neihardt, not yet eighteen years old but a normal school graduate, began teaching outside Hoskins, Nebraska, twenty miles southwest of Wayne.[81] He was paid thirty dollars a month for four months.[82] "The district would furnish corncobs for fuel, and I'd do the janitor work myself," he remembered.[83] John was young and small for a college graduate, and he was even younger and smaller for a schoolteacher, barely five feet tall and weighing no more than 120 pounds.[84]

The start of the District 77 school year was postponed until December because a number of the students were needed in their families' fields until corn husking was finished.[85] During the last night of November 1898 it began to snow, and the next morning, the first day of school, as John walked to the one-room schoolhouse building set at "a lonely crossroads," the snow continued to fall. Later in life he remembered worrying about how he was going to deal with the older boys who would be in his school, students he expected would be bigger than he was. "I felt much better after I had started a fire in the schoolhouse," he remembered. "There was something reassuring about the oversize cast-iron stove that stood in the center of the otherwise cheerless schoolroom."[86]

More than twenty boys and girls attended the school, assigned to desks of increasing size from the front of the room to the back, and John was expected to teach them the full range of elementary school subjects. And yet, when he looked back on his time as a country school teacher many years later, one of the few stories he chose to tell about the experience was how, on this first day, he had gained and maintained control over the boys who stood taller than he did. The snow had continued to fall, and, feeling he was losing control of the students, he took them outside for an impromptu snowball fight. The bigger boys challenged John, of course, testing him, but by capitalizing on his strength and a trick wrestling move he knew, he was able to subdue the boys and win their respect. As John remembered it, from that time on, he was in charge of the schoolroom.[87]

He returned to teaching the following fall at another Wayne County country school, District 55, first a two-month term beginning in August 1899, then a four-month term beginning in December, all at a raise in pay. But before he moved to District 55, John tried again to find a publisher for *The Divine Enchantment*. He targeted the Macmillan Company in New York, and wrote, in pencil, a letter in which he asked them to read the manuscript "with a view to publication at your hands." Macmillan passed.[88] John then turned to James T. White and Company, another New York publisher, which agreed to publish the book at John's expense: five hundred copies for $250. John had $50 saved, and his uncle George co-signed a note at one of the local banks so that John could borrow the other $200, roughly equivalent to $4,000 today, which it took John several years to repay.[89] John wrote a brief preface and glossary, and early in 1900 *The Divine Enchantment* by "J. G. Neihardt" was published. Bound in yellow with gold lettering, the five-by-seven-and-a-half-inch book contained forty-six pages.

Though the book was not widely reviewed, such criticism as appeared— for example, the *Albany Times-Union* in New York found it to "speak exceptionally well for his imagination," and the *Pittsburgh Times* in Pennsylvania found the poem "lofty in tone"—was good enough to persuade John, who had not really enjoyed teaching in a rural school, to give up his day job.[90] His sister Lulu was teaching school in Bancroft, Nebraska, less than forty miles away, and John's mother and other sister were moving there as well. He decided to join them. He was going to devote himself to writing.

In the summer of 1898 while John was on his Kansas City adventure with John Chaffee, a letter had arrived from his father. "I desire not to create emotion, or a pathetic strain of thought," Nicholas wrote to his son, "but have spent many a sad hour in the seven last years." After leaving his family, Nicholas had lied about his age, lowering it by twelve-and-a-half years, and had enlisted in the Fifth Missouri Volunteer Infantry with hopes of seeing action in the Spanish-American War. He signed the letter, on stationery from Camp George H. Thomas in Chickamauga Park, Georgia, "your ever-loving Pa-pa, pop-oo, dad, nickie &c, &c."[91] Nicholas wrote to his daughters too, and it is clear that John at least wrote back, beginning a sporadic correspondence.

That fall, less than two months after John returned to Wayne, Nicholas was back in Kansas City. "I am having a good time, nothing to do, plenty to eat and I have a really good cot of my own upon which to sleep and plenty of good cover, too," Nicholas wrote. The only thing that would make his life even better was if his son would come to see him. "Johnnie, I wish you were here a few days to see me and the soldiers."[92] John did not go. When the Volunteers were mustered out in late 1898, Nicholas quickly signed up with the Twenty-Second Infantry headed for the Philippines.

The next February, before John was finished teaching his first country school term, Nicholas was on his way to Manila. When his troop transport stopped in Honolulu, he wrote again to his children, offering first a travelogue extolling the exotic beauty of Hawaii: "The cocoa tree grows tall and slender, having few limbs if any, but the leaf is from a foot or so, to 6, 8, 10, 12, even 14 ft or more . . . in length, about a foot broad or so." But mostly he wrote about his love for the military, an idealized view that he passed on to his son, and in one passage he offered an ode to a battleship: "That magnificent, that glorious, that heroic craft, that great traveler, the *Oregon*, is anchored here, and with about four hundred sailors welcomed us with a salute, and a thousand voices echoed from the *Ohio*. O, how I love that, one of the greatest of ships, the *Oregon*."[93]

Once *The Divine Enchantment* was published, John sent a copy to his father, then stationed in San Luis. They corresponded about the possibility of John visiting Nicholas as part of a tour of the Far East, but neither could afford such a grand trip. Nicholas, who still thought of John as "little Johnnie," was proud of his son and concluded his letter by saying so: "I am so filled with awe, and wonder, to learn of your wonderful stride in education, and your literary work, that I know scarcely what to think or write."[94] But he chastised his son for not including more in his letters about his sisters, who clearly were not writing to their father. What John may have written in response is lost. After two years of letters, Nicholas once again fell silent. John, then only nineteen, never heard from him again.

If John had wanted to do so, he could have reported at least one piece of personal news to his father. John had discarded one of the few things his father had given him: his middle name. When he decided to try to make his way in the world as a poet, he did not want to wear another poet's name as part of his own. He had discovered he might be related to a Prussian field marshal, August Graf von Gneisenau, and he liked the idea of being connected to a military hero.[95] Since boyhood, stories had been a part of John's life. He had heard them from family, tales of his ancestors' westward migration, of the hardships they faced, of the battles in which they had fought. He had heard them in Kansas City, tales of the old Northwest from the former trappers and traders along the Missouri River docks and classic tales of Greece and the Far East from the parents of his first friend, Dick Scammon. At school in Wayne he had read more stories, tales of heroic men like Roland and Sigurd. Now, nearing the end of his teenage years, he was determined to become a writer, a poet, a teller of stories of his own making. A middle name may be of limited value, most often represented by nothing more than a single letter. But to young John Ncihardt, the change was profound. He was moving to Bancroft as a new man: John Gneisenau Neihardt.

3   A BIG-CITY ADVENTURE

To the Omaha Indians who lived nearby it was Unashta Zinga, the "little stopping place," because trains paused there to refill their water tanks. In the late 1870s, when Ford and Deborah Barber, homesteaders from Maine, decided they were too modest to let the town growing up around their cabin be called Barberville, residents chose instead to call it Bancroft. No one has ever been quite certain whether it was named for George Bancroft, the American historian and former navy secretary, or George Bancroft, a civil engineer who lived nearby while the railroad was being extended through northeast Nebraska.[1] In 1900, when John Neihardt moved there with his mother and sisters, the town's population was still nine years away from reaching its peak of one thousand residents. Nestled atop the rise of a low hill, Bancroft, like Wayne, had half a dozen churches and an opera house. Though it also had a wood-planing mill, a flour mill, and wagon makers, it was best known as a rather rough reservation town, being situated on the edge of the Omaha Indian reservation. Neihardt would remember it as "a fighting town," where on Saturday nights arguments would spill into the streets. "It was at the edge of the old pioneer period. . . . When the West was the West."[2]

Lulu Neihardt, now twenty-three years old, secured a teaching job at Bancroft High School in 1900, and that September, Alice rented a house big enough for the whole family just a block and a half from the school. Grace was about to turn twenty-two, and John, fresh from his third term of teaching and having published his first book, was nineteen. Though Neihardt was cheered by the reviews of *The Divine Enchantment*, he soon found it flawed and embarrassing. Within a year of publication John burned most of the copies, just as he had burned his earlier "Stubble-Haired Boy" and "Cave Man Trilogy." "They kept the kitchen stove going for about two weeks," he later told a friend.[3]

While he found the work he had produced so far to be substandard, he had no doubt it was the work he was supposed to do. His apprenticeship now in ashes, John wasted no time getting started on both new poetry and prose. In and around Wayne, even as he taught school and worked on *The Divine Enchantment*, John had continually written short lyric poems and experimented with writing short stories. Now a full-time writer in Bancroft, he focused on lyric poetry as his most promising path.

He had barely settled into his family's new home in Bancroft when he received word that a poem he had written the summer before he left Wayne, "The Song of the Hoe," had been accepted for publication in the *Youth's Companion*. The tabloid newspaper had offered him fifty cents a line for it—thirty-six lines meant eighteen dollars—and for the first time he was a paid poet.[4] The main audience of the *Youth's Companion* was young people, and at the turn of the century it boasted more than half a million subscribers, more than fifteen thousand of them in Nebraska.[5] John would have recognized it as the journal that published stories by Laura Everingham Scammon, mother of his Kansas City playmate Dick Scammon, as well as such well-known writers as Jack London, Sarah Orne Jewett, and O. Henry, and such poets as Edwin Markham and Katherine Lee Bates. It would soon publish a poem by another writer with a Nebraska connection, Willa Cather.[6]

In "The Song of the Hoe," published that fall, John imagined a day's work in the potato patch as told by a hoe being wielded by a young man, with a wife and children. The idea for the poem came to him while he was hoeing potatoes, the rhythm of the work suggesting to him the music of verse, and he tried to capture the sounds of slicing, shuffling, and scraping

made by the hoe. He later told a newspaper reporter he had written the
first lines of it on the blade of the hoe itself, not having any paper handy.[7]

> "Chugity, chug, chugity, chink!
> Now that was the sound of a stone, I think;
> But there's many a stone on which to catch
> In life's half-acre potato-patch;
> Chugity, chinkety, one more row."
> > This was the merry lilt of the hoe,
> > All of a sultry day.

> "Chug, swish;
> Oh, how I wish
> That the sun would tumble faster;
> For I almost crack with the weight on my back
> Of the hand of my sturdy master!
> But ah! he has measured the length of my shade,
> He is cleaning the clay from my ringing blade,
> And now for the cottage that we well know."
> > This was the cry of the happy hoe,
> > Under the fading day.[8]

The rhythm of motion and the accompanying sounds of slicing steel
inspired John again one bitterly cold night that winter while he was
ice-skating with friends. The stars shone bright enough to cast shadows
but apparently not bright enough to let John see a hole where the town's
icemen had already cut out blocks to sell. John fell through the ice into
the frigid water. In the poem he wrote later, "Skating Song," the skater
suffers no such humiliation:[9]

> "Clink, hiss, O flight, O bliss,
> The frozen winds are slow;
> The spirit of Speed from Heaven is freed,
> To frolic to-night below;

"I have breathed a god into mortal feet,
And whispered a song in their pulses' beat,
And they shall be fleet, for flight is bliss,
Clink, clink, hiss."

Into the empty calm we rush,
With the weight at our backs of the heavy hush;
And we fly like gods of the wingèd heel
Through the stinging air on the singing steel.[10]

The *Youth's Companion* bought and published "Skating Song" as well.

Being paid for two poems in such short order strengthened John's confidence. These poems, less ambitious than *The Divine Enchantment*, solidified his focus on shorter lyrics. He must have believed his poetry was improving because, though he never included either "Song of the Hoe" or "Skating Song" in his later collections, neither did he burn them. In these two poems Neihardt had worked from personal observation, and he tried to build on that foundation.

In a third poem, also soon published in the *Youth's Companion*, "Song of the Turbine Wheel," John once again imagined himself as an inanimate object, this time a water turbine wheel deep beneath a flour mill, working where "nobody sees it, it never sees the sunlight, but it makes flour."[11] In this poem, written nearly a year after John moved to Bancroft, he moved beyond simple sounds and rhythms and embodied the turbine wheel to make a larger point about society: the workers responsible for progress often miss out on the fruits of their labor. The water that turns the wheel comes through with stories of green grass, blue skies, and whistling fishermen, but the turbine wheel is stuck below in the dark, working without break, without light, without a chance to enjoy the things the water has seen. It marked his first step out into the larger world, one where he found "the will of the Mill be done," and it contained the initial rumblings of his interest in socialism. For the wheel, the real worker in the poem, there is no enjoyment, only back-breaking labor.

Hearken the bluster and brag of the Mill!
The heart of the Mill am I,
Doomed to toil in the dark until
The springs of the world run dry;
With never a ray of sun to cheer
And never a star for lamp!
It cries its song in the great World's ear—
I toil in the dark and damp.[12]

In each of these early poems John took his personal experiences—an afternoon in the sugar beet fields, a late-night skating party, the idle musing about the mill's wheel—and set them to the ancient music of rhythm and rhyme. They were still the work of a beginner and easily forgettable. But "Turbine Wheel" served as a dividing line: Neihardt wrote it as a teenager, and it was published for young people. But it was also the earliest of his work that he would include when a collected volume of his poetry was published. He was now twenty years old, his rough and impoverished childhood and adolescence behind him. He was still living with his mother and sisters, but he was in a new town, one where no one remembered him as a boy.

During his first months in Bancroft, Neihardt worked on a lengthy poem—103 stanzas—called *Twilight of the Gods*. Neihardt believed that man created God, not the other way around, and in this poem, which he had started while living in Wayne, he had all the gods of history parade by in review. "I can see it now," he remembered years later, "the flowing host of gods that lonely man, lost in the cosmic mystery, created in his need. . . . Slowly they passed before me, one by one."[13] That October, Neihardt wrote to the Macmillan Company in New York about publishing the poem.[14] He reminded the publisher again the following February about the work, but Macmillan chose not to publish it.[15] A short time later, discouraged, Neihardt destroyed the manuscript.

That fall, 1901, had begun as a pleasant time for Neihardt. A friend, Willard Sinclair, owner and editor of the *Bancroft Blade*, had helped him get a job at the *Omaha Daily News*, one of the daily newspapers in Nebraska's largest city. Neihardt rented an attic room in downtown Omaha, and with oil lamps and a skylight for illumination, he wrote in his free time and imagined himself Victor Hugo in Paris. He recalled it as "a romantic adventure in the big city."[16] The *Bancroft Blade* routinely reported on Neihardt and his city job. "John Neihardt returned to Omaha Sunday morning where he will continue his work on the *Daily News*," the *Blade* announced one week. "Here's success, John."[17]

Neihardt was proud of his job and his town's interest. One night during his first month in Omaha, while a gentle rain fell, Neihardt, who had not lived in a city since he was a boy, tried to capture the images in a poem he called "Rainy Evening in the City," which the *Omaha Daily News* soon published. In it he relished the rain as it helped to quiet the busy city, leaving horses standing asleep in the twilight and a woman hurrying through the streets, trying to keep from getting wet.

I like to have the rain begin
　　When lights are being lit;
The slow rainfall that ushers in,
　　A hush along with it.

I like to see the street become
　　A stream of hazy light;
That issues from the dusk, and dumb,
　　Flows on into the night.

The snarling trolley grumbles past,
　　Its snapping wire glows;
Again where yon pale light is cast,
　　The hackman's horses doze.

In vain the bargain windows wink,
　　The passersby are few;

The lone streets stretch away and shrink
  In dull electric hue.

A footfall! hist! My eye reverts
  Adown the glinting street;
And lo! beneath a storm of skirts,
  The twinkle of shy feet![18]

The poem was a romantic vision of Neihardt's life that fall, but this idyllic life would not last. Almost from the start, his work at the *Omaha Daily News* did not go well. Sinclair had recommended him for the city hall reporter's job based on his ability to write, not report. "I got scooped every day," Neihardt recalled. "I'd wandered about the corridors, a lorn, lost soul, thinking about some character sketch, or some humorous squib for a poetical column, while my competitors went about the offices in a business-like way gathering the news of the day. . . . And when the evening papers came out, I'd learn that there had been a fight over water, or gas, or street paving, and I'd never heard a word of it!"[19] Finally editor Joseph Polcar had had enough, and he fired Neihardt.[20]

Years later Neihardt was certain it had rained the night he was fired. If it did, it was not a gentle, calming rain like the one he had recounted in "Rainy Evening in the City." This was "a slow, chill, sighing rain," and Neihardt spent the evening of his firing alone in his garret room, rewriting his earlier poem, recasting many of the images. In this poem, which he called "Lonesome in Town," a homesick narrator looks out to see only a bleak, uninviting cityscape.

The long day wanes, the fog shuts down,
  The eave-trough spouts and sputters;
The rain sighs through the huddled town
  And mumbles in the gutters.

The emptied thoroughfares become
  Long streams of eerie light;
They issue from the mist and, dumb,
  Flow onward out of sight.

The snarling trolley grumbles past,
　　Its snapping wire glows;
Again where yon pale light is cast,
　　The hackman's horses doze.

In vain the bargain windows wink,
　　The passersby are few:
The grim walls stretch away and shrink
　　In dull electric blue.

A stranger hurries down the street,
　　Hat dripping, face aglow:
O happy feet, O homing feet,
　　I know where mine would go!

For oh, far over hills and dells
　　The cows come up the lane,
With steaming flanks and fog-dulled bells
　　A-tinkle in the rain.[21]

The poem was a rare instance in which Neihardt, who generally did not rewrite, dramatically reworked a poem. In both versions he applied the rain to the evening city scene, but in one it left the downtown cool and quiet, while in the other it became dark and mournful. The light, instead of being "hazy," became "eerie," and it issued not from the dusk but from the mist. And these streams of light, no longer stretching infinitely into the night, now moved quickly "out of sight." Neihardt, by changing these opening lines, altered the mood of the entire poem. The next two stanzas—with the exception of one line—were identical. The only change Neihardt made for "Lonesome in Town" was in the third line of the second stanza: the "lone streets" stretching away became "grim walls." He also ended the poems very differently. In "Rainy Evening" the narrator heard something and looked up. A woman hurried down the street, fast enough that the raising of her skirts displayed just a glimpse of her feet, the final stanza extending the pleasure of the rainy night with the tiniest hint of the sensuous. In "Lonesome in Town" Neihardt switched the gender of the stranger on the street from female to male. Where "Rainy Evening" offered the narrator, who is alone, at least a suggestion of an encounter with this shy-footed woman, "Lonesome in Town" contrasted the narrator, not only alone but lonely, with the wet and scurrying businessman happily hurrying home, presumably to his family. Neihardt then added another stanza, offering in opposition to the dreary city street a portrait of the small-town alternative, an image he recalled from being on his uncle's farm outside Wayne when the cows came in at night.[22]

Before being fired Neihardt had managed to get a few pieces of newspaper poetry published in the *Omaha Daily News*. Two of the poems, "To William McKinley" and "The Man: Funeral Ode to William McKinley," were published a week apart in the *Daily News* and memorialized the U.S. president who had been assassinated that September. The first poem, nineteen lines long, mourned the president and at the same time celebrated the fact that the murderous act brought the country together, even if only in grief.

> Not with the voice of party do we cry,
> Not with the lips that prate of cross or creed
> Nor with the accents of a certain tongue.
> Today we are one party, speak one speech![23]

In "To William McKinley" Neihardt relied on classical references, an approach that would become characteristic of his poetry, comparing McKinley to "Enceladus of the Titan brood" and suggesting that "Time shall roll an Aetna o'er your name." Five days later the *Bancroft Blade*, now Neihardt's hometown newspaper, reprinted the poem, but neither publication must have elicited any comment. "I do not recall the slightest indication that anybody ever read it," Neihardt observed years later. "But I did have the satisfaction of seeing it hiding in the midst of the loud world's recorded agitations."[24]

Neihardt sought to catch the rhythm of the funeral march in the second poem, the twenty-five-line "The Man: Funeral Ode to William McKinley," and in it he offered a glimpse of his ideas about life and death, which would continue to shape his writing. "It is the form that passes, not the man," he wrote. The spirit, he continued, "pines / For new existence that cannot grow cold." Like his first McKinley poem, "The Man" was soon forgotten, and Neihardt never included either poem in any collection. But when the president's assassin, who had been quickly captured and convicted, went to the electric chair that October, Neihardt wrote "Czolgosz," a poem that he would later include in a hardbound collection. This poem, unlike the earlier two, derived its power from a central theme: that both assassin Leon Czolgosz and the state of New York failed to kill what they intended. Czolgosz, a newly minted anarchist, believed the wealthy in the United States were exploiting poor workers. But by killing McKinley, Neihardt believed, "He missed the tyrant's heart at which he struck." Likewise, in executing Czolgosz, the state of New York did nothing to calm the anarchist spirit. "Nor do we kill the Thing that struck the blow!" Though Neihardt could not resist reaching for a historic reference, it was at least an original one: Francois Ravaillac, who stabbed to death King Henry IV of France in 1610.

He murdered! Hasten! Let the Nation kill!
A godly State, we wield the chastening rod.
Dumb in the chair he waits—Oh hush, be still!
Once more a priest insults our patient God!
* * *
The pistol ball wounds not the vaporous mark,
Nor can the dagger pick our prison lock!
Strike Night!—you stab some brother in the dark;
And Henry Fourth survives poor Ravaillac![25]

Neihardt knew people in Bancroft had been following his career, and he was ashamed to return home a failure. "I knew that my fine job in the city had occasioned much comment, kindly and otherwise, around our town," he recalled. "And what would be said if I came slinking home like a beaten dog with dragging tail?"[26] To delay returning to Bancroft, he found work as a busboy at a café downstairs from his apartment, but he was no more successful as a busboy than he had been as a newspaper reporter. One day a number of his former colleagues from the *Daily News* were eating at the restaurant, and Neihardt, naturally, was embarrassed. The situation became unbearable when his boss at the café criticized his work loudly enough for the patrons to hear. As Neihardt later told the story, he stormed out, not even stopping to collect the wages he was due. By Christmas he was back at home in Bancroft.[27]

4   A SENSE OF ALIENATION

Inshtamaza, or Iron Eye, the last recognized chief of the Omaha tribe, was generally known by the name of his father, Joseph La Flesche, a French fur trader. Born in 1822, roughly a hundred years after the Omaha first settled in what would become Nebraska, and later adopted by Omaha chief Big Elk, La Flesche understood the Omahas' predicament. "Before the white people came we thought that the land was ours," he wrote to a Methodist minister in 1878. By then La Flesche knew that white settlers were not going away and that the white way of life would prove powerful. La Flesche worked hard for his tribe, trying to ensure that the Omaha were not mistreated. He argued strenuously that the Omaha had a distinctive culture and manner of living and that white Americans should recognize that all Indians were not the same. "[W]e are unlike," he wrote to the minister. "We Indians are of different nations."[1]

La Flesche continually walked the line between accommodation and defiance, encouraging his people to farm as the neighboring whites did but, at the same time, working to preserve Omaha traditions. "I did not say, 'Abandon your Indian life,'" he told his brother in 1878. "I did not say, 'Live as a white man.' Nor did I say, 'Live as an Indian.'"[2] He believed his people, especially his own children, should respect the traditional Omaha life, but he wanted them prepared to live in a world he felt certain would be dominated by Euro-American culture. He saw to it that his children were educated in white schools; carrying further his ideas of respect for the past and acceptance of the future, they grew up to be some of the most influential Native Americans of their time, among them a doctor, a nationally known lecturer, and a respected ethnologist. Several of the La Flesche descendants lived in or near Bancroft when Neihardt moved there, and as he became acquainted with the family, they introduced him to the life and culture of the Omaha.

Rosalie Farley, the second of La Flesche's daughters, served as the tribal banker. She and her husband, Edward, both taught for a time at the Mission School outside Bancroft, and their home was a meeting place for Indians and whites.[3] Soon after moving to Bancroft, Neihardt met and became friends with their sons Jack and, especially, Caryl, both about his age. With Caryl as his guide and interpreter Neihardt was introduced to some of the older Omaha, and through them he learned about tribal legends and history. He came to admire these elderly Omaha, writing years later that they "were truly pious in the fine old Virgilian sense of love for their land and people and profound reverence for the great Mystery that is central to all religion. Such men were still true to the tribal conception of ethics—a very high conception—and had refused to adopt the white man's vices as they had refused to accept his civilization. They were not 'romantic' beings. They were intensely human, and, if one really knew them, lovable. Certainly they commanded one's respect."[4]

While at Nebraska Normal in Wayne, in late 1896, Neihardt had written a short story, now lost, called "Hot Wind," which was published in the *Sunflower*, a magazine of limited circulation out of Eureka, Kansas. The plot is unknown except that it was inspired by a summer of brutal heat from John's boyhood. "The 'story' did not amount to much," he later admitted, "but it grew out of my experience in northwest Kansas on the upper Solomon when I was with my grandparents."[5]

Now, inspired by the stories he was hearing from the Omaha, he began creating fictionalized accounts for white readers, and he soon sold a series of short stories to San Francisco's *Overland Monthly*, the best-known and most respected literary magazine then published in the West. Beginning with "When the Snows Drift" in August 1901, the magazine published one of Neihardt's short stories every month for six months. Soon after, he began publishing stories in *All-Story*, *Munsey's*, and H. L. Mencken's *Smart Set*. By April 1902 he had written enough stories to seek a publisher for a hardcover collection he planned to call *A Bronze Ophelia*. Once again he wrote to the Macmillan Company in New York. "These stories are taken from the lips of the old Indians," he wrote to the publisher, "and considering the fact that the Omaha Tribe is almost unknown in fiction, I believe you will find some interest in the stories."[6] Macmillan declined.

At a time when Indians were usually stereotyped in stories as either sentimental or murderous, Neihardt's early stories focused on characters who were neither. Generally set in times before Plains Indians first came into contact with whites, Neihardt's stories dramatized the Omaha's everyday lives. His Indians were not simply noble or savage: a generally sympathetic character became resentful, and a cruel warrior ended up showing pity for a bested rival. When Neihardt's stories included white people's interaction with the Omaha, the Omaha liked some of them, mistrusted others, and were taken advantage of by still others. Though he humanized his characters, Neihardt made it clear that the Indians in his stories were not simply white people with darker skin: these people had a different system of justice, a different conception of religion, a different way of looking at the world.

The stories showcased Neihardt's strengths: his affection for the Omaha and his attempts, no matter how imperfect, to bring their culture and religion to light respectfully. But they also highlighted his weaknesses: his veneration of classical allusions; his inclination, no matter his closeness to and fondness for the Omaha, to portray them as primitive and childlike; and his almost exclusive focus on male characters. The action in some of Neihardt's early stories occasionally stopped for what were almost ethnographic details of traditional tribal life, observations of an interested but detached narrator: "On the banks of a creek the Omahas had built their winter village. The tepees were constructed by driving trimmed willow boughs into the ground in the shape of a cone, about which buffalo hides and bark were securely fastened, leaving an opening at the top, through which the smoke of the winter fire might pass."[7] He described ceremonies and rituals: "The drums were placed in a small circle; before each an old man, who had seen many battles ere the eagle glance faded from his eye, sat cross-legged, holding a drumstick in either hand. About these the braves gathered in a larger circle."[8]

He tried, roughly at first, to fashion a voice and style that would allow the Omaha speech to resonate in English. Neihardt's short story characters do not speak broken English, and they are not monosyllabic. He worked to create a sentence structure that mimicked the way the Omaha elders sounded to him and to capture what he viewed as the gripping imagery that colored their language. In "The Look in the Face," published in *Munsey's Magazine* in July 1906, Neihardt writes of a romance involving a man named Half-a-Day, who is so in love with a young woman that he can barely think. "I could not hear the bugs nor the running of the spring water nor the wind in the willows, because my heart sang so loud."[9]

Neihardt did not simply transcribe Omaha legends. He took the raw materials from his conversations with the tribal elders and, by incorporating his own ideas and background and relying at times on his own memories of life on the Great Plains, created his own stories to explore the themes and subjects that represented the most memorable experiences in his life. Chief among these subjects was the power of dreams, especially those experienced by young men. It was at this time that Neihardt began to see similarities between his own fever dream at age eleven and the visions young Omaha boys sought at about the same age. In these early stories, in which characters relied on their own mysterious visions to guide their lives, are found his earliest attempts to make use—and sense—of such dreams. One character, finding himself near defeat, remembered what had once been strong in him: "Ah, it was the Great Dream!"[10] Another found strength in his vision, his eyes growing big "with the dream he was dreaming."[11] And yet another reacted to his dream in much the same way as Neihardt had done: "And then one night I dreamed—or was it a dream? It was rather like waking from a dream."[12] Neihardt's characters often found that a powerful dream could make them feel like strangers among their own people, that they now were going to experience life alone. "Only the Dream walked with him," he wrote in "The Singer of the Ache," and "he sang the songs that ache."[13] Neihardt introduced that story with a line he undoubtedly believed was true of himself as well: "Now this is the story of one who walked not with his people, but with a dream."[14]

Taken as a whole, Neihardt's stories of this time revealed his fascination with isolated characters, his sensitivity about his small size, and his conflicted feelings about the treatment of indigenous peoples caught in the path of what he and many others then considered the natural and unstoppable westward migration of white people.

Neihardt clearly felt an affinity for his Omaha friends. But though he treated the Omaha and other Indians humanely in his writings, he did not rise above all his own preconceived ideas about American Indians. "The Spirit of Crow Butte," a tale of self-sacrifice and honor, epitomized Neihardt's conflict when Europeans and Indians came into contact. He began the story, which related the legend of a band of Crow warriors trapped atop a butte by a group of Sioux warriors, with an intrusive statement attacking the racial prejudices of whites. "Should a European fashion a personification of Martyrdom, it would have a white face. This is a reproach to the blind egotism of individual races."[15] Yet in the same story, which contains no white characters, Neihardt revealed his own stereotypes and his own belief in the monolithic "Indian." "In his own rude and picturesque manner, an Indian loves his home, his squaw, and his brown-faced papooses; but more than these he loves the freedom of the plains, the dash of the hunt, the ecstasy of fight—all that is unrestrained he loves. It were easy for him to die with the shout of the foe in his ears; for this requires animal fury rather than courage."[16]

Neihardt believed that the white race had gone through a similar "primitive" stage much earlier, and that the American Indian tribes—a "child-like people"—were simply well behind on the road to civilization. When Indian characters in his stories came into contact with white characters, the whites easily took advantage of the Indians—though the Indians were almost always in the right. Though Neihardt believed that

Indians had been mistreated by whites—and that at the opening of the twentieth century they were still being mistreated—he also shared the widespread belief that their race was vanishing. "I love the poor devils," he wrote to a friendly editor. "I can not bring myself to see fun in them. They have their rude jokes, it is true; but to me their laughter is ghastly—they are passing away."[17] Neihardt made it clear in one story especially, "The Last Thunder Song," that whereas he admired the Omaha elders, he had less use for the younger members of the tribe. When people in the story gathered to watch a rain dance, the generational difference was obvious: "The old men went to a shrine," he wrote, "the young men went to a show."[18] One of Neihardt's overworked images in his short stories was a stereotypical lone Indian, standing atop a hill, hand to his brow, scanning the horizon.

Neihardt's stories were also weakened by his continual use of classical allusions and archaic language that he had so loved in Tennyson's poetry. Words like "smote," "verily," "vulpine," and "metempsychosis" are sprinkled throughout the stories, as are such references as "a wild Cassandra chorus" and "a bronze Colossus." Reviewers, when they eventually offered opinions on collected editions of Neihardt's stories, criticized him for the "grandiloquent style" in which his characters often spoke, and a *New York Times* review once suggested that in a few years, he might want to reread the stories "with a blue pencil in hand."[19]

Nearly all of Neihardt's stories—whether about the Omaha or not—were written, as he often described it, in a "minor key." The stories, personal tales of love and betrayal, of the aftermath of acts of bravery or cowardice, are mournful and melancholy, and the men—Neihardt's dominant characters were almost always men—are lonely, reflective creatures. Two of his stories, "Mignon" and "The Look in the Face," revolved around the reminiscences of old men, and the tone, not surprisingly, is wistful. Even when a story seemed to call for lightness, Neihardt chose not to answer that call. A "glad song" was sung "in sullen tones."[20] Harvest time, which might have been associated with bounty and celebration, was instead a time of despair, "the brown, drear time."[21] In Neihardt's imagination, even the air was lonesome.[22] And children played "beside the singing streams and in the lonesome places where the silence lingered."[23] Characters rode their horses mournfully; people wailed for lost power "like a fitful night wind."[24] Trails were inevitably long, even "endless."[25] When he gathered his first stories into a collection in 1907, he called it *The Lonesome Trail.*

This melancholy rose, to some extent, from the dark moods that occasionally came over Neihardt. "[A]ltho' I fight against them," he wrote to a friend in 1906, "the blue devils do come at times."[26] The tone also effectively reflected the isolation and seclusion experienced by Neihardt's main characters. Whether he was writing about Indians or mountain men, his other frequent short story subject, Neihardt tended to feature cast-offs, loners, and miscreants. In one story a fleeing criminal, described as "a man of no race," took refuge with a female wolf in a wintry cave, and Neihardt called the story "The Alien."[27] In his stories men were betrayed by women, by other men, even by their religion, and they were left feeling pitted against the world. Sometimes a man's shortcomings—his cowardice, egotism, or hatred—caused him to be cast out from his people. "In lonesome places shall I walk with my hate," Neihardt's character Rain Walker says in "Dreams Are Wiser Than Men"—"I have no longer any people!"[28] And other times a man's misdeeds—often murder—led to his banishment.

Neihardt's fascination with outcasts was personal. "[D]id you ever notice the alien cry in most of my stuff that you have read?" he once asked an editor. "There's a reason for that."[29] Sometimes he felt inferior because of his small size—he was about five feet, one inch tall—and he occasionally explored this theme in his fiction. In "The Revolt of a Sheep" a "little man shook with a passion that seemed grotesque, because it was too big for him."[30] In "The Beating of the War Drums" the primary character was born "no bigger than a baby coyote" and was bullied for his small size—a circumstance Neihardt had undoubtedly experienced himself.[31] Often, though, Neihardt's sense of alienation came simply from the fact that he felt he had nothing in common with the other residents of small-town Nebraska. "You know what these Western towns are, don't you?" he wrote to a friend. "The people are all right, but they have nothing to do with my business. I don't think for a minute that I am so lofty that I am misunderstood; I am simply out of place here; I'm an alien, and always have been."[32]

This idea of feeling foreign to those around him would always wear on Neihardt, and this feeling contributed to his affinity for the Omaha and other Indians, whom he recognized as being likewise isolated from the mainstream. His sense of alienation often led to feelings of superiority—writing was a higher calling in his mind than simply working for a living—but it is clear from these early stories as well as from later writings that being set apart carried a heavy price. Some years later, writing about another author, Neihardt offered a hint of regret: "Likeness is the cement that holds a society together; and to be different is always, in one way or another, a perilous adventure for the individual."[33]

In March 1902, just three months after returning to Bancroft following his failure as a reporter in Omaha, Neihardt accepted a position with J. J. Elkin, a Bancroft lawyer, insurance salesman, and Indian trader.[34] For thirty dollars a month he became a stenographer, clerk, and bookkeeper for Elkin's various businesses. He spent most of his time collecting overdue bills from the Omaha Indians. (Elkin, who would at various times also serve as Bancroft's water commissioner and village clerk, also managed to get some of the Indians' land: when the land allotments on the Omaha reservation were opened for sale in early 1903, he bought the first parcel for thirty dollars an acre.)[35] Neihardt convinced himself the Omaha understood that although he was working for a collector, he was not out to take advantage of them. "The Omahas knew I was not skinning them, that I was just making my living," he told an interviewer years later, "and they liked me."[36]

Neihardt had already come to know many of the older Omaha through the Farley brothers, and many of his best Indian stories had been written before and during his time at the newspaper in Omaha, well before he went to work for Elkin, so it is unlikely that his job offered him new insights into the lives of the Omaha or their interactions with their white neighbors. But his work for the trader likely led to one short story, "A

Political Coup at Little Omaha," published in *Tom Watson's Magazine* in December 1906. Most of Neihardt's Indian stories were somber in tone and set in the days before the Omaha had come into contact with white people. "A Political Coup at Little Omaha," though, is set in the early years of the twentieth century and represents Neihardt's solitary attempt at satire. By creating mischievously outrageous and overdrawn characters, Neihardt seeks to get at the truth of the times. The story is set in a reservation town in Nebraska's third congressional district—which would have included Bancroft—in the weeks leading up to an election. The white voters of the district are evenly split between Democrats and Republicans, forcing the candidates to campaign on the reservation for the deciding votes.

The story is told from the viewpoint of the white majority. "For practical purposes," the narrator explains, "the intelligent white voter ceased to exist, and there was only a slothful, ignorant band of semi-savages who should choose by chance the national representative of educated thousands." The parties' path to victory is simple. "The typical reservation Indian is primarily a stomach," the narrator reports, "and secondarily nothing in particular. Let him fill his belly and he is easily handled."[37] The Democrats distribute meat on the reservation, and it looks as though they have the election in hand, until the local Indian agent, appointed by a Republican administration, announces that a land payment being held in trust by the federal government will be paid just before the election. In the story Neihardt defined such a "big payment" tactic "as the spectacular bow of the Present to the Past, with which Civilization lowers its proud plume and says to the Savage Age: 'Sorry I swiped your land; take that and don't feel sore!'"[38]

By the time Neihardt finished the story and published it, he had long since left Elkin's employ, and he does not spare his former employer's line of work. "These were the inevitable collectors who hang about an Indian payment like a crowd of crows scenting a carcass."[39] All the white men in the story are scoundrels, and the Indians are slyly in control, pretending not to understand English when it suits them and knowing that they stand to be handsomely compensated for their votes by the greedy, unscrupulous white politicians. When the Republican contender eventually speaks to the chief, a young Indian boy is tossed a coin to translate what he has to say. Here, finally, Neihardt gets serious. "These new times are not like the old times. When we old men were young and the bison still bellowed on the prairies, we were strong and swift and wise. Now we are weak and slow and not wise. I cannot understand. It is all like a day when there is fog everywhere. When we were young and fought the Pawnees and the Sioux, there were not bigger, wiser men than Nuzhee Mona [Rainwalker] and Shonga Ska [White Horse]. Look at us now! We are old and slow and we cannot see far to-day."[40] In the end this story of racial politics, as Neihardt tells it, proves that the Indians can connive just as well as the white candidates.

Even at thirty dollars a month, Neihardt must quickly have grown uncomfortable collecting debts on the reservation. He continued to seek writing jobs, helping out at the *Bancroft Blade* from time to time and applying for a position at the *Tribune* newspaper in Sioux City, Iowa, forty miles to the north. The *Tribune* offered him a reporting job, but by the time Neihardt got to Sioux City, the reporter he was to replace had changed his mind about leaving, and no opening existed.[41] "Mr. Neihardt will remain in Bancroft until his services are again needed on the *Tribune*," the *Blade* reported.[42] Apparently they never were.

In January 1902, again not long after Neihardt had returned to Bancroft, Nicholas Neihart, absent from the family for ten years, was discharged from the military, though his family knew nothing of it. If Nicholas had stayed with the Twenty-Second Infantry, father and son would at least have had one last chance of being reunited. The month after Nicholas's discharge, L Company, the unit of which he had been part, was reassigned to Fort Crook in Omaha. That summer the men were marched seventy-five miles from Fort Crook to the Omaha Indian reservation, where the U.S. Army had a rifle range.[43] On their trip back to Omaha late that August, the men spent the weekend camped on the edge of Bancroft, and Neihardt visited the camp. Many of the men remembered his father, a small man they all knew as Nick. Neihardt recorded that the men had nothing but good things to say about his father that day. "He was a good guy," Neihardt later told an interviewer, "and he knew a hell of a lot. . . . They thought he was an educated man." Neihardt gained new knowledge of a father who had finally found himself in his most desired of professions, that of a soldier. Nick's former comrades told Neihardt that when the other soldiers would go on drinking binges, Nicholas would go along, but he would not drink or smoke. Years later Neihardt was clearly proud to report that such wholesomeness had not turned the other men against his father. "[I]nstead of hating him or despising him," he said, "they liked him. He was an independent cuss."[44] When the men of the Twenty-Second Infantry marched off toward Omaha the next day, all traces of Nicholas Neihart once again vanished from his son's life.

In April 1903 *Overland Monthly* published "The Voice of the West," a twenty-seven-line poem Neihardt wrote extolling what he saw as the rise in importance of the American West. The second word of the poem is "destiny," and Neihardt made it clear that he believed the justified and inevitable battle for the West was between humankind and nature, not between people newly arrived and the people who already lived there. In the "fermenting depths" of the western half of the United States, Neihardt wrote, "fervescent futures" awaited. Neihardt believed that the prominence of the "queenly East" was now past, about to be replaced by the "sunrise" in the West. "I feel / The strength for brilliant battles!" he wrote, offering the only suggestion in the poem that the conquering of the West had involved military action. All that keeps it from being a poem about conquest is that those being conquered are not mentioned. Though the viewpoint expressed in the poem was certainly not unusual for the time, Neihardt never included the poem in any collection. Later in life, he could recall only the vaguest details of it, so it is possible he thought little of the poem. Yet it offers an indication of his acceptance, at that time, of this prevailing opinion regarding the settling of the West.

Neihardt, though, was not without experiences to counter this conception. Neihardt had become friends with Thomas Henry Tibbles when

Tibbles and his wife returned to live on a farm outside Bancroft. Neihardt had been drawn to him in large part because nearly everyone else in Bancroft seemed to dislike the man. "[W]e readily became friends," Neihardt wrote, "for he was a lonely man."[45]

Then in his early sixties, Tibbles had been a journalist and lecturer. The next year, in 1904, he would be the Populist Party candidate for vice president of the United States. But what had brought him to Bancroft was his marriage to Susette La Flesche, known to the Omaha as In-shta-the-amba, or Bright Eyes, one of Joseph La Flesche's children. For a time, this woman was likely the most famous American Indian in the United States. She had been born on the Omaha reservation in 1854 and had attended the Omaha Presbyterian Mission School. She then graduated from the Elizabeth Institute for Young Ladies in New Jersey, before returning to teach at the reservation school.

In 1877 the Ponca, a peaceful and prosperous tribe living in South Dakota near the Nebraska border, were forcibly removed and marched to Indian Territory in what became Oklahoma. When their chief, Standing Bear, led a group of Ponca on a return to their homeland to bury his son, he was arrested and jailed. Though Brig. Gen. George Crook, commander of the Department of the Platte headquartered at Fort Omaha, was charged with bringing Standing Bear to justice, he was moved by Standing Bear's predicament and tried to countermand the orders to return him and the other Ponca to Indian Territory. Crook enlisted the help of Tibbles, then an Omaha journalist, to focus the nation's attention on Standing Bear's story.

On May 12, 1879, District Court Judge Elmer Dundy famously declared Standing Bear a man in the eyes of the law, the first time an Indian had been so designated. As such, Standing Bear could decide where he wanted to live.[46] Standing Bear's supporters, hoping to capitalize on the court decision to reform the country's Indian policy more fully, asked Tibbles to undertake a lecture tour of the East Coast. Eventually the tour included Standing Bear himself, with Bright Eyes along as an interpreter. Soon Bright Eyes began lecturing herself, impressing audiences everywhere. While Tibbles was on the speaking tour, his first wife died of peritonitis. Two years later, only months after Neihardt was born, Tibbles and Susette La Flesche were married.

The couple had lived in Bancroft, off and on, for twenty years. In late May 1903, while once again in Bancroft, Susette La Flesche died. Tibbles sent word to Neihardt, who had known Tibbles for about a year, asking if Neihardt would keep him company as he sat with his wife's body at their home. "Of course I went," Neihardt said, and as the body lay in a bedroom, Neihardt spent the night listening to Tibbles recount stories of his life.[47] "Often he would become garrulous, forgetting, for the time, why we were there together," Neihardt said. "At such times he would even recall funny incidents and laugh heartily. Then suddenly he would remember what had happened and we'd go into the bedroom to look at her again."[48]

Tibbles had written an account of Standing Bear's trial, *The Ponca Chiefs: An Indian's Attempt to Appeal from the Tomahawk to the Courts*, in 1879. Nearly one hundred years later the book was reprinted, with an introduction written by Neihardt. In that introduction Neihardt explained how he had known Tibbles during his later years in Bancroft. "I greatly admired his indomitable, crusading sprit," he wrote. "When his Omaha Indian wife, the once famous Bright Eyes, died, it was my privilege to spend with him and his dear one the long last night before the burial. During that time of bitter-sweet remembering I heard from his own lips how the two had worked together for the rights of a people in the dear dead days when this valiant little book was new."[49]

Neihardt held onto these conflicting ideas about American Indians and their place in the nation's history for years, never appearing to struggle to make sense of the conflict. At this point in his life, he admired many of the Indians he knew and respected their traditions and their religion, and yet he still accepted—even believed in—the idea of Manifest Destiny.

5 A POWERFUL
   ENDORSEMENT

During the first ten years of the twentieth century, Bancroft's population peaked at nearly one thousand residents. John Neihardt, in his early twenties, tried hard to fit in. He joined the Masons and in 1903 was among the men chosen to represent the local lodge at a reception in nearby Beemer, Nebraska.[1] Later that year he was elected secretary of the Bancroft Republican caucus and selected, along with seven others, as a delegate to the Republican county convention in West Point, the county seat.[2] As chronicled by the poetry he wrote at the time and by frequent coverage in the *Bancroft Weekly Blade*, it was clear that he had plenty of friends among the young men and women of the town.

Neihardt was enjoying himself, but he had yet to find consistent employment. In September 1903 he was set to become editor of the *Democrat*, a weekly newspaper in nearby West Point, but the job offer fell through.[3] Then two weeks later came an announcement in the *Bancroft Weekly Blade*: a group of local businessmen, including Neihardt's old boss J. J. Elkin, had joined together to buy the *Blade* and install Neihardt as the new editor and manager.[4] Neihardt announced in the newspaper that same week that the *Blade* would remain a Republican paper. "It will, however, endeavor to be a newspaper first of all," he wrote, "and a political organ after."[5]

Immediately he made changes: he shortened the name to the *Bancroft Blade*; he moved to the front page the "Local News," the country weekly staple that chronicled the routine visits and activities of local residents. He began to feature local articles on the front page, including coverage of the town baseball team and the county's state fair entries; and he added a paid column of business cards down the left side of the front page. The newspaper still carried many standardized state, national, and international articles, but now it had a slogan—"Better is one jolly than one hundred knocks"—suggesting it was likely to favor good news over bad.[6]

Neihardt was quick to trumpet his editorial independence. "The fact that a man's father voted the straight republican [sic] ticket ever since he wore long pants," Neihardt wrote in an editorial only three weeks after promising to remain a Republican newspaper, "is not admissible evidence that that man will be an excellent public servant."[7] He used his editorial page to tackle issues of all sorts: He pushed for an opera house in Bancroft and called attention to the eighty-fourth birthday of Susan B. Anthony, writing that "never in the history of the world have so many years of a woman's life been spent to such noble ends."[8]

Neihardt's editorials afforded him his first opportunity to address an issue that he promoted throughout his life: what he came to call "the higher values." In praising the establishment of a musical and dramatic club in Bancroft, he wrote: "The predominating commercial spirit of the time has a fatal tendency—it encourages the too prevalent neglect of the pursuit of the beautiful. . . . What a man is, makes him happier than what he has."[9] Neihardt was unafraid to take stands that must have been unpopular among his readers, as when he praised a Nebraska Supreme Court decision that ordered a school teacher to stop reading the Bible to her students, writing that "unthinking church people" were likely to be upset by the decision. "However," he continued, "it would seem to be directly in accordance with that attitude toward religious liberty which has characterized our country since the landing of the Pilgrim Fathers."[10]

As the editor of the *Blade*, Neihardt received invitations to celebrations in Omaha commemorating the fiftieth anniversary of Nebraska's statehood and in Fort Calhoun, Nebraska, to mark the visit, one hundred years earlier, of the Lewis and Clark expedition. There Neihardt and other attendees met Z. D. Clark and S. Arion Lewis, descendants of the famed explorers, and heard a speech extolling the virtues of Manifest Destiny.[11]

Being a full-time newspaper editor did not mean Neihardt had given up on poetry. Just in time for Christmas 1903, he took advantage of his access to the hand-fed press at the *Blade* to print five copies of a little book of poetry he called *A Bundle of Myrrh*, the title of which came from a line in "Song of Solomon": "A bundle of myrrh is my well-beloved unto me; he shall lie all night betwixt my breast."[12] He typeset the poetry himself, ten lyric poems he had written since moving to Bancroft three years earlier, and bound the collection in chamois skin.

Though they were much better than his earlier verse, the poems were still clearly the work of a young poet. In this short collection Neihardt's persona was already available in sharp relief: his worshipful attitude toward women, his allegiance to the classics, and his unbridled ambition. In some of the poems, especially one he called "I Would Sing as the Wind," he heralded his entrance as an energetic poet, announcing he would sing "as the Storm whipped by Lightning" and seek to create poetry as "Artless as Winds in their gladness or Winds in their anger!" He continued: "For I am a part of the Prairie—part of the Wind and the Lightning! / I love as the Prairie would love: as the Storm would hate, I hate!"[13]

Neihardt made it clear from this first poem that he intended to write forceful poems: he had big dreams. He had lived on the prairie, and he had seen storms form in the distance, then roll ever closer. Power poured across the prairie, dark and desperate, but the persistent winds also carried rejoicing relief. He wanted his poetry to command the strength of those extremes. Poetry was a serious undertaking for Neihardt, who continued at times to fight despair, and he questioned, in another *Bundle* poem called "Lines in Late March," whether truth, at least a poet's truth, inherently held such bleakness.

I used to seek the dark and found much of it.
Is there in truth much darkness?

Have the meadow larks lied to me?
Have the green grass and the blue sky testified
  falsely?

Spring would always refresh Neihardt, and he would come to write many poems about it. "Lines in Late March" called him outdoors and sought to brighten his outlook with its maple buds and meadowlarks. The poem started off defiantly—"I whistle: why not?"—but softened before the last lines to an almost pathetic uncertainty:

I want to trust the sky and the grass.
I want to believe the things I hear from the
  fence posts.
Why should a maple bud mislead me?[14]

The most memorable poems in *A Bundle of Myrrh* are the ones that focus on Neihardt's "fevered blood and selfish lust," as he would eventually characterize his search for love and meaning.[15] Neihardt was not quite twenty-three years old, and he was enjoying being a young man. In one poem, the erotic "A Witless Musician," he examined what occurs when a young man first touches a woman, "with that divine thrill in my finger tips, / That reverent nervousness of the fingers."

I am a musician for the first time!
I have found an instrument to play upon!
She is my violin. She is my harp.[16]

Again, Neihardt opened the poem with a strident certainty: The narrator, a young man, is a musician, the young woman merely an object, an instrument upon which he can play his tune. A melody has lain dormant in the woman and he—only he—has found it. Soon, however, this young musician discovers he has awakened a song he does not fully understand or control. He is "a witless musician," stumbling only by chance on the melody, which then carries him away, overwhelmed. "A Witless Musician" and others of these early poems were simple, often overstated, but they captured the reckless innocence of young love.

Neihardt kept one copy of the self-made book and gave copies as Christmas presents to his mother and two sisters. The fifth copy he gave to Bancroft's pretty young assistant school principal, Emma Engle, then the primary object of Neihardt's ardor. She had returned to Bancroft that fall, after spending the summer with her parents at their home in Michigan, and she and Neihardt remained a couple for much of the next two years, until their relationship failed to survive her move a hundred miles south to Plattsmouth, Nebraska, where she became assistant principal in the fall of 1905.

Neihardt found many of the activities of small-town life—and chronicling them in his newspaper—mundane. After less than a year and a half as editor and manager of the *Blade,* he announced on January 20, 1905, that he was resigning. "I was not fashioned for the pleasant and flowery path of a country editor," he wrote. "I can not bring myself to place an epochal significance upon the fact that Miss Somebody 'went to the next town Saturday' or that Willie Brightboy 'has been very ill with the mumps.' I concede that this peculiarity amounts to incapacity." A friend recalled that Neihardt simply did not like the job very much. "Neihardt didn't fancy going down to the train to see who had gone away or who was coming in," his friend said.[17] Serving as the newspaper's editor, Neihardt told his readers, meant struggling between pleasing the public and pleasing himself. "Months ago I was conscious of failing miserably in both."[18]

Neihardt fired off a final shot before giving up the soapbox of the editorial page, however. In a front-page editorial published in his last edition on January 27, Neihardt viciously attacked what he saw as the negative side of small-town life, likely one of the reasons he felt so alienated living there.

> You, who profess religious principles, do you ever go about among your neighbors and peddle hurtful gossip? If you do, then you are a despicable hypocrite and hell is too good for you! . . . You rake up all that is low in the neighborhood. . . . You are like crows, always found near something putrescent. . . . You have HEARD something! You rush over to your neighbor and tell it. You do not wait to learn the

truth. You might thereby lose a chance for malice. And malice is your business. . . . And then the very next Sunday you are seen sitting in your pew in church with a come-to-Jesus look plastered all over your inferior physiognomy! Who has not heard you pray? How can a malicious gossip have the face to talk to God?[19]

Neihardt's anger suggests he had been the subject of such gossip, and the editorial must have stirred considerable discussion in Bancroft. In those years it was common for weekly newspapers to trade complimentary copies—"exchanges"—with other papers, and the newspapers occasionally wrote summaries, based on the exchanges, of what was going on in other communities. The editor of at least one other Nebraska newspaper, the *Wausa Gazette*, surmised, too, that Neihardt was speaking from personal experience. "Editor Neihardt of the *Bancroft Blade* gave the gossip mongers who profess Christianity a hot shot last week. J. G. evidently has met a few of them from the way he goes after them."[20]

By the first issue of February, the stockholders of the *Blade* had picked a new man to run the paper, and Neihardt devoted himself once again to writing poetry and short stories.[21] In his poetry he continued to seek a focus, bouncing from "To a Cat," in which he pondered the connection between a feline image he had once seen on an Egyptian urn and his own "scratch-scarred" pet, to "It Might Be," a twenty-line lyric in which he explored the eventual loss of youth. In this poem, which he later renamed "It May Be," he wonders, if he were to meet a former lover many years later, whether they would be able to conjure up any of their old feelings and let the "love light up the shadows."[22]

If at age twenty-four Neihardt was still searching for an identity as a poet, he remained comfortable as a writer of short stories. He continued to spend time with his Omaha friends, writing stories that grew out of his conversations with them. In the fall of 1905 he spent a month among them, and in September San Francisco's *Overland Monthly* published another of his stories, "The End of the Dream," in which Neihardt examined the life of an outcast who sounded much like the author himself.[23] Nu Zhinga—Little Man—was an Omaha boy being raised by his mother.

The boy's father, who is absent, was a brave fighter killed in battle. The boy's mother hopes her son will grow up to take after his father, and she keeps his weapons to give to the boy someday. She becomes despondent as the boy grows up, though, because "his heart was not the warrior's." Even as a young man, Nu Zhinga is noticeably small. "His legs were short and bowed, his hips narrow, and upon shoulders of abnormal breadth sat his monstrous, shaggy head," Neihardt wrote. "It was as if he were the visible body of a black spirit's joke, save for his lustrous eyes, that were like two stars that burn big in the air of evening through a film of mist."[24]

The Omaha Indians around Bancroft called Neihardt Tae-Nuga-Zhinga, or Little Bull Buffalo, and the description of Nu Zhinga could have been of Neihardt himself. Like Neihardt, Nu Zhinga "lived in a little world of his own." For Nu Zhinga it was a world of outcasts that included only himself, his mother, a tame wolf, and a crippled girl named Tabea. Nu Zhinga and Tabea, inseparable since childhood, are unable to meet anyone's expectations—in his first battle with the Sioux, Nu Zhinga cries when his horse is killed—and the rest of the tribe scorns them. A terrifying disease hits the tribe, and by the time the tribe's medicine man determines that only a tuft of hair from the head of the white bison can save the tribe, those brave enough to try to obtain the hair are too weak to do so. After a powerful dream, Nu Zhinga, taking his father's weapons and followed by his pet wolf, sneaks off in search of the white bison. Defying all expectations, he succeeds. Though his actions do not come soon enough to save his mother and Tabea, he does save the surviving members of his tribe. Nu Zhinga's people had learned they had been wrong to underestimate the small strange fellow in their midst.

By late 1905 Neihardt had built up a fairly large catalogue of both short stories and poems. Magazines east and west were still happily publishing them, but what Neihardt wanted was a collection between hard covers. He wanted those stories "which contain the most of me" to reach a wider audience.[25] That fall he mailed a collection of his poems to an editor at *Munsey's Magazine* in New York, Robert Davis, and stumbled onto a lifelong supporter. Though Neihardt did not know it when he first wrote to Davis, the New York editor had been born in Brownville, Nebraska.[26] When Davis was just a boy, shortly after Custer's defeat at the Little Bighorn in 1876, his father, a missionary, had taken his family west to live among the Sioux, and Davis grew up to become an ardent supporter of American Indians. Part of his initial willingness to help Neihardt was based on their mutual respect for the country's original inhabitants, and he told Neihardt he was "interested in any man, friendly to the Indians."[27] For Neihardt, Davis became critic, adviser, and, though only twelve years older, father figure. He coaxed Neihardt to make changes in his stories, turned down poems he disliked, and through years of correspondence helped Neihardt refine his own ideas about the craft and business of writing. Neihardt would remain forever grateful. Early on, Neihardt dashed off a short piece of verse to Davis:

> I was a stranger roaming in literary sin;
> Your light shone through the gloaming; I knocked—
>   you let me in:
> You warmed me at your fire, you sat me down to
>   chew,
> And I'm a bloody liar if I don't cherish you![28]

When Neihardt complained about not fitting in in Bancroft, Davis consoled him. "No matter where you are, my friend, you will find the lice of civilization crawling around annoying you," he wrote. "A restless spirit never really gets among his own people, because his own people are equally restless, hustling along the Riviera of life, seldom stopping or looking backward."[29] Throughout Neihardt's long life, he wrote to and received letters from a growing number of editors, writers, poets, and friends, but he tended to concentrate on one primary correspondent at a time. Between 1904 and 1908, the years when Neihardt was gaining a foothold in the literary world, that correspondent was Robert Davis.

Davis had previously worked at the *New York Sun* and at the *New York Daily News* before moving to Frank Munsey's stable of magazines, which then included *Munsey's*, *All-Story Magazine*, and *Scrap Book*. He knew Mark Twain, Stephen Crane, and O. Henry and was credited with having discovered Edgar Rice Burroughs and Max Brand. Years later he ranked Neihardt among his finds. "I don't expect to live a thousand years," he wrote Neihardt, "but when I do pass on I shall recall a few luminous, flashing, permanent stars that I saw come out of the haze in the east and reach the zenith. You're one of them."[30]

Thinking highly of Neihardt's work did not keep Davis from criticizing it when he saw fit. Neihardt sent Davis one of his early short stories, "The Alien," in which the half-Omaha, half-French protagonist Antoine, running from the law, stumbled into a cave to find not only a female wolf but her litter of pups as well. Davis found the wolf pups extraneous and told Neihardt they had to go. Throughout his career Neihardt had difficulty taking criticism, and he resisted making the change. But he trusted Davis enough that he soon eliminated all mention of the pups. "Your letter of late date concerning the wolf story has done me more good than all the other letters I have ever received," Neihardt responded. "I will gladly undertake the changing of the wolf tale, and will drown the litter as soon as they get back from New York. . . . I did like those pups, though."[31]

Neihardt and Davis argued about another of Neihardt's stories, "Mignon," especially about the title character. Davis's half of the argument is lost, but it is clear from Neihardt's response, which Davis kept, that Davis had objected to the characterization of the young French woman Mignon and her seduction of the Indian Yellow Fox as he travels with a wild west show in Europe. "I want you to see why I don't believe what you said about my dear wanton little girl, Mignon," Neihardt wrote to Davis in early November 1906. Neihardt compared Mignon to Flaubert's Madame Bovary, arguing that no one cares for the personality of such a person—"a silly hussy of a country town"—but that it is the creation of the character that readers admire. "In the name of God, my friend, is Literature to be merely a catalogue of the Virtues?" Neihardt implored. "What are we going to do with the other 99% of humanity?"[32]

In the end Davis chose not to buy "Mignon," and it was eventually published in H. L. Mencken's Smart Set magazine. Ten years later Davis tried to take some of the sting out of their disagreements over this and other Neihardt stories. "I never read a story of yours in my life that I didn't think came spontaneously from you, and I know how difficult it will be for you to write, any time in your existence, a particular story to suit particular requirements."[33] Even about "Mignon," when it was eventually included in Neihardt's first collection, Davis found a way, being careful, to say something nice. "I shall read this book all over again and recall some of the unkind things that I said about 'Mignon.' I may be induced to retract. I am willing now to go this far, to wit: If 'Mignon' is the worst story in the book, it is the best collection of short stories between covers."[34]

Davis was no less critical about Neihardt's early poetry. For example, when Neihardt first sent him some poetry in November 1905, a selection of love poems that were fairly racy for the time, Davis's response, while light-hearted, was mostly negative. "A cursory inspection of a few of the verses leads me to the impression that parts of it ought to be fumigated," he wrote to Neihardt. "I know that warm, passionate nature of yours is difficult to suppress, but I think you had a tremendous gall to send this through the United States Mail." Later in the same letter he allowed that two of the poems—"If This Be Sin" and "Let Down Your Hair"—"look like the real thing to me."[35] Over the years Davis would go on to publish a number of Neihardt's poems in various of the Munsey magazines, including two of the early poems that Neihardt sent him in that first group.

Despite his misgivings about many of the early poems, Davis circulated them among his New York friends, including men who became significant Neihardt supporters. Chief among them was Volney Streamer, who had been an actor in the company of Edwin Booth, the greatest American actor of his time—and also the older brother of Lincoln assassin John Wilkes Booth. In the late 1800s Booth deeded his Gramercy Park home to The Players, a gentlemen's club designed to bring the best actors of the day together with the captains of industry as a way of raising the status of the acting profession. Streamer became the club's librarian and curator. Although Streamer wrote literary criticism, he spent much of his time compiling material for small gift books: collections of religious poetry, definitions of friendship, and the 120 British and American novels and seven plays that had drawn their names from the verse of William Shakespeare.

After Streamer first read Neihardt's short poems, in early 1906, he became an immediate and enthusiastic fan. When it appeared, for a time, that Neihardt's poems would not find a publisher, Streamer offered to publish them at his own expense.[36] Neihardt declined the offer, but he and Streamer corresponded frequently that year. In Streamer, who was nearly thirty years older, Neihardt found another father figure—in their correspondence Streamer even addressed the young poet as "Cub" and signed his letters "Dad." In May 1906 Neihardt celebrated his already close friendship with Streamer with a poem, in which he asks rhetorical questions to try to understand the speed with which they became so close: "Were we two souls in the aether / Flung from a central Soul?" and, later, "Oh, how and when / Did we come to the Now and Here?"[37]

By summer Streamer was working hard to find a publisher for Neihardt's poems. "I have discovered," Neihardt wrote to Davis at the time, "that he intends making it the object of his life to see me placed."[38] In August 1906 Streamer took the train from New York to Bancroft to meet Neihardt, staying with him and his mother for two weeks. The two men sat on the lawn outside Neihardt's mother's house in the evenings, and Neihardt was able to hear a trained actor recite not only passages from Shakespeare but also some of Neihardt's own poems. "I learned something about the projecting of a voice from being around him," Neihardt said many years later. "When he'd recite my poetry, I'd think, 'My God, did I write that? . . . [H]e'd make it sound so beautiful.'"[39] Before he left, Streamer gave Neihardt a copy of his book *In Friendship's Name*, with the inscription: "A friend is a fellow who knows all about you but likes you."

Streamer decided that the publishers in New York needed to meet Neihardt, and he offered to pay for Neihardt's train ticket. In January 1907 Neihardt accepted his offer, bought a new suit, and traveled to New York for the first time, staying nearly a month. Streamer and Davis saw to it that Neihardt made the rounds. He ate at Sherry's Restaurant on Fifth Avenue, one of New York City's finest establishments, where he could enjoy Little Neck clams, broiled Spanish mackerel, and Egyptian quail. He frequented the Turkish baths. He dined at The Players club and the Authors Club, which made a special impression. "Looking about the modest quarters," Neihardt recalled twenty years later, "one noted aging faces of famous writers known from childhood. . . . Save for the power of the faces, it might have been a meeting of ordinary farmers. There were cob pipes in that company."[40]

Neihardt also spent time at another gentlemen's club, the Century Association, where he met Louis V. Ledoux, an author, poet, metallurgist, and recognized authority on Japanese prints. Less than a year older than Neihardt, Ledoux quickly became a close friend and confidant; the two spent time together in New York and wrote to each other frequently after Neihardt's return to Nebraska. "When you bring two beings with such different lives as ours have been, into contact, there is apt to be some fire struck," Neihardt wrote to Ledoux only months after meeting him. "But fire fuses."[41]

Early in their correspondence the two men argued about the virtues of free verse, poetry that contains no strict rhyming scheme. Free verse, though it had a long history, was becoming popular in the United States, and at that time Neihardt was a proponent, while Ledoux was opposed, favoring instead a more structured, traditional approach. Ledoux saved the correspondence, and within a couple of years a publisher expressed interest in publishing the give-and-take. Upon re-reading the letters, however, both Neihardt and Ledoux declined to have it published. "My letters do not represent any stage of my development," Neihardt wrote to Ledoux. "They bore me intolerably."[42] Ledoux, in looking over his half of the conversation, decided they had come from "a stilted young prig."[43]

Those weeks in New York were a heady time for Neihardt. "There is a charm about that place that no western city has," he wrote to Davis after returning to Bancroft. "I don't know what it is. I don't believe the New Yorkers know either."[44] While he was in the city two New York magazines published his poems: *Munsey's* used "Come Back," and *McClure's Magazine* printed "Youth's Prayer," later renamed "Let Me Live Out My Years." The poems showcased two of Neihardt's enthusiasms at the time: romance and ambition. "Come Back" begs a lover who has left to return with "the summer in your eyes" and "peace of evening in your quiet ways." "Youth's Prayer," on the other hand, asks that the writer be allowed to "live out my years in the heat of blood," to "go quickly like a candle light," to "let me be a tune-swept fiddlestring / That feels the Master Melody—*and snaps!*"[45]

Although Neihardt was most interested in obtaining a publisher for an expanded version of *A Bundle of Myrrh*, he was also circulating his short stories. Another of the men he met in New York was Rutger Jewett, managing director of the American branch of the British publisher John Lane. Jewett agreed to publish a collection of twenty of Neihardt's stories, to be called *The Lonesome Trail*. At age twenty-six Neihardt was about to move beyond magazine publication. He proudly returned to Bancroft only months away from being the author of a book. For Neihardt, having a strong belief in himself was always paramount, and his success in New York had seriously bolstered his self-confidence.

When *The Lonesome Trail* was published in April 1907, the publisher advertised it as the "most virile and original note since Jack London."[46] The *Washington Post* reprinted one of the stories, "The Nemesis of the Deuces," in full.[47] Reviewers generally found the stories vivid, even charming, but depressing: the *Arena*, a literary and political magazine published in Boston, cautioned, "It is not a volume to be read through at a sitting." The *New York Times*, in a three-paragraph review, agreed that the collection should not be read all at once—"unless one likes to sup on horrors."[48]

But if these reviewers believed that Neihardt's stories were too grim in their portrayal of the people of the American West, another reviewer thought Neihardt had gotten the portrait exactly right, and her opinion came to matter much to him. Susan La Flesche Picotte, another of Joseph La Flesche's daughters and a physician in Bancroft, had read some of Neihardt's stories, and she invited him to come and see her. Greeting him with the name by which he was known among the Omaha, Tae-Nuga-Zhinga, Little Bull Buffalo, she told him she liked his stories.[49] When Robert Davis later asked Neihardt what the Indians thought of his short stories, Picotte was happy to repeat what she had told Neihardt. "As a race," Picotte wrote to Davis, "we have suffered many things of many writers—writers who, with only a superficial knowledge of the Indian character, may have given to the public something 'readable,' but not true to Indian nature. Mr. Neihardt's delineation is accurate and admirable, for not only has he drawn his information from authentic *Indian* sources, but his sympathetic insight into the mysticism and spiritual nature of the race gives him a true understanding of Indian character."[50]

After *The Lonesome Trail* was published, Picotte repeated her praise yet again, in a letter to the *New York Times*. She introduced herself in the letter as a "representative of the Indian race," and she argued that in Neihardt's stories, "there is no overdrawing." "[H]is Indian," she wrote, "is not a bizarre creature of the imagination; neither does he place him on a pedestal, based on sentimentality, investing him with attributes he does not possess. The Indian is flesh and blood, with the same cardinal virtues and the same cardinal sins, and so possessed with the same amount of human nature as the rest of human kind." Picotte noted in particular the story "A Political Coup at Little Omaha," Neihardt's satirical look at the life of the reservation Indian, praising him for this portrait of "the Indian after he has been brought into contact with the white people."[51]

Picotte's endorsement proved to Neihardt, and to his friends in New York, that he was getting the Indian right. He never forgot her support and referred to it often. She was only one person and her unqualified support only one person's opinion, but to Neihardt she was a person who truly counted. Her recommendation gave him a sense of confidence that he would come to rely on in the years—and in the work—ahead.

In April 1907, the same month that *The Lonesome Trail* was published, Neihardt spoke to the Bancroft Woman's Club on the poetry of John Keats, the English Romantic poet of the early nineteenth century. Neihardt had first spoken publicly the year before, when he returned to Nebraska Normal College in Wayne to speak on "Nature and the Significance of Poetry."[52] No record exists of what he said that day, but for his second engagement, the *Bancroft Blade* took the opportunity to cover the young poet's address, in which he focused on ideas he retained for the remainder of his life. Neihardt argued that enjoying nature was what made a complete life. "Those having an abundance of this world's goods may be paupers," he said, "while those in the humblest place may be rich in being able to see beauty in the hills, the sunset, the clouds, and music in the bird's song and rustling of the leaves."[53]

The next month, still buoyant from his success in New York and the publication of *The Lonesome Trail*, Neihardt took his mother to southwestern South Dakota to spend the summer in a cabin near Spearfish Falls. Their cabin was near a place called "The Crossing," ten miles from the town of Deadwood, and Neihardt thought the scenery could be outdone only by the Grand Canyon. "We have a small, rude cabin," he wrote to Davis, "but it keeps the rain out and we have clean beds and good grub."[54] He planned to do no writing while in South Dakota, though New York magazines were still asking him for more stories, instead using the time for reading—Sophocles, Euripides, and some of Trollope, he said—and for hiking. "When one can act, one does not think, and I have walked over 500 miles," he wrote to a friend two-thirds of the way through his stay. "This was all done on wild mountain trails, and there is much to brood over on such walks when one knows the history of the country. I have much material stored away, and faith I shall need it, as I have orders for more stories than I can write."[55] Among the places Neihardt hiked was Harney Peak, the highest point east of the Rocky Mountains and only a little more than ten miles from his cabin.[56]

Although he was not writing during his vacation, he was researching. He had agreed to write a series of articles on the Missouri River for the sporting and adventure magazine *Outing*, published in New York, and he spent some of his time seeking out the history of early steamboating and of the men who helped develop the old Northwest.

By mid-August Neihardt had had enough of vacationing. "I have been having a blue fit," he wrote to Ledoux. "If I were at home, I might make something. But I have established too firmly the precedent of doing no work in the canyon, and my muse is just now giving me the heartless ha ha. But let her beware. I shall hitch her to some big jobs this winter, and she shall work like an Irish washerwoman."[57]

Neihardt had continued to write short lyrics, and he now had nearly three dozen poems he wanted to issue as a book. But he still needed a publisher. Just before leaving South Dakota he wrote again to Ledoux, and for the first time mentioned having consulted a fortune teller. He had seen one shortly after returning from New York, and she told him he had a book of verse in hand that would soon be published. "Now I don't believe in prophecies except as they suit my desires—and this one does!" he wrote to his friend. Her prediction turned out to be correct: in December 1907 the Outing Publishing Company published a hardbound version of an expanded *Bundle of Myrrh*, a selection of thirty-three poems. Neihardt sent copies to his friends in New York, among them Streamer, Ledoux, and Davis. "It does me good to see this little collection between covers," Davis wrote to Neihardt. "When rereading it, I am not prepared to change my opinion, except to confess that I see more beauty now than I did even in the beginning—although it got under my skin in the days gone by."[58] Robert Frothingham of *Everybody's Magazine*, in a letter to the book's publisher, called Neihardt "truly great," and added: "His lines lay hold on the eternal verities. I don't know when I have read anything that has thrilled me as his stuff does."[59] Caspar Whitney of *Outing* magazine sent his copy to Neihardt for an autograph. "I am not, as a rule, a reader of verse," Whitney wrote, "but I must say I have read this little book of yours from cover to cover,—and that isn't merely polite language but the actual fact."[60]

Writer and historian Agnes C. Laut, reviewing the book for the *New York Times*, recognized it as a poet's first collection but said: "You are conscious in every line of great passion and great beauty, as well as the technique that is good because it is unconscious of itself."[61] The frankness of the poems attracted much of the attention, and some reviewers found the poems too daring. "It is hoped," a reviewer for the *Outlook* wrote, "that he will not make the mistake of thinking that nudity is strength, and that in order to show that one is independent and virile he must exhibit all his emotions unclothed rather than clothed upon the imagination."[62] *Putnam's and the Reader* agreed that some readers were going to be put off by Neihardt's explicit poetry. "I suppose that John Neihardt's verse will seem at first, too free," the reviewer wrote. "It seems to be a little antagonizing to some of us who have become very cultivated and thoughtful, to see a man having his own way so, with anything in this world, even with his words." But the reviewer found the poems timeless, imagining how Neihardt's poetry would be read "five hundred years off, with John Keats, Wordsworth, Sidney Lanier, Whitman and the Songs of Solomon."[63]

Neihardt now had two books published to good reviews. As he described the time to a friend years later, "the world was my oyster!"[64] That spring he published two more short stories: "The Brutal Fact," based on a true tale of fur trappers Mike Fink, Will Carpenter, and Frank Talbeau, who for sport used to shoot a tin cup off the top of one another's heads, and "The Parable of the Sack," a cautionary tale of a young greenhorn who heads west to find gold. Neihardt stayed active in Bancroft, serving on the executive committee of the Bancroft Athletic Association and helping to remodel a two-story brick building into a gym.

He also learned that *A Bundle of Myrrh* had earned yet another positive review, this one from a young artist recently returned to the United States. She had written to Neihardt to praise the book, as had a number of other young women, but something about this one piqued Neihardt's curiosity. "Do you know a young lady by the name of Mona Martinsen?—a sculptor, I believe," Neihardt asked Ledoux in May. "It seems she got several works in the Salon last spring. . . . Said to be young and—my imagination adds—very beautiful."[65]

6 A PARTNER IN ART
AND MARRIAGE

Mona Martinsen was a sculptor who in 1908 had recently returned to New York, the city of her birth, after studying for two years in Paris with the renowned Auguste Rodin, creator of "The Thinker" and "The Kiss" among many other pieces of sculpture. She was three years younger than Neihardt, having turned twenty-four just about the time he first mentioned her to Ledoux, and she had experienced a life as different from Neihardt's as could be imagined.

Mona's father, Rudolph Vincent Martinsen, had died when she was only eight years old, just days before Christmas in 1892. At the time of her father's death at age forty-one, Mona's parents had two homes, one at 58 East 54th Street, just west of Park Avenue in New York, and the other, as the *New York Times* described it in an article about her father's death, "a handsome chateau at Gernsbach, near the Black Forest" of Germany. Rudolph Martinsen, born in Russia into an aristocratic German family, had been a financier most of his adult life, working primarily for Boissevain & Company, a firm headquartered in Amsterdam. Later he joined the board of the Canadian Pacific Railway; formed a syndicate that reorganized the Maxwell Land Grant Company, which owned nearly two million acres in New Mexico; and served as president of the Missouri, Kansas, and Texas Railroad. In the spring of 1892 he resigned all his positions except one—he remained president of the Consolidated Coal Company of Wyoming—and spent most of the year in Europe on business. He had taken ill on the steamship home and died of heart disease ten days later in New York. His wife, Ada Ernst Martinsen, and his three children were immediately summoned to New York from the German chateau.[1]

Mona's mother did not have the financial acumen of her husband, and in the years after his death the family fortune dwindled. Still, there was money for Mona to study sculpting. In 1902, at age eighteen, she began her training under sculptor F. Edwin Elwell, curator of sculpture at the Metropolitan Museum in New York. The next year she completed a statue for Elwell called "Motherhood," which he praised in an article he contributed to the magazine *Arena*. "It is a wonderful statue," he wrote, "not unlike Rodin in treatment, but yet thoroughly original, and her own: it has the stamp of her own individuality."[2] Elwell taught her to attend personally to all aspects of her art—even the chopping of clay and the washing of the studio floor, to destroy and forget her inferior work, and to strengthen her hands. He was more than satisfied with the results. "They are the hands of a woman who is doing her own thinking and can destroy as well as create," he wrote. "They are the servants of a brain that sees clearly the larger forms in art, and they do not tire in the search for those forms."[3]

In 1905 Elwell advised Martinsen to study with the best sculptor she could find. She chose Rodin in Paris, and a family friend helped pay for her time abroad.[4] Martinsen recalled her first meeting with the great sculptor: "I walked over to him and said, 'I have come across the Atlantic to see you.' He smiled and said, 'I am all yours, Mademoiselle.'" After examining several of her sculptures, Rodin accepted her as a student. As she studied with Rodin, she mostly worked alone in her tiny, skylit studio just off the Montparnasse and learned to sculpt from memory. "It was Rodin's policy to work with a model in the morning," she later told a reporter, "then rely on memory in the afternoon."[5] In 1907 she was invited to exhibit two works at Le Salon des Beaux Arts, widely viewed as a rite of passage for any artist hoping to work successfully as a sculptor or painter.[6] One was a life-size sculpture called "The Maiden" and the other a bust of a Cuban sugar planter. After the Salon she gave the summer to touring Italy, spending most of her time in Florence and Rome admiring the work of Michelangelo.[7]

That fall Martinsen returned to New York to find her mother, who was searching for ways to make money, trying unsuccessfully to arrange a German-language edition of a collection of short stories she had come across that were written by a young author from Nebraska. When this young writer—John Neihardt—published a book of poetry at the end of the year, Ada Martinsen, uninterested, passed it along to her daughter. Mona, like a number of other young women, was moved enough by the poems to write approvingly to the author, and by the middle of 1908 John Neihardt and Mona Martinsen were writing to each other often. She later said she had been "lured by the *Bundle of Myrrh*."[8] As for Neihardt, he was quickly smitten, and he continued to hound Ledoux to reach out to her.

"Louis, you could do this Mona Martinsen a great deal of good by calling," Neihardt wrote in mid-May. "She is trying to get established in New York, having just come over from Paris where she has lived for some time. . . . I take it that she is very much alone in New York, and if you would call, mentioning my name (we seem old friends) I know she would feel a great uplift."[9] Ledoux, always the faithful friend, called on Martinsen, but he did not fill Neihardt in on the visit fast enough. "I understand you called on Miss Martinsen," Neihardt wrote impatiently before the end of the month. "What the devil did you do to her? What have you to say to me about her?"[10]

Ledoux apparently had done right by his friend. "You certainly did me a good turn," Neihardt wrote soon after in thanks, "and I love you—for this and many other things."[11] As his poems in *Bundle* had made clear, Neihardt believed he was experienced when it came to women. Though his poems of the time were frank about his young, lustful attitude, he almost never mentioned women in his letters to friends. This changed with Mona Martinsen. "Louis, about Miss Martinsen," he wrote late in June, "When I asked you what you had done to her, I was merely being merry in a meaningless way. I know what you did—you told her about me among other things."[12] Neihardt must have been sorely tempted to return to New York to meet Martinsen, but he already had plans for his summer.

Most of Neihardt's short stories had focused on the Omaha and their life near the Missouri River. Many of his non-Indian stories dealt with Missouri River fur trappers and traders. But none of his early writing better established the significance of the Missouri River in Neihardt's personal and literary life than *The River and I*, the book that grew out of a series of magazine articles he wrote in 1908 and 1909, chronicling his boat trip down the river from Fort Benton, Montana, to Sioux City, Iowa. *The River and I* is at times philosophical and reflective and at other times humorous and exaggerated. Written in the days of Teddy Roosevelt, the book reads like a story told around a campfire, punctuated frequently with cries of "bully!"

A group of wealthy sportsmen, led by well-known hunter and leading outdoors writer Caspar Whitney, had purchased *Outing* magazine in 1900 and quickly transformed it into an intelligent, attractive, and lively journal.[13] In early March 1908 Whitney hired Neihardt to travel the Missouri and write a series of articles, offering him eight-hundred dollars for forty thousand words. What excited Neihardt, much more than either the money or the serial magazine publication, was an agreement that the articles would be collected into his first volume of nonfiction.[14] Almost as soon as Neihardt signed the contract, however, Whitney and his partners began to lose interest in magazine publishing. By the time Neihardt finished the trip, the magazine had changed hands, and the articles were published instead in *Putnam's Monthly*, a better magazine with more than 100,000 readers.

Neihardt wrote the first article, "The River of an Unwritten Epic," before he left for the trip, writing of the larger-than-life men who had traveled the Missouri in the early nineteenth century—"big men," he called them, "mighty travelers, intrepid fighters, laughers at time and space," descriptions that seemed to echo those of the men he and his father had met years earlier in Kansas City.[15] Once he had finished the opening article he began planning for the voyage itself. "My head is full of power boats these days," he wrote to Ledoux. "Very soon I will be up in the Rockies getting ready for my toboggan slide down the roof of the continent!"[16]

Neihardt took with him a friend, photographer Will Jacobs, and as an aide a boy from Bancroft, Chester "Chet" Marshall, who would turn sixteen on the river and would be known in the articles and in the book simply as "the Kid." Ironically, Neihardt, who so loved the idea of the westward migration, chose to go to the northwestern end of the river and then to follow it eastward. He and his crew took the train to Great Falls, Montana, a four-day ride from Bancroft, then walked for two days to Fort Benton, the head of Missouri River navigation. They had shipped their baggage—including food, cooking utensils, and an Edison phonograph and cylinders—and the boat they would use. In Bancroft Neihardt had built a motorboat of half-inch oak ribs and cypress planking. "I wanted a boat that would be swift and that would be maneuverable and also able to stand the blow of rocks."[17] He christened it "the Atom."

When Neihardt arrived in Fort Benton that July, he met the captain of a government snagboat, a riverboat that plied the shallow Missouri removing obstructions, who warned him that he would not find a channel that would carry him down the river in his motorized canoe. "He was very stiff and proud," Neihardt wrote in *The River and I*. "He awed me. I stood before him fumbling my hat."[18] Sixty-five days and sixteen hundred miles later, Neihardt looked up from his boat to see the snagboat again. "Crossing her bows and drifting past her slowly," he wrote, "I stood up and shouted to the party in the pilot house: 'I want to speak to the captain.' He came out on the hurricane deck. . . . He was still stiff and proud, but a swift smile crossed his face as he looked down upon us, half naked and sun-blackened there in our dinky little craft. 'Captain,' I cried, and perhaps there was the least vain-glory in me; 'I talked to you at Benton.' 'Yes sir.' 'Well, *I have found that water!*'"[19]

Neihardt had taken to the river that summer hoping to trace the paths of some of his heroes, but he was surprised when he was able to meet one. Grant Marsh, whom Neihardt delighted in calling "the Grand Old Man of the Missouri River," was working that summer as captain of the steamer *Expansion*, hired to carry supplies upriver for an irrigation dam project. In 1876 Marsh had been captain of the *Far West*, the boat that carried to safety the cavalry and Crow survivors of the Battle of the Little Bighorn. Spotting Neihardt in the little boat, Marsh invited him to come aboard the *Expansion*. "A large elderly man, dressed like a farmer, with an exaggerated straw hat shading a face that gripped my attention at once, was looking down at me," Neihardt wrote. "It was the face of a born commander; it struck me that I should like to have it cast in bronze to look at whenever a vacillating mood might seize me."[20]

Another man who merited mention in *The River and I* was Doane Robinson, secretary of the South Dakota Historical Society. Robinson did not figure in Missouri River history, but he certainly figured in Neihardt's appreciation of it. When Neihardt first received the *River and I* assignment, he had written to Robinson for help. "I want historical works on the Black Hills," Neihardt wrote to him in 1907. "Works giving the anecdotal side of the men who developed the Northwest would suit my purpose better than the purely historical." Robinson's response is lost, but later correspondence between the two men makes it clear that he promoted two names above all others: Jedediah Smith and Hugh Glass, both members of the famed Ashley-Henry expeditions of the early 1820s. In *The River and I* Neihardt recounts pulling into Pierre at sunset for a reception given by Robinson. "I felt again the warmth of the great heart of the West."[21]

The summer of 1908 was hot and dry, and as the river levels fell during Neihardt's trip, he and his tiny crew continually jettisoned cargo to keep their boat afloat. When the boat's engine stopped working partway through the journey, the little party resorted to driftwood paddles.[22] Neihardt had counted on the breezes being helpful, but the prevailing winds were from the south, and "progress was slow and difficult."[23] He replaced the Atom midway through the trip with a steel-hulled boat and ordered a new engine—which did not come. "The gods wish to try me, it seems," he wrote to Robinson. He also lost his photographer during the trip. "Way up in the Bad Lands his nerve left him and he got very homesick. At the Yellowstone he left me—went home."[24]

On September 21, after Neihardt and his companions had rowed 1,400 miles against an almost continual head wind, finishing 2,000 miles in a little more than two months, he and the Kid pulled into Sioux City. The river had become his home in a way no town ever had. "Up river when the night dropped over me, somehow I always felt comfortably, kindly housed. Towns, after all, are machines to facilitate getting psychically lost."[25]

In those early years of the twentieth century, America's waterways were a popular topic for authors. G. P. Putnam's Sons, which published *The River and I*, also published books about the Columbia, Mississippi, Ohio, and Colorado rivers as well as the Chesapeake and Narragansett bays and the Great Lakes. Neihardt's conversational narrative, which contained his usual classical references, was the only one of the waterway books of the time in which the author looked at himself as well as the river. "When I started for the head of navigation a friend asked me what I expected to find on the trip. 'Some more of myself,' I answered."[26] In addition to explaining the Missouri and its history, the book shows a man consciously creating a persona for himself. When he sat overlooking the Great Falls in Montana, for example, he wrote: "Most men, I fancy, would have enjoyed a talk with a civil engineer upon that ledge. I should have liked to have Shelley there, myself. It's the difference between poetry and horse-power, dithyrambics and dynamos, Keats and Kipling!"[27]

When *The River and I* was published in 1910, the reviews were generally good. The *New York Times* found it "thoroughly admirable in style and story," but thought it would have been better illustrated with Neihardt poems than by the fifty-one photographs made by his departed friend.[28] The *Nation* disagreed, finding the book "generously illustrated" and arguing that *The River and I* offered a world seen through rose-colored glasses: "[A] balky engine, boiling rapids, sand-banks, mud-bars, head winds, hunger, cheerless days and nights, serve only to spur his enthusiasm, and to add a lustier zest to his song in praise of life in the open."[29] Poet and professor Richard Burton, writing in the *Bellman*, called it "a delightful outdoor book, enjoyable, every page of it, and making you feel that a panoramic sweep of country properly calls for epic treatment."[30] Yet another literary magazine expected the book to "give the conventional city-dweller a wholesome jolt."[31]

One reader who was reacting personally to *The River and I* was Nicholas Neihart, unheard from for years. Although his son did not know until years later, for a time Nicholas lived only 250 miles away at the Soldier's National Home in Leavenworth, Kansas. Nicholas wrote to a brother in January 1910, telling him about John's recently published magazine articles on the Missouri River and proudly noting, "In the magazines he is called The Nebraska Poet!"[32]

Neihardt was gone nearly three months on his river trip, and his mother, who missed him terribly while he was gone, was in Sioux City to meet him when he returned. "I have felt with John's going that the machinery of all the world had stopped," she wrote to her son's friend Louis Ledoux early in August. "His absence makes our little home seem a big empty hall and the silences are deathlike."[33]

Undoubtedly Neihardt himself must have missed his newest correspondent, Mona Martinsen. While he had spent his summer months traveling down the river, she had spent hers on the island of Nantucket, south of Cape Cod, Massachusetts. Neihardt and Martinsen, who each returned home about the same time that September, nonetheless managed to make plans during the summer months. "As to Miss Martinsen—I have some startling information which will be divulged at the psychological moment," Neihardt wrote to Ledoux just four days after finishing his trip.[34] Neihardt continued to be coy with Ledoux about his romance and was slow to tell the whole truth of what he and Martinsen had planned during their fevered correspondence. "Mona intends to come back West with me this winter," Neihardt wrote Ledoux. "We may start for the arctic with the spring breakup—by way of the Mackenzie—or we may go to a ranch in Montana. Write out your sensations upon reading this—if indeed it gives you any—and feel free to write at length and as philosophically as you please."[35] Indeed, when Ledoux finally received the news, it was Martinsen who delivered it. She wrote to Ledoux's wife, Jean: "Do you know that John Neihardt and I are betrothed? Well, we are, though we have never met, materially speaking!"[36]

Their correspondence, in which they discovered that Mona shared

John's views on art and the "higher values," had culminated in a marriage proposal. On Saturday, November 28, 1908, they finally met when Martinsen's train—No. 112 from New York—arrived on track thirteen of Omaha's Union Station. Neihardt was there with a marriage license in his pocket. All he had to go on were photographs she had sent him, but they were enough to tell him that the third person climbing down was his Mona. "A stately young woman of more than average height stepped gracefully through the coach door," he wrote more than sixty years later. "She wore a velvet cape and her hat of like material was almost ample enough to serve as an umbrella, I thought."[37]

Neihardt and Martinsen were married the next day at the apartment of a friend, Keene Abbott, a feature writer for the *Omaha World-Herald*. In addition to the Abbotts and the minister who officiated at the wedding, which Abbott's newspaper described as "an informal event" and as "a partnership in art as well as a nuptial partnership," only one other guest attended: John's mother, Alice.[38] According to Neihardt family lore, Alice had initially opposed the marriage, fearing that Mona, who had been raised with so much, would never fit into their simple lives in Bancroft. John was also the last of her three children who remained at home, Lulu and Grace both having married and moved out of Nebraska, and it is possible that Alice wanted to delay losing him. But she always supported John, and before long he convinced her that he and Mona would make it work.[39]

After the wedding the couple stayed in Omaha until Wednesday evening, when they took the train to Bancroft, where Mona joined John in his mother's house. Neihardt remembered years later that the young man who drove Bancroft's public transportation—a spring wagon fitted with a canvas roof and seats—took them the long way home, down Main Street, so that the townspeople could see the beautiful young New Yorker as he delivered them.[40] After the wedding Robert Davis was sure "that the classic young poet now walking in the town of Bancroft, Nebraska, looks a good deal better with a sculptress by his side than he did when he was accompanied only by a few rhymes in his head."[41]

Eventually Neihardt found an offhand way to confirm the news to his friend Ledoux, finally: "I have been very busy of late on my River series and several short stories. Am working steadily, and enjoying it immensely," he wrote. "By the way, I was married in Omaha Nov. 29th."[42] No matter how hard he tried to downplay the change Mona had caused in him, however, Neihardt could not hide that he was a happy man. Two weeks later he wrote to Ledoux again: "I trust you had a merry Xmas. I think mine was the best Xmas I ever spent."[43]

Immediately after marrying Mona, Neihardt began to consider leaving Bancroft to find a quieter place for a writer and a sculptor to work. Before his first Christmas as a married man, Neihardt told Doane Robinson he and his bride were thinking of moving to western South Dakota. "We want to take up some land in the White Owl country with the idea of creating a permanent place of quiet for our work," he wrote in late December.[44] In 1909 the state of South Dakota was looking for a sculptor to create a statue for the capitol rotunda in Pierre, and Neihardt pushed Robinson to consider Mona for the job. When it became clear that South Dakota was likely to show a preference for a South Dakota artist, Robinson queried Neihardt about their plans to move, and Neihardt was forced to tell him they could not yet afford to do so. "It would be childish to tell you that we would become South Dakotans, as a further inducement to the Committee," he wrote. "Nevertheless, if the commission should be given to Mrs. Neihardt, we would be able to carry out our plan with regard to a home up there."[45]

Mona did not win the commission, and the Neihardts did not move to South Dakota. In the intervening months, John and Mona had changed their minds and were now thinking of moving to Missouri. "I am intending to buy a certain nice little forty acres down in the Ozarks soon," he wrote to Ledoux. "Plenty of woods, springs, fruit trees—peace. And the living is cheap."[46]

Even before he left on his Missouri River trip, Neihardt knew Martinsen was having an impact on his work. "She has had more influence already on me than any woman ever had before," he wrote to Ledoux in June

1908. "I have been doing verse that surpasses everything I have ever done. I am almost superstitious about her."[47] Nine months after their wedding Neihardt remained ecstatic about his marriage. The two had acquired a cat, Bobet, and he was writing poetry, short stories, and nonfiction magazine articles. "Mona and I are perfectly matched," he told Ledoux. "Never a more congenial pair."[48]

Not long after coming under Mona's influence, Neihardt finished an unusual poem in which he recounted a visit he and a friend made to a brothel. In the poem, initially called "House of Death" but retitled "A Vision of Woman," he recounted how he was attracted to a young prostitute when he first saw her in a room loud and garish with light. When they retreated to the privacy of a room and she undressed, however, Neihardt, perhaps thinking of his budding romance with Mona, lost his nerve. Standing there naked, the woman suddenly represented to Neihardt Every Woman, Every Mother. In the poem he tells the prostitute to go to sleep, and he uses the moment to envision a march of all the great women who have lived, an idea very similar to his youthful "Twilight of the Gods."

> I touched you—and 'twas Helen that I touched;
> And in my blood young Paris lived again;
> And all the grief and gloom of Ilium,
> Her wailing wives enslaved to foreign lords,
> Her stricken warriors and her gutted fanes,
> Her song-built towers falling in the smoke,
> And all the anguish of her tragic Queen,
> Seemed naught for one round burning kiss from you![49]

Years later he declined to read the poem for an interviewer, saying it was not representative of him or his work. "I pitied her," he said, "and I lay there wide awake thinking about her."[50] Though "A Vision of Woman" still idealized women, they had ceased to be mere objects, and the poem represented a more mature view than he had conjured in *A Bundle of Myrrh*. When the poem was eventually published, Harriet Monroe, who was about to start her own poetry magazine, called it "vivid and powerful," and cited it as evidence that Neihardt and another emerging poet by the name of Ezra Pound were the leaders of a new movement in poetry, "aware, both of them, of the angel and the dragon, and high-hearted enough to welcome the one and grapple with the other."[51]

The 211-line "Vision of Woman" opened Neihardt's next poetry collection, *Man-Song*, published by Mitchell Kennerley in the fall of 1909. In what would become a lifelong pattern, Neihardt believed this, his latest book, was the best thing he had done. "[E]very line of it surpasses the *Bundle*," he wrote to Ledoux.[52] Mona sculpted a daring design in high relief, which was then photographed and affixed to the book's cover. The cover showed a nude woman and a man wearing only a breechcloth, and it is clear they are John and Mona Neihardt. Their bodies face forward, and she turns her head shyly toward her right arm, which reaches out to touch him, while he raises his head proudly to the heavens. They are standing on a block that reads "NEIHARDT" and are holding up a similar block that says "MAN-SONG," a design suggesting that the two of them, together, are supporting his poetry. The design, Neihardt told Ledoux, "is certainly attractive, and, incidentally, a work of Art."[53]

Among the twenty-seven poems in the book were some he had published in various magazines as well as recently written unpublished pieces, including one written only three weeks before his wedding. Originally called "The Cry of Eros" but renamed "Love-Cry" in the collection, the poem covers some of the same ground as "A Vision of Woman," depicting man's cry of love for woman, suggesting he is all powerful and part of an ancient, unending story. The final lines of the poem read almost like a wedding vow:

Ancient and ending never,
This is the Law and the Plan.
Oh, you are the Woman forever—
I am the Man![54]

Neihardt also included a poem that the *Smart Set* had published the month he was married, a short lyric originally called "The Poet." Renamed "Outward" in *Man-Song*, the poem is about the poet who, unlike a sailor who at least knows a home port awaits him after a sea journey, moves endlessly forward into the unknown. The sailor is always being called back—perhaps, Neihardt suggested, by his mother—but the poet is only called further outward: "Onward, outward I must go / Where the mighty currents flow."[55]

Man-Song was notable for another poem that Neihardt had written a few years earlier, at a time when he "was down and out," with "no money, no fuel in the house."[56] In the poem, "Battle Cry," essentially a prayer offered up in the heat of struggle, the narrator asks not that he win the battle, only that he be allowed to continue to fight: "Fighting the fight is all," he argues. It is no sin to lose, but it is a sin to not try. And the narrator, clearly, is losing; he is "breathless and reeling, but tearless," and "bleeding, half beaten." As Neihardt often did, he invoked the man's mother: "Grant that the woman who bore me / Suffered to suckle a Man!"[57] Much more than any of Neihardt's other short poems, "Battle Cry" had staying power. Over the years the poem was praised not only by poets and critics but also by social activists of the time. San Francisco union leader Olaf Tvietmoe quoted the poem in a pivotal meeting with famed lawyer Clarence Darrow.[58] American Federation of Labor leader Samuel Gompers frequently used it in speeches, reprinted it in the AFL's publication *American Federationist*, and usually carried a copy of it in his pocket.[59] In 1924 Neihardt sued Los Angeles oil speculator C. C. Julian, who the year before had published "Battle Cry" in an ad for his oil company and claimed to be the author. In writing about the lawsuit, the *Los Angeles Times* judged Neihardt's poem to be better than Rudyard Kipling's "If" and William Ernest Henley's "Invictus."[60]

In large part because of "Battle Cry" and a few similar poems in *Man-Song*, the book garnered better reviews than had *A Bundle of Myrrh*. Bliss Carman, the Canadian critic and poet who had collaborated with Richard Hovey on the popular *Songs of Vagabondia*, wrote in the *New York Times* that in the book Neihardt appeared "as a champion of the robust—to have attempted to put in verse much the same spirit that Mr. Jack London so relentlessly puts in prose, the spirit of the primitive fighting man."[61]

London himself was drawn to Neihardt's work. Jim Tully, who wrote hard-boiled novels in the early twentieth century, admired Neihardt's poetry and reported that London did as well. "I met Jack London years later and found in him also an intense admirer of the Western poet," Tully reported, noting that London especially liked "Let Me Live Out My Years" and "Battle Cry."

London used the opening stanza of "Let Me Live Out My Years" as the epigraph to his novel *Martin Eden*, although, as Tully noted, he "was thoughtless enough not to add Neihardt's name to the poem."[62] Charmian London, in her two-volume biography of her husband, *The Book of Jack London*, quotes the same stanza, crediting it to Neihardt and saying it expressed London's own exuberance.[63] H. L. Mencken, writing in his magazine the *Smart Set*, seemed unaware that the magazine had published a number of Neihardt's poems and short stories. "I don't know who John G. Neihardt may be—what a label for a rhapsodist!—but this I do know, that he writes blank verse of quite remarkable excellence. . . . It has clang and clash in it and gorgeous color."[64] Two decades later some critics found the poems in *Man-Song* still resonated. In 1927 the *Saturday Review of Literature* recalled the book's impact: "I remember the late John Reed, the most striking young rebel of that time, a man with brilliant journalistic gifts and poetic, who left magazine work to espouse the cause of Labor and finally to die in the Russia that held for him a great vision, reading and applauding *Man-Song* by Neihardt."[65] And Fred Lewis Pattee, in his *New American Literature: 1890–1930*, placed the book—and Neihardt—in the company of Vachel Lindsay and Edwin Arlington Robinson, writing, "There was virility in the poems, at times even fire."[66]

A decade into the twentieth century Neihardt had published a collection of short stories, two collections of poetry, and a volume of nonfiction. He continued to write short poems, and he had tried poetic drama—*Man-Song* had included two attempts, "The Fugitive Glory" and "The Passing of the Lion," both unmemorable. Now, though magazines in New York continued to clamor for more stories, he decided to stop writing them.

He was still unsure what kind of writing he wanted to do, though the success of *Man-Song* gave him confidence in his poetry, but he knew he had tired of writing short stories. He wanted to do something bigger. When "The Discarded Fetish," one of Neihardt's early, non-Indian tales, was published in the *Smart Set* in July 1907, Broadway producer George C. Tyler of Liebler & Company expressed interest in staging a play based on the story, and Neihardt traveled to Chicago that November to meet with him. After their negotiations came to nothing, Neihardt chose to spend much of 1909 and 1910 turning the story into a novel, *The Dawn-Builder*, published by Mitchell Kennerley in 1911.

Set in 1862 at Fort Calhoun, Nebraska Territory, the original story contained a hint of autobiography, with its young tow-headed and fatherless boy and his devoted mother. The plot focuses on a one-legged printer who becomes a friend and father figure to the boy, falls in love with the mother, then loses her when her long-absent husband returns from seeking gold in the West. The story, which Neihardt recycled almost verbatim as the opening to the novel, ends with the despondent printer removing his new artificial leg, bought to impress the boy's mother, and tossing it into the Missouri River.

In expanding the story, Neihardt chose to follow the printer rather than stay with the newly reunited family. He tacked on parts of another non-Indian story, "The Man Who Saw Spring," which had just been published in *American Magazine*. He added two characters, the elderly Ambrose Ambrosen, an either crazy or brilliant man living on an island in the Missouri, and his beautiful, innocent daughter Diana, who then serves as a romantic interest for the printer.

The Dawn-Builder allowed Neihardt for the first time to state publicly his thinking about the relationship between facts and truth, an idea that would echo through his writing. Neihardt's work to this point had included poetry, fiction, and nonfiction, and he sometimes blurred the lines between the disciplines; some of his short stories exhibited an almost journalistic detachment in observation, and in his nonfiction—which at this point consisted only of *The River and I*—Neihardt occasionally aimed for a truth that did not require him to be absolutely accurate in all the smallest details. In *The Dawn-Builder* he has the narrator meditate on the true meaning of rain. "Should you ask a scientist to explain the matter to you, he would weary you with discussions concerning the thermometer and barometer. He would be correct, no doubt. But giving you the facts without the truth, he would make the mistake of leaving the heart out of the thing."[67]

Though some sections of the book showcased Neihardt's robust writing and others allowed him to explore his take on issues as diverse as isolation, nature, and the human need for religion, it read like several too-small pieces stitched together, each piece with its own characters, plot, and setting. Some of Neihardt's personal experiences found their way into the book. Ambrosen, like Neihardt, has an epiphany after a vivid childhood dream. Neihardt gave the town's busybody his maternal grandmother's tendency to invent words.[68] Finally, he included his belief that too many self-styled religious people looked for God only inside churches, whereas he preferred to take his spiritual exercises outdoors. He had written poems about the idea, most notably one called "The Temple of the Great-Outdoors" in *A Bundle of Myrrh*. In *The Dawn-Builder*, when Ambrosen's daughter Diana arrives in Fort Calhoun and is questioned by the town gossips about where she worships, she answers as Neihardt would have: "In the still night out under the stars; at the burning of the dawn; in the quiet evening; in the thunder-storms and when the snow wailed through the bare branches." When the shocked women tell her that "decent folks" worship in a church on Sunday, she asks, "Do they keep God in a house?"[69]

Critics generally ignored the book, though a review in the *Dial* praised Neihardt's "poetical imagination" and his skill in making Waters somewhat believable as a romantic protagonist.[70] A second novel, *Life's Lure*, which Neihardt started as soon as he finished *The Dawn-Builder*, suffered the same fate when it was published in 1914. Built from material he gathered during his summer stay in South Dakota in 1907, *Lure* explored the sin of greed through tales of placer miners searching for gold. Reviewers found it relentlessly grim but captivating—"a merciless picture of a merciless life—a merciless life that is alluring still."[71]

Neihardt would one day come across a collection of prose by Walt Whitman that, although the stories contained distinct Whitman touches, Neihardt categorized as being part of the poet's "blundering stage of his development."[72] *The Dawn-Builder* and *Life's Lure* represented a similar stage in Neihardt's development. Within a few years, Neihardt himself remembered both as unremarkable.[73]

7 A FATAL ROW

John Neihardt had been attracted to the idea of epic poetry since he first encountered Tennyson. He had called the first chapter in his *River and I* "The River of an Unwritten Epic," and some reviewers had agreed that the Missouri River and its environs were worthy of epic treatment. The writing of epics remained on his mind in the early months of 1911, when he began reviewing books as a freelancer for the *New York Times Book Review*. He began by critiquing Charles A. Hanna's *The Wilderness Trail: Or, the Ventures and Adventures of the Pennsylvania Traders on the Allegheny*, which explored the westward migration of the early Pennsylvania traders. In his review Neihardt explained the significance of the epic by using an idea from Lyman Abbott, historian and author of *The Life and Literature of the Ancient Hebrews*, that "universal history" contained three divisions: the factual, the philosophical, and the epic. America, Neihardt argued, had the necessary raw materials for a universal history, and in the biographical sketches of Indian agents and traders in Hanna's book, Neihardt saw the stuff of America's epic. "In reading of the romantic lives of such men as these and their prototypes in the fur trade of the Northwest," Neihardt wrote, "one wonders that America has not produced a full-sized National epic."[1]

In the same article, Neihardt also reviewed Walter McClintock's *The*

Old North Trail: Or, Life, Legends, and Religion of the Blackfoot Indians, which allowed him to express his views on the nation's original inhabitants and what he saw as their imminent disappearance. "For in the American Indian we have a living race of the Stone Age, with its religion, its customs, its traditions, its literature, its music," he wrote. "A bit of prehistoric life perishing in the strange, tense twentieth century! With the passing of the present generation the racial consciousness of the Indian will be lost."[2] Neihardt lamented the inaccurate image of Indians that predominated at the time, and he blamed "our two best-known generalizers in that direction," James Fennimore Cooper and William F. Cody. "Interpreted by the former," he wrote, "it must be confessed, however reluctantly, that the Indian is a painted and befeathered white man lending himself to the manipulation of a masterly storyteller. Interpreted by the latter, he is a pseudo-picturesque exponent of robbery, arson, treachery and murder. Untrue as these extremes necessarily are, a compromise between them is quite as untrue. The difficulty lies in the point of view." To portray Indians accurately, Neihardt argued, would require an author to undergo a "soul-change," a transformation that would require the writer to be both artist and ethnologist, to combine the two approaches to get at the Indians' religious consciousness, a task that he allowed would be immensely difficult. "Unlike his white brother, the Indian does not wear his religion on his sleeve, nor has he ever attempted to thrust it upon any one. It was never a dogma to be discussed or defended; but a self-evident portion of life itself, to be lived—quite as much a part of everyday existence as water and air."[3]

Although it would be the first of many he wrote for the *Times* that spring, the review was significant in that it afforded Neihardt the opportunity to work out in print the philosophy he had spent a decade establishing as he lived and worked among the Omaha. He quickly became the reviewer of all things Western for the *Times*. He was, for example, critical of Charles Alexander Eastman's *Soul of the Indian*, which he generally liked but found "too limited in scope." In the review Neihardt wasted no time making two points he continued to make most of his life: that Indian religion was the real thing and that he found himself living in a shallow time. "One wonders," he wrote, "while reading the Indian's conception of worship, as compared with the average white man's, whether or not the charge of barbarism has been rightly placed!"[4]

By the fall of 1911 John and Mona had been married for nearly three years. John had continued to write, and Mona, who had not cooked or kept house before moving to Bancroft, had immediately begun to learn both from a mother-in-law who prided herself on her accomplishments in both areas. Mona had also quickly returned to sculpting, in the unattached "summer kitchen" when it was not too cold and in the dining room when it was. She had completed the relief for *Man-Song* and a bust of John. Mona also played the violin, and she soon contributed to the family finances by giving lessons to local children. When the house next door became available, John and Mona bought it and started their own home.[5]

That October Neihardt wrote to Louis Ledoux to apologize for having recently sent him so few letters. Neihardt, thirty years old and normally a prolific letter writer, had virtually ceased all correspondence. "You see," he wrote to Ledoux, "when a man is expecting a baby and two books, he has a very good excuse for being silent!"[6] One of the books was his novel *The Dawn-Builder*, published earlier in 1911, and the other was *The Stranger at the Gate*, a third collection of short lyrics that was scheduled to be published early in 1912. The "stranger" being celebrated in the poems was John and Mona's first child, and the expectant parents spent the summer quietly preparing.

Calling it their "summer of enchantment," John and Mona slept most nights in the yard outside their house, as was common in the days before air-conditioning, lying in hammocks amid the hollyhocks, grape vines, and plum and cherry trees.[7] This flora, along with the nearby cattle, wheat, and corn and the nighttime sights and sounds of Bancroft made their way into Neihardt's meditations on becoming a father. From this mix, he fashioned a sequence of eleven poems that opened *The Stranger at the Gate*. At times, Neihardt, who tended to see the darkness in things, struggled to focus on the joy of impending parenthood. Viewing the flickering lights of Bancroft at night and the dark spots that were the unlighted meadows, and hearing the wind rustle the wheat fields on the edge of town, he imagined the ghosts of all the people who had gone before. Life, it seemed, was so difficult for the living and so full of the dead. In "In the Night" he asks:

> Is it the night wind sobbing
> Over the wheat in head?
> Is it the world-heart throbbing
> Sad with the coming years?
> Is it the lifeward creeping
> Ghosts of the myriad dead,
> Livid with wounds and weeping
> Wild, uncleansing tears?[8]

As one reviewer wrote, it is not, of course, any of those things, "but the poet is licensed to suggest them, for his revelation is not of nature but of his own soul."[9]

Most of that summer Neihardt was able to fight his own dark nature and remain optimistic. After all, a child—"the blessed Comer," as he called her in the poem "In the Night"—was on her way. In the poem that best sets the tone for the sequence, "The Weavers," Neihardt realizes that plants and animals, even the stars in the sky, are in a state of constant preparation for birth and rebirth. Using mostly short, everyday words, he creates the rocking rhythm of a loom, providing the central metaphor for the poem.

> In the flowing pastures,
> Where the cattle feed,
> Such a hidden love-storm,
> Dying into seed—
> Blue grass, slough grass,
> Wild flower, weed![10]

The poem, like others in the book, is occasionally marred by archaic word choices; amid the sun and moon, the corn and cattle, is the mother "wrapt in visionings" and the sound of the "god-flung shuttles of a loom" humming. As poet Joyce Kilmer wrote in a review in the *New York Times*, the poem was "a glorious vision" but one "clouded with a mist of words."[11]

Volney Streamer, Neihardt's New York champion, had predicted the child would be a boy, and Neihardt promised Streamer that if he were right, the boy would be named Volney Neihardt.[12] Streamer, however, turned out to be wrong, and John and Mona named the baby Enid, to honor his favorite Tennyson character, the loyal wife of the knight Geraint in *Idylls of the King*.[13] They fashioned a middle name, Volnia, to honor Streamer.

It was not the poems written in the months before the baby's arrival that made *The Stranger at the Gate* a memorable collection. The second half of the book collected Neihardt's most successful previously published short work, including such poems as "The Poet's Town," which the *New York Times* review described as "already known and loved."[14] The poem had originally been published in *Forum* in November 1910, and the *Dial* had also drawn attention to it. "We are much impressed with 'The Poet's Town,'" its reviewer wrote, "describing the boy who is at heart a poet, living his own life amid commonplace surroundings."[15] Though Neihardt would argue late in life that the poem was not just about him but about any young man trying to find grace and beauty in a small provincial town, the poem was clearly autobiographical. Neihardt was telling people what it was like for him, a poet, to live amid the farmers and shopkeepers in the small Nebraska towns of Wayne and Bancroft. "The poem expressed my world-view when I was about 26 years old," Neihardt told a friend many years later, "and it still has a poignant meaning for us."[16] In the poem townspeople look down on the young poet because he has no paying job, the only way they seem to know how to judge a person's value. The young poet is seen as something of a joke, but beneath the surface he is no comedian. At times he wishes he were just like everyone else—just a man, not a dreamer. But he is what he is: a poet for whom the distant past and the far future combine into one heady present.

Lover of golden apples,
Munching a daily crust;
Haunter of dream-built chapels,
Worshipping in the dust;

Dull to the worldly duty,
Less to the town he grew,
And more to the God of Beauty
Than even the grocer knew![17]

As was so often the case for Neihardt, the most profound impact of the publishing of "The Poet's Town" was personal. Julius T. House, a young college professor at Neihardt's alma mater, Nebraska Normal in Wayne, was impressed when he read the poem in *Forum* and was then surprised to learn that the poet lived only thirty-five miles away. At the time House believed that American poetry was in decline, he said later, and "The Poet's Town" changed his mind. "I have always thought I was pretty good at 'picking a winner,'" he wrote to Neihardt years later. "I picked you before I ever saw you, and have always felt good about that fact. It was not friendship that made me yell for the 'Poet's Town.' I had never seen you."[18] House and Neihardt quickly became friends, and House began spending weekends in Bancroft. He would prove to be a sounding board for Neihardt for decades to come.

Key to the success of "The Poet's Town" and others of the later poems in *The Stranger at the Gate* was Neihardt's less self-centered focus. Though autobiographical, "The Poet's Town" was more objective, more socially conscious than most of the poems that had come before it. Collected with the deeply personal poems about his impending fatherhood, these poems stood out all the more. Eventually Neihardt himself recognized the difference that made these poems stronger. "I was able to generalize my experience, giving them impersonal and enduring significance."[19]

This change in Neihardt came, at least in part, from his burgeoning interest in socialism. World War I and the Russian revolution were still a few years away, but the war between capital and labor was raging, and

Neihardt, usually uninterested in writing about current events, included in *Stranger* several poems that commented on the worldwide uprising he believed was coming. In the poem "Money" he fashions a passerby criticizing a ditch digger for working only for pay, calling money "the graven symbol of your ache" and "the minted meaning of your blood."[20] In "Cry of the People" Neihardt foresees a revolution in which working-men rise up and take what is rightfully theirs.

> We are the workers and makers!
> We are no longer dumb!
> Tremble, O Shirkers and Takers!
> Sweeping the earth—we come!
> Ranked in the world-wide dawn,
> Marching into the day!
> *The night is gone and the sword is drawn*
> *And the scabbard is thrown away!*[21]

The poem was widely praised and anthologized. Poet Edwin Markham said it stirred "like bugles above the battle."[22] Upton Sinclair, the well-known novelist, journalist, and political activist, included the poem in an anthology of social protest, and thirty years later the BBC used it in a program on India.[23]

Although less celebrated, "The Red Wind Comes" seemed even more prophetic. Again Neihardt saw a revolution coming, and he criticized the "bombast" of Fourth of July celebrations and the hypocrisy of religion that fell into step behind a system that made some people poor while others got rich. He reminded readers that the working people of the United States were the ones who "built the cities, fructified the lands," and he called on them to rise up and take back "the product of our hands." Years later Neihardt said "The Red Wind Comes" and "Cry of the People" expressed his response to what he saw as the social injustice of the time, "when a good man would work a hard, ten-hour day for a dollar or less, if he could only find work to do."[24]

Of the remaining poems in *The Stranger at the Gate*, one more stood out, not for its exploration of current events but for its explanation of the childhood event that continued to have profound meaning: the night-marish epiphany Neihardt had suffered as an eleven-year-old boy. He always pinpointed that fever dream as the moment he chose to become a poet, as the moment his life took on an additional mystical meaning. Nothing ever dissuaded him from this belief; in fact, throughout his life, events continued to underscore his faith in this defining dream and cause him to expand on it: by 1911 Neihardt believed not only that something had called him to a life of poetry but also that whatever or whoever had called to him continued to watch over him.

When Neihardt wrote the poem early that year, he called it "The Calling Brother." He constructed within it a dialogue with a spirit—the "brother"—who seems to demand that he connect with the mystical mystery of the universe. When Neihardt published the poem in *Forum* that June, he renamed it "The Ghostly Brother." The poem chronicles the times when he tries, unsuccessfully, to shut this brother out, to live only in the real world, to accept it and be "content with little things" like he thinks everyone else is. But his "ghostly brother" will not let him be and implores the poet to join him.

> *I am you and you are I!*
> *When the world is cherished most,*
> *You shall hear my haunting cry,*
> *See me rising like a ghost.*
> *I am all that you have been,*
> *Are not now, but soon shall be!*
> *Thralled awhile by dust and din—*
> *Brother, Brother, follow me!*[25]

The sense that someone was looking after him, watching over him, had bothered Neihardt for years. Shortly after he and Mona were married he told her about this feeling, and she urged him to try to write a poem about it. At first Neihardt felt the idea was too vague to tackle, but a couple of years later he suddenly felt the need to try to put it down on paper. In working out the poem, Neihardt discovered that this "brother" not only pushed Neihardt always to do better, to do more; he also claimed half the glory from anything Neihardt did. As he wrote in the poem,

> Do I love? You share the kiss,
> Leaving only half the bliss.
> Do I conquer? You are there,
> Claiming half the victor's share.

The character of the "Ghostly Brother" remained only vaguely character-ized in the poem and seemed to represent to Neihardt something more like a spirit than any actual human presence. The year after the poem was published, however, the brother became a more concrete character. Spiritualism, the belief that mediums could communicate with the dead, was at the height of its popularity in the United States, and in the spring of 1912 Neihardt visited such a person in Omaha. She told Neihardt he was doing good work and that it was beginning to have an influence on others. Then, as Neihardt later recounted to a friend, she told him she could see his brother standing behind him. "He is tall, has dark hair and dark eyes; he was a Scotch minister and died a long while ago. He says that when you were eleven years old you had a fever and nearly died, that you were often out of the body, and that he then got control of you and has controlled you ever since."[26] Many years later Neihardt would say only, "Everything in this world is an echo of something greater. . . . And it weaves in and out, makes echoes, all the time."[27]

Having his freelance book reviews published in the *New York Times* gave Neihardt confidence that he had something of value to say about the cur-rent state of literature and that he could read and write about others' books while still finding time to write poetry. The *Times* reviews also gave him examples of his work to show others, and in the spring of 1912 he used those samples to secure a position as literary editor of the *Minneapolis Journal*, the "Great Daily of the Great Northwest." W. H. Jones, the *Journal*'s edi-tor, gave Neihardt until September 1 to plan a weekly books feature and move his family to Minneapolis. For the first time since being married, Neihardt had a writing job that would provide a regular paycheck.

To gather background information for a series of profiles he planned to publish, Neihardt immediately wrote to a cross section of America's poets and writers, among them Sara Teasdale, John Jay Chapman, Edwin Arlington Robinson, and George Sterling. Sterling was born in Sag Harbor, New York, but he now lived in Carmel, California, and was known unofficially as the poet laureate of San Francisco, where he also kept a room at the Bohemian Club. Tall, athletic, and charismatic, Sterling had been mentored by critic and short story writer Ambrose Bierce and was friends with poet Robinson Jeffers and writer Jack London, serving as the model for Russ Brissenden in London's autobiographical novel *Martin Eden*, the same book for which London had used Neihardt's "Let Me Live Out My Years" as an epigraph.[28]

Neihardt admired Sterling's poetry and for months had talked of him with Mona. Eventually, at Mona's urging, Neihardt wrote to Sterling, and the two men began a correspondence that would last a dozen years and influence both of their careers. They shared poems or pieces of poems and were always mutually supportive. Each did not necessarily like everything the other had written, but they chose to focus more on what they liked about each other—and each other's work—than on what they disliked. Neihardt believed that poetry, to be great, must be timeless, and it was this element that he found in nearly all of Sterling's work. Before the end of his first month at the *Journal* he published a 1,600-word article about his new friend. "He brings us nothing more nor less than a new reading of beauty," Neihardt wrote. "He shows us the ancient sea, the ancient stars, the ancient mountains, dawns and days and nights, but he makes us see them as parts of that ego that is included vaguely in the name, George Sterling—haunted with the mystery of his own soul, the questionings of his own mental processes, the austere music of his own dreaming."[29]

Sterling was equally taken with Neihardt's poetry. After Neihardt had sent him copies of his books, Sterling responded: "I've put in several happy evenings this month with your *Man-Song* . . . . I'm still thrilling to much of its beauty, sweetness, strength. I like best the splendid, vital 'Vision of Woman.' That's a noble, unforgettable thing! . . . To have caught such a thing justified raising all sorts of Hell."[30] They disagreed on economics and politics—Sterling considered himself a materialist and Neihardt thought himself a socialist—so they generally avoided those topics. They devoted most of their correspondence to their writing and that of other contemporary writers and poets. Especially for Neihardt, nearly a dozen years younger and geographically and socially much more isolated than Sterling, their correspondence afforded him an opportunity to try out ideas on a sympathetic reader and to learn about the wider world of American poetry in the early years of the twentieth century.

Late in August John and Mona and baby Enid moved to Minneapolis, finding a house south of downtown; Mona was now six months pregnant with their second child. The next month Neihardt began his "Reviews of New Books" column, opening with a 1,500-word essay that explained why he believed America, perhaps much to its surprise, was on the verge of an exciting time for poetry. "If you say 'Ivory Soap' to the average American, he will immediately either say or think, 'It floats,'" he wrote. "Likewise, if you say the word poetry, the same man will either think or say, 'There are no longer any poets worth reading.'"[31] Neihardt argued that on the contrary, the country was ripe for great poetry. As he worked through his argument—that all great literary ages seemed materialistic at the time—he cited his influences: Homer, Shakespeare, Victor Hugo, Aristophanes, Aeschylus, Tennyson, and Swinburne. "Science has been likened to a river, art to an ocean. Science is progressive—it advances. Art does not progress—it rises and falls," he argued. "Once again the wave is rising, and it is safe to say that we are now in a remarkable lyrical age."[32] What great poetry required, he argued, was imagination, and he found the early years of the twentieth century full of imagination. "[N]ever in the history of man has there been such a time for dreaming and for realizing dreams," he wrote. People could now fly, light their homes by the push of a button, talk to friends and family thousands of miles away. "We have taken our poetry in the form of skyscrapers and aeroplanes and ocean liners and limited trains and automobiles and wireless telegraphs and the like. The trouble is not with the singers, but with those who have not yet listened."[33]

Neihardt was not alone in thinking that the world of poetry was ready to boom. In Chicago fifty-two-year-old Harriet Monroe was preparing the first issue of *Poetry: A Magazine of Verse*, a journal devoted to a new crop of serious poets. As a young woman Monroe had been a drama critic for the *New York Herald Tribune* before returning to her hometown of Chicago, where she became art critic for the *Chicago Tribune* and a freelance journalist for the *Chicago Times-Herald*.[34] She had written some poetry herself—in 1893 she was named laureate of the Chicago World's Columbian Exposition—but her goal with the new magazine was to promote the work of others rather than her own.[35] Like Neihardt, Monroe spent much of 1912 writing to America's poets, announcing her venture and soliciting their work for her new magazine. That August, just as Neihardt was packing for his move to Minneapolis, Monroe wrote to him about her magazine and to solicit a poem or two for it. "It is a brave and a beautiful undertaking," he quickly responded, "and I shall do whatever I can to help it along." He offered to send her the poem he had just spent four months writing, "The Death of Agrippina," a 700-line poetic drama about the final hours in the life of Julia Agrippina, mother of the Roman emperor Nero. As usual, he believed the poem was the most important thing he had yet written.[36] "I believe it hits hard," he told Monroe. "I believe it would attract attention."[37] A few days later, she responded enthusiastically. "I hope very much that you may send us your tragedy, 'The Death of Agrippina,'" she wrote, "as the publication of a short drama, written by a poet of your quality, would be exactly what I most wish for. It would, of course, occupy an entire number except for the few pages of prose, and I think we can make satisfactory terms. Please send it as soon as possible."[38]

Monroe was certainly predisposed to value whatever Neihardt sent her. She had just finished writing an essay on modern American poetry that would be included that fall in the *Poetry Review*, a magazine published in London. In the article she featured Neihardt and Ezra Pound, the poet who was then founding what would become the visual movement in poetry known as Imagism. Both poets, Monroe wrote, were among the leaders of "the younger crowd" of American poets and possessed "delicately tempered weapons." While she found "boyish insolence and brag" in some of Neihardt's poems, she wrote, she also found "a high spirit in them, and sometimes a grand marching movement."[39]

But she was terribly disappointed when "The Death of Agrippina" arrived late in August. Though her initial response has been lost—Neihardt may have chosen to dispose of it—their subsequent correspondence makes clear that she was not impressed with his latest work. "I have your note regarding 'The Death of Agrippina,' which you wrote after a hasty reading of the play," Neihardt responded. "I rather think you will find it deserves several readings."[40] Ten days later Monroe wrote to apologize for not having written since "that first harsh letter," saying she had been busy getting out the first issue of *Poetry* and moving.[41]

Monroe and Neihardt continued to correspond weekly about the long poem, both remaining civil even as they remained committed to their positions. Monroe tried diligently to get out of her promise to publish the play in full without directly criticizing Neihardt or the poem. She suggested Neihardt choose a passage or two from the poem for her to publish but, sensing that he would not go along with such an idea, told him she could not use the entire play. "After very careful consideration, I feel that we can not venture at present to print the whole play, as it would mean a much larger number than usual, which we can not now afford."[42] Instead of completely closing the door on the poem, however, Monroe kept it open just a crack. "Some months hence, when we have a larger subscription list and when we can tell better what we can afford to do, I should like another chance at this play if you have not done anything else with it."[43] Neihardt wanted Monroe to have the poem. "If you can assure me that you *can* use it," he wrote her, "I shall hold it up for you, tho' I have never had much trouble in placing my stuff. To be frank, I prefer having it appear in your magazine, and I believe it would make a successful number."[44] Monroe soon offered a hundred dollars for the poem but did not commit to publishing it in a single issue.[45] Even so, at this point Neihardt still believed in her magazine. "Miss Monroe," he wrote in the *Minneapolis Journal* in November, "has cried out against a blindness that has characterized all generations."[46]

On December 1, 1912, Mona gave birth to a son, Sigurd Volsung, names Neihardt had taken from William Morris's poetic retelling of the Icelandic epic *The Story of Sigurd the Volsung and the Fall of the Niblungs*.[47] As his older sister was linked to Tennyson's epic poetry and her father's New York friend Volney Streamer, Sigurd was now tied to Morris's epic poetry and his father's California friend George Sterling: Sigurd was born on Sterling's forty-third birthday.

Now, as Neihardt and Harriet Monroe continued to correspond, the tenor of their disagreement grew harsher and more pointed, in part because of Sterling. He too had been writing to Monroe, in part to criticize Ezra Pound and his poetry. In January Sterling began to share those criticisms with Neihardt, writing that in his most recent letter to Monroe, "I told her that Pound is beginning to make an ass of himself."[48] Two weeks later Sterling wrote to Neihardt again: "Pound makes *my* face worse than ache. He seems eager only for new forms, which in this year of our Lord are no forms at all. An ass, John."[49] Neihardt and Monroe had already clashed politely about free-form verse—*vers libre*—and now with Sterling's example and encouragement, Neihardt began to push harder. In January Neihardt argued again against breaking his poem into smaller, more easily publishable pieces. "If it is separated and loaded in with a bunch of 'vers libre' (that shoddy makeshift of those who do not *love* enough to *work*!), it will be passed over as only another effort by another phrase-monger."[50] Late in February Neihardt drew Monroe's attention to an essay he had just written for his book page in the *Minneapolis Journal* titled "The Inevitability of Form in Art," which made his position clear. He wrote: "There is a strong tendency in contemporary painting, sculpture and poetry to repudiate form as being outworn. There are futurists, cubists, post-impressionists, imagistes; and they all talk so loudly and with such a show of earnestness that many innocent people are beginning to listen seriously."[51] Neihardt went on to call free-form verse "that slap-dash, haphazard, lawless kind of composition" and argued that no such thing could actually exist: "Form is not free, and cannot be so conceived," he wrote. "It was not through whim or chance that poets first chanted in rhythm; it was not through mere whim that rhyme was invented. Rhyme and rhythm came about naturally, in accordance with the universal tendency of power to return upon itself, to make cycles."[52]

Finally, that spring, Monroe relented, asked for a couple of small changes, to which Neihardt quickly agreed, and published the poem in full. In the May issue she devoted thirty-four of fifty-two pages to "The Death of Agrippina." (The issue also included a four-page essay on "Tradition," written by Monroe, and a shorter one on "Poetic Prose and Vers Libre" by Alice Corbin Henderson, whose second poetry collection, *The Spinning Woman of the Sky*, Neihardt had just panned in the *Minneapolis Journal*.[53] Henderson also briefly reviewed Robert Frost's *A Boy's Will*, Maurice Hewlett's *Helen Redeemed and Other Poems*, and John Masefield's *The Daffodil Fields*.) The issue generated almost no comment, and what did emerge was negative, something Neihardt found hard to believe. When he learned that poet and critic May Sinclair had written to Monroe critical of "Agrippina," he demanded to see the letter and any others she had received. "I don't know whether I ought to send you May Sinclair's letter," Monroe responded. "It is very drastic, but her comments were intended for a friend and I like to have her write me candidly." As for other letters, "We have received very few."[54]

Monroe, while she continued to be polite to Neihardt, stood her ground. "I suppose it comes down at last to a question of innate preference," she wrote. "I find that my instincts are rather with the radicals than with the academicians. This feeling is so emphatic that I devoutly hope a man of your caliber will not spend any more time over Roman tragedies. I feel that that sort of thing is not for our modern world."[55] Given his devotion to the classics, this would have been a bitter pill to swallow, and Neihardt did not back down. In fact, once "Agrippina" was published, Neihardt stepped up his attacks on Monroe and the magazine, always supported by Sterling—"I'm in *entire accord* with what you say as to form and 'modernity' in art," he wrote to Neihardt that summer.[56] "Why do you take so much trouble to yourself by way of fighting sincere work?" Neihardt asked Monroe the month after "Agrippina" appeared. "We can not banish our ancestors with a fiat. Important changes are not abrupt. . . . Real growth is imperceptible. You and Pound can't change natural laws. . . .

Why make your magazine a freak?"[57] Monroe, naturally, was insulted by the characterization. "I don't see why a few poems or editorials that we print should place it in that category, even if they seem to you freakish, for surely we have been hospitable to all kinds and have not confined ourselves to any one school. You, at least, ought not to accuse us of limiting ourselves to the radical group."[58]

Monroe and Neihardt's fight over "The Death of Agrippina," though brief, marked the beginning of a decades-long breach that did no harm to Monroe or her magazine, which went on to become one of the leading monthly poetry journals, but which set Neihardt on a course of opposition to virtually all the modern trends in poetry. The two would move only further apart in the years to come, ensuring that Neihardt was always outside the mainstream.

Soon Neihardt's fight, like Sterling's, seemed to be more with Pound than with Monroe. Early in 1913 Neihardt had referred to Pound in the *Journal* as "a milder sort of Walt Whitman," but just a few months later he had changed his mind.[59] "Ezrapoundism simply drives me wild," he wrote to one friend. "One can not hate an ass, but one may be considerably irritated by its braying."[60] Monroe summed up her side of the incident in a letter to Pound in the midst of her fight with Neihardt:

> I accepted Neihardt's play in the very beginning of the enterprise. I think it was before number one came out, and I was gratified to have a man of his strength offer me what he considered his best work. Even then I was terribly disappointed to find it a Roman tragedy of Elizabethan origin. Of late, I asked him to release me from my promise to print it in a single number, but he declined, so I am fulfilling the promise. It has some strong passages, I think in Nero's soliloquies, but much of it is bombast, and it isn't drama. However, we will get it off our hands and off our files and will never do such a thing again, please God.[61]

Though Pound laughed it off at the time, decades later he said it had been a "secular crime" to devote an entire issue of *Poetry* to Neihardt's poem.[62]

Neihardt never backed away from his traditional approach, though he did soften his stance toward the vers librists, even calling Pound "one of our most promising formless, time- and spaceless bards." And within a decade he came to realize the mistake he had made with Monroe. "Hattie and I got into a row very soon after *Poetry* started," he wrote to a friend in 1922. "The row began as soon as I saw which way she was blowing. I think it was that ass, Ezry, who cooled my ardor. After that the braying was deafening, and my love never returned." Then he added a telling handwritten postscript: "When *Poetry* was started, the lady gave me every opportunity to become immortal, but the row was fatal."[63]

1. Young John Neihardt, left, with his mother, Alice Neihardt, and two sisters, Grace and Lulu (kneeling). WHMC

2. Mona Martinsen in 1907, shortly after she returned to New York from her studies in Paris. WHMC

3. Neihardt during his *River and I* trip down the Missouri in 1908. WHMC

4. Neihardt (left) and George Sterling traveled to Muir Woods in California in 1917. WHMC

5. Neihardt (center) with a group of Nebraska dignitaries after the laureate ceremony in 1921. WHMC

6. Neihardt (left) sits with Black Elk (center) and Standing Bear during
interviews for *Black Elk Speaks* in 1931. WHMC

7. Black Elk prays atop Harney Peak in South Dakota at the end of his 1931 meetings with Neihardt. WHMC

8 AN UNTOUCHED EPIC

A year in Minneapolis was enough of city life for the Neihardts. Neihardt offered to take a reduced salary in return for less writing and to be allowed to do his writing and reviewing back in Bancroft. W. H. Jones, the *Journal*'s editor, agreed, and by the fall of 1913 Neihardt had moved his family back to Nebraska, arranging to submit a weekly article by mail.[1]

The *Journal* paycheck was enough to cover Neihardt's expenses, allowing him to devote himself to a new project. He had planned to write yet another poetic drama, this time on the French Revolution. "I was very much interested in the social question and knew quite a bit about it," he wrote later. But once again, Mona, just as she had pushed him to contact Sterling, steered him toward a different subject: mountain man Hugh Glass. "One day I was talking to her, just happened to be telling her about Hugh Glass, and she said, 'Oh, John, you want to save that old man for posterity.' She said, 'There is your theme. . . . You don't need to write about the French Revolution. . . . This is right under your feet.' And I thought, why, she's a wise woman."[2]

Neihardt was coy in announcing his new venture to his friends, seeming almost afraid to say too much about it. "Something has happened to me & I feel tremendously fortunate," he wrote to Louis Ledoux. "I have discovered a field that is entirely untouched—one that my whole experience has fitted me to handle to the best advantage."[3] He kept even Sterling in the dark at first. "What you say of your new body of epic material is as interesting to me as it is mysterious," Sterling wrote. "I can't imagine what it can be."[4]

Hugh Glass had been a trapper on the Ashley-Henry fur-trading expedition of 1823, during which time he was badly mauled by a bear and left for dead by two colleagues. Glass survived and, living primarily on roots and berries, made his way down the Grand River in what would become South Dakota, crawling on his hands and knees much of the way, until he reached Fort Kiowa. Neihardt may first have heard of Hugh Glass as a boy as he and his father listened to the men on the Kansas City docks, but it is certain that Glass was one of the men Doane Robinson had suggested to Neihardt during his *River and I* research. Neihardt was attracted to Glass's story because he believed "it made it possible to comment on every phase of life."[5] He was especially drawn to Glass's near-death journey to Fort Kiowa, in which he saw represented the difficult striving he believed each person faced in life, an idea that recurred throughout his writings. Life might be difficult, nearly impossible at times, but, he believed, people must not give up.

Neihardt worked on his newspaper column early in the week, reserving Fridays, Saturdays, and Sundays for what he came to call *The Song of Hugh Glass*. Each night before going to bed Neihardt would read aloud to himself what he had written that day, trying to make it his last waking thought, hoping his mind would ponder the poem as he slept. Then first thing in the morning, he would start again. He started work on the poem in October 1913 and immediately began obsessively to chronicle, in letters to friends, his weekly production, a habit he maintained for more than twenty-five years. "Have 500 lines now—and I believe I'm succeeding," he wrote to Sterling early in December.[6] Two months later he reported, "Have reached line 900 in *Hugh Glass*. It moves slowly, but it is *constructed*, I think."[7] Nearly a year later he reported, "2,100 lines with 900 to do. No padding either—no slovenly work. So it seems to me."[8]

The previous year's correspondence with Harriet Monroe and George Sterling, coupled with the research and writing he had done for his weekly book page, had left Neihardt more loyal than ever to traditional rhythm and rhyme in poetry. He had experimented with forms in many of his earlier lyric poems, trying blank verse and mimicking chants he had heard on the Omaha reservation, but he had always been most comfortable with the forms he had grown up with, like those used by his early poetic heroes, especially Tennyson. Now, having defended tradition for more than a year in his fight with Monroe, Neihardt had turned his preference into a philosophy. "I am growing more & more in love with rigid form," he wrote to Ledoux. "I know that one can be free only within fixed boundaries."[9] For *Glass* Neihardt had chosen to write in pentameter because "for sustained narrative, it best suits the genius of the English language—as hexameter suited that of the Greek," he explained later. "My verse method in handling rhymed pentameter is essentially that of blank verse. The unit is not the line ending in a rhyme, as I write it. The unit is the *breathing length*, determined by the handling of caesuras."[10] As for the rhyme, even Sterling had questioned Neihardt's use of rhyme in "The Death of Agrippina," and as Neihardt began work on *The Song of Hugh Glass* he tried to explain to his friend his attachment to it. "You once asked why I used rhyme instead of blank verse. Because one may use the *method* of blank verse in rhyme, and the latter acts as a necessary limitation. Rhyme makes for economy & speed & gives a sort of 'come on' to a tale."[11]

The following spring, in April 1914, Sterling traveled from California to New York and stopped in Bancroft to meet Neihardt. The two walked out into the countryside, rested on a farmer's haystack, and talked for hours. Though Neihardt did not record what they talked about, he never forgot their time together. "I can see him still rolling in the hay and laughing," Neihardt wrote years later. "When he laughed, his ears went back and he looked like a *faun*."[12] Sterling enjoyed meeting Neihardt, too. "I've thought often, since leaving Bancroft, of broad-breasted Nebraska and your cozy home there," he wrote soon after. "I envy you more than I dare say."[13] Neihardt felt down after the visit. "After you left I had a slight touch of homesickness, or something like it," he wrote to his friend.[14]

For the next year Neihardt maintained his weekly routine: four days of work for the *Minneapolis Journal,* three days on *Hugh Glass.* He took time off from the long poem to write a short story, "The Red Roan Mare"—"I needed the money, dammit!" he told Sterling—and two short poems.[15] The story, which appeared in *All-Story Weekly* that summer, was a supernatural tale set at the time of the Little Bighorn battle between the Lakota and the U.S. Cavalry under the leadership of Lt. Col. George Armstrong Custer. Once again Neihardt told a story of betrayal, this time two friends falling out over a woman. His mystical approach took center stage, with the narrator comparing the feeling he gets in recounting the story to what one might feel on a rainy night in a new country, when a flash of lightning can offer up a surprising landscape: "And after that he believes in considerably more than the ground under his feet, for he feels that world all about him silent in the shadow."[16] His classical allusions to such names as Xenophon and Homer marred the otherwise restrained narrative. Even in a tale told sympathetically from the side of the white soldiers, Neihardt found a way to praise the Lakota warriors, calling them "a body of cavalry that had not a superior in the annals of war-craft."[17] Reaction to the story was favorable, the *New York Herald Tribune* finding it "pleasantly reminiscent" of work by Ambrose Bierce.[18] The *Saturday Review of Literature* called it "an exceptionally vivid performance."[19]

The two poems "The Farmer's Thanksgiving" and "Katharsis" were unusual for Neihardt in that they commented on current events, in this case World War I. Even during the war, and later during World War II, Neihardt rarely concerned himself much with national or international issues; his correspondence was always much more focused on his work and that of other writers and poets. In 1914 the *Country Gentleman,* the nation's leading agricultural magazine, asked Neihardt to write a poem on the war, and he used "The Farmer's Thanksgiving" to compare farming to warfare.

> Prepare the feast and let us sing
>   Of how the foe we slew;
> How on a bleak frontier of Spring
>   We ran our trenches true.[20]

In manner and meter, if not in the comparison to war, at least one critic found similarities to "The Corn Song," a poem within a poem written in the mid-nineteenth century by Neihardt's original namesake, John Greenleaf Whittier. In the other poem, "Katharsis," Neihardt more directly confronted the causes of the war—which he saw primarily as greed—as well as the misguided direction of modern artists.

> Lo, how they made a fetich [sic] of caprice,
> And worshipped with aberrant brush and pen!
> What false dawns summoned by the crowing hen!
> How toiled the lean to batten the obese!
> What straying from the sanity of Greece
> While yet her seers and bards were fighting-men![21]

Eventually Neihardt himself would dismiss the poems as "more like newspaper verse."[22]

For most of 1914 and the first half of 1915, though, he remained devoted to his long narrative poem. "Am still busy on my *The Song of Hugh Glass* after 18 months of work," he wrote to Ledoux in January 1915. "It will be finished in the summer, I think.[23] By the end of June it was complete, now totaling more than three thousand lines. Within a month, the Macmillan Company in New York, the publishers of Jack London and Edwin Arlington Robinson and the firm Neihardt had first written to fifteen years earlier, agreed to publish it.[24]

The Stranger at the Gate had heralded the arrival of John and Mona's daughter Enid. Now it was young Sigurd's turn, and Neihardt dedicated *The Song of Hugh Glass* to his son, introducing the book with a poem titled "To Sigurd, Scarcely Three." In the poem Neihardt, now thirty-four, promised to teach his son how to make a kite, a boat, and a bow if, in return, Sigurd would remind him of "the goodly art of being ten." Neihardt said that on rainy days, when they could not play, he would work at the other thing he knew how to do: writing poems "that strive to build for you the mood of daring and of fortitude." For he wanted to preserve for his son some sense of the fur trade's "wonder-days

/ When first you glimpse the world of men / Beyond the bleaker side of ten."[25]

Having lost his own father when he was ten, it is not surprising that Neihardt chose that age as the end point of boyhood. In choosing a member of the Missouri River fur trade as the subject for his historical poem, Neihardt was reaching back to the day he and his father watched from a Kansas City bluff as the Missouri overreached its banks. In a "Note" that introduced *The Song of Hugh Glass*, Neihardt characterized his attachment at that early age to the Missouri: "It was for me what the sea must have been to the Greek boys of antiquity."[26] He believed that the period following Lewis and Clark's expedition in the early 1800s was "one of the most enthralling in the entire story of the human race, and yet the very names of its principal heroes are practically unknown except to specialists in Western History."[27] These heroes, he thought, were direct descendants of Achilles, Hector, Aeneas, Roland, Sigurd, and the knights of King Arthur's court.[28] He saw *The Song of Hugh Glass* as helping to bring to light this "overlooked and forgotten" phase of U.S. history and believed he needed to relate his hero's tale through a traditional form.[29]

Neihardt considered the book "a meditative poem," and "a poem of ideas," and he worked to make Glass larger than life:[30]

Large of bone,
Deep-chested, that his great heart might have play,
Gray-bearded, gray of eye and crowned with gray
Was Glass.[31]

In the section of the poem he called "The Crawl," which detailed Glass's struggle to travel southeast from the Grand River to Fort Kiowa, Neihardt tried hard to link his latest work with the epic stories of the past. In *Hugh Glass* Neihardt has his hero essentially die—he was, in fact, left for dead—and then be reborn, undertaking a treacherous journey of self-discovery and pain, eventually emerging at the other end a new and better man. Because Neihardt, at the time he wrote the poem, had not traveled to the area, he relied on his South Dakota friend Doane Robinson to get the place right. "I wish you would give me a general idea of the country lying along a line drawn from the forks of the Grand to old Fort Kiowa near Chamberlain," Neihardt wrote to him. "What would be the condition of the rivers in the Fall—how hard would they be to cross? Would any special features be encountered on the way? What roots would be edible? How about wild cherries as food? Is there another name for the bull-berry beside buffalo berry?"[32]

The reaction to *Hugh Glass*, at a time of polarized camps in poetry, was mixed. One critic, writing for a regional literary magazine, thought the poem should "take rank with, if not precedence over, Scott and Tennyson in our schools."[33] Another, Jim Tully, the writer who had been a fan of Neihardt's early lyrics, praised Neihardt's "power of epic writing": "Beside his terrific bombardment and corralling of beauty," Tully wrote, "Longfellow's 'Hiawatha' and 'Evangeline' are pretty tales told by old ladies at Chatauqua."[34] The *New York Times* called the poem a "book of virile quality," and said, "Mr. Neihardt has uncovered a rich mine in the annals of the explorer and fur trader and tells his story with dramatic effect."[35]

But if the narrative elicited mostly positive response, the archaic form did not. Harriet Monroe personally reviewed the book for *Poetry*. "Of course Mr. Neihardt is an accomplished craftsman, and there are in his poem passages of fine simplicity and stately music," she wrote. But she soundly criticized Neihardt for the form. "He has fitted the story to the measure instead of letting it choose its form, and somehow the nobility and high-sounding rotundity of the poem do not satisfy us. . . . Such art smells of the old-time theatre."[36] She was not alone in her criticism. The *New Republic* found the traditional form of rhymed couplets "most antipathetic to the modern mood." Though the magazine credited Neihardt with trying to invent ways to avoid the "flat-wheel thudding" of the couplet, it found he had not fully succeeded. "He has in fact added to the unavoidable archaic quality of rhymed pentameter by the inclusion of a number of figures, words, phrases, and allusions that were part of the poetic stock in trade in the days of Pope and Addison."[37]

As usual, though, Neihardt's trusted correspondents supported him. Regardless of whether he was able to convince Sterling of the appropriateness of rhyme, once Sterling read the finished poem he offered nothing but praise. "This is to state, declare and asseverate that I've received and read *Hugh Glass*," he wrote soon after Neihardt sent him a copy, "and thank you heartily for the book *and for writing it*. Some of my friends have read it too, and we are all agreed that it is splendid stuff, nobly American, and a *real* addition to the literature of our country."[38] Doane Robinson, too, praised the book. "I am struck with the great number of quotable lines in *Hugh*," he told Neihardt. "There is scarcely a situation pertinent to the western life that does not have its illuminating line."[39]

The book also sold well. "The first two months' sales of *Hugh Glass* buys my winter's coal," Neihardt wrote to his sister Lulu, "not so bad!"[40] In Bancroft, townspeople had taken notice too. Frank Luther Mott, a writer and editor, visited the Neihardts in 1915. As he was preparing to leave by train he bought a soft drink from a young man working behind the depot's counter, and he noticed that the young man was reading *Hugh Glass*. Mott, discovering that the man knew Neihardt, asked what he thought of the book. "It's pretty good," he told Mott, "even if it is poetry."[41]

From the moment he began writing *Hugh Glass*, Neihardt envisioned it as only the beginning of a much larger project. "*Hugh Glass* is the first in a series of heroic poems built on northwestern history," he wrote to Ledoux in November 1915. "When the series is completed, I think there will be something like an epic cycle—and genuinely American. I see ten more years of work ahead in that direction."[42] The next month he presented a slightly more specific plan to George Sterling, suggesting that the epic cycle would be broken up into smaller collections. *Hugh Glass* and the next one he was about to start would be part of the first "saga." "Within four years I should have *The Rocky Mountain Saga* complete," he told Sterling, "then even those who lack imagination will see what I'm trying to do."[43]

For his second volume in this first cycle of narrative poems, Neihardt chose another true story from the Ashley-Henry expeditions. Like *The Song of Hugh Glass*, his new poem, *The Song of Three Friends*, told the story of real people, though as he had done in the first book, Neihardt changed some of the few known facts to dramatize the tale. "[The story] had already circulated for years around the campfires of the West," Neihardt said, "and was, therefore, in the nature, almost, of a folktale. But it was true."[44] Mike Fink had been a Mississippi Valley keelboatman before joining the expedition up the Missouri River in 1822. He was a larger-than-life character and after his death in 1823 became a folk hero and the subject of two early biographies. His companions on the expedition were Will Carpenter and Frank Talbot. Fink and Carpenter, both crack shots, were known for performing a death-defying trick: they would fill a tin cup with whiskey and then shoot it off the top of each other's heads from sixty yards away. One day, after a disagreement, the two undertook the trick, flipped a coin to see who would shoot first, and when Fink won the toss, he shot Carpenter out from under the cup, killing him instantly. An angry Talbot some time later avenged Carpenter by shooting and killing Fink with the gun Carpenter had bequeathed him.[45] Neihardt knew of the episode from Hiram Chittenden's *American Fur Trade of the Far West*, and he also researched the story in the periodicals the *Western Souvenir*, *Western Monthly Review*, and *Missouri Intelligencer* as well as in letters collected at the Kansas Historical Society.

In 1908 Neihardt had written a short story, "The Brutal Fact," that told the tale of the same incident, though he changed the names of the principal characters. Chittenden's account had Fink, drunk some months after the shooting, admit he had intended to kill Carpenter, and at that point Talbot shot and killed him. But Neihardt, in his short story, stretched the aftermath of the tin cup shooting into a journey of self-discovery for Fink and Talbot: Talbot, upon hearing a drunken Fink admit the killing, orders him, at gunpoint, to run, then follows him, keeping him from water, food, and shelter. The days that follow give both men a chance to examine their acts and motivations. By the time Talbot decides he has gone far enough in punishing his old friend, Fink has died on the trail. Neihardt told the same story in *The Song of Three Friends*, though he added a prairie fire to introduce the climactic scene in which Fink admits to intentionally killing Carpenter and chose to use the men's real names—only spelling Talbot as Talbeau to make sure readers used the French pronunciation. He started writing in February 1916 and by summer was issuing his regular production reports. "I'm sailing along nicely with *The Song of Three Friends*—the second piece of my epic cycle," he wrote to Sterling in July. "After the *Friends* there are two other pieces, & I have six years of work laid out clearly."[46]

Writing *Friends* was not all that kept Neihardt occupied in 1916. Money was tight for John and Mona, and he needed to supplement his income. The same month he undertook the new poem, he started lecturing and reading his work publicly, beginning what would become a lucrative sideline. "I don't especially like the stunt," he said, "but it pays very well, & helps in several ways."[47] He started his speaking engagements in Wayne, Nebraska, at the normal school he had attended, then traveled to Indiana, where he read one of his poetic dramas, parts of *Hugh Glass*, and an assortment of his early lyrics. Throughout the year he continued to speak whenever he could, at one point putting together a tour in which he spoke fourteen times and earned eight hundred dollars. He and Mona had borrowed some money, but as he wrote to his sister Lulu, the engagements—along with the success of *Hugh Glass*—would get him out of debt by winter. Still, he thanked her for sending hand-me-downs for him and an ever growing family: on December 6 Mona gave birth to another daughter, Hilda, giving the Neihardts three of what they lovingly called "Wubs."[48] "Quite satisfactory!" Neihardt announced. "Mona is very well."[49]

One speaking engagement in particular drew Nebraska's attention to its poet. In late January 1917 Neihardt read from his poetry at a meeting of the Society of Fine Arts in Omaha. It must have been especially gratifying for him that among those attending the reading was Joseph Polcar, the former editor of the *Omaha Daily News* who had fired him from his reporting job in 1901, and that the *Daily News* published an article about the event under the headline "'Fired' by News, Now He's Famous."[50] The *Omaha World-Herald* published an editorial praising— and expressing surprise at—Neihardt's success:

That we could actually bring forth a poet, a real poet, one exceptionally gifted, is difficult for us to believe. If he is a child of the prairies, breathing the wholesome winds of our open spaces; if he interprets the significance of our daily life, weaving into the wool of his verse our corn, our sunflowers, our wheat; if he celebrates the orioles and thrushes we can see in our own backyards; if he tells the epic story of adventure which our own pioneer kin may have experienced in the early West; why, then we wonder whether he can really be a poet. Can we possibly have hatched a swan?[51]

A few days after the event, the *Daily News* reported in a front-page article that local bookstores were reporting large sales of Neihardt's books and that Omaha's library was experiencing a run on its copies.[52] That June the University of Nebraska awarded honorary doctor of letters degrees to Neihardt and fellow Nebraska author Willa Cather, a writer Neihardt believed was earning her place in American literature. "Miss Cather appears to be a novelist well on her way toward permanent distinction," he wrote in a review of her novel *The Song of the Lark* in 1915. As to receiving an honorary doctorate himself, "My own state seems to be waking up," Neihardt told a friend. "For ten years I have been rather widely known among readers of contemporary literature; but Nebraska discovered me only last winter."[53]

Neihardt continued to write for the *Minneapolis Journal*, and he used the platform to carry on his fight against the new trends in poetry. Edgar Lee Masters had just published *Spoon River Anthology*, a series of monologues spoken by dead men and women populating a midwestern cemetery. Given his own experiences with small-town hypocrisy and narrow-mindedness, which Masters ruthlessly attacked, Neihardt should have enjoyed the book, but he did not, calling it a collection of "slapdash, though occasionally inspired, effusions." In another article Neihardt compared poets to birds, saying that among the vireos, orioles, thrushes, robins, mockingbirds, and wrens were a number of crows, "croaking hopefully though raucously." But he suggested readers should be thankful for these crows. "When even the crow wishes to be a singer, how shall the nightingale keep silence?"[54]

Some traditionalists certainly agreed with Neihardt, but many modern poets and readers did not. By 1917 critic Louis Untermeyer wrote that "the 'new' poetry was ranked as 'America's first national art.' . . . People who never before had read verse turned to it and found they could not only read but relish it. They discovered that for the enjoyment of poetry it was not necessary to have at their elbows a dictionary of rare words and classical references; they no longer were required to be acquainted with Latin legendry and the minor love-affairs of the major Greek divinities. Life was their glossary, not literature."[55]

The turmoil over embracing or rejecting the new poetry grew loud enough that Lloyd Morris, an author, critic, and social historian, solicited poets to explain their positions on the matter and then published them, in 1917, as *The Young Idea: An Anthology of Opinion Concerning the Spirit and Aims of Contemporary American Literature.*[56] Based on their responses, Morris categorized the poets into one of five groups: Empiricists, Romanticists, Idealists, Pessimists, and Traditionalists. Not surprisingly, Neihardt, one of the thirty poets who responded to Morris's call, ended up, along with Edwin Arlington Robinson and Louis Ledoux, in the Traditionalist camp, whereas Harriet Monroe joined Vachel Lindsay and others in the Empiricists. Monroe and Neihardt, without mentioning one another specifically, made public their private discussions, with Monroe arguing against "close observance of the well-worn formulae of rhymes and iambs" and explaining how her magazine, by publishing some of the new poetry, was trying to tear down the walls that limited verse to traditional forms. "We have printed not only odes and sonnets, blank verse dramas and rhymed pentameter narratives, but imagistic songs, futuristic fugues, fantasies in *vers libre*, rhapsodies in polyphonic prose—any dash for freedom which seemed to have life and hope in it—a fervor for movement and the beauty of open spaces—even if the goal was vague and remote, or quite unattainable in the distance."[57] Neihardt, in his contribution to the book, criticized what he saw as a "democratic" movement in poetry, "in the sense that nearly everyone seems to be engaged in writing it." To him it looked as if the difficulties of writing poetry had been removed, allowing new poets to forgo the "long and faithful apprenticeship" once necessary. Neihardt believed that modern poets should be connected to those who came before them and that "by ignoring the Past the poet deliberately sacrifices the chief source of poetic power." "For it is mainly by appealing to memory that poetry works its magic," he wrote, "and the individual memory is too brief, too fragmentary."[58]

At the end of the book Morris offered his own conclusion that contemporary literature, "and particularly contemporary poetry," was expressing "a social content." Poets at this point were appealing to the public "less as lovers of art than as lovers of life," he concluded, and were bound by no traditional conceptions of beauty. What surprised him, he said, was how little discussion of poetic form he had elicited from the gathered poets. In the book Monroe and Neihardt were nearly alone in confronting form, and Morris made it clear that he had expected a more fervent conversation. "The emphasis of the poets seems rather to be in the direction of content," he wrote, "as though they believed that content shapes its own form."[59] The *New York Times*, in reviewing Morris's book, described the "reawakened spirit of true poetry" as "a protest against the artificialities, the essentially untrue, conventional, sentimental interpretation of life of the verse dominating the age of Dryden and Pope."[60]

Neihardt briefly served as an example of the changing poetry landscape when the first collected edition of his early verse was published that same year. He had first contacted the Macmillan Company about such an edition four years earlier, sending the publisher copies of *A Bundle of Myrrh*, *Man-Song*, and *The Stranger at the Gate* as well as the issue of *Poetry* magazine that contained "The Death of Agrippina." "It seems to me that, considering my standing among American poets, and the fact that there seems to be a revival of popular interest in verse, my proposition ought to be of interest to you," he wrote the company, "and I hope the matter will be given careful consideration."[61] Macmillan agreed to publish the book, which it titled *The Quest*, and Neihardt chose seventy-three of his poems. He dedicated the book to the women in his family: "mighty givers, meagre takers, mother, sister, wife." The collection afforded readers and critics the opportunity to look again at Neihardt's lyric poetry. The *New York Times Review of Books*, for one, was impressed. It reviewed *The Quest*, Amy Lowell's *Men, Women, and Ghosts*, and Edgar Lee Masters's *The Great Valley* on its front page, illustrating the three with engravings of each poet and presenting them all under the headline "The New Movement in American Poetry." The review said Neihardt "has renewed for us the incomparable note of his youth . . . the *Bundle of Myrrh*. It contained lyrics that have not been equaled by any of our modern poets. . . . The volume traces a fine spiritual crescendo, opening with youthful abandonment and rising to a dramatic climax."[62] The literary magazine the *Dial* found that "abundant egoism" remained in Neihardt's poetry but thought it might be necessary for self-preservation in "that prairie country in which he lives and sings."[63]

But the *Times* and the *Dial* did not represent the entirety of the critical reception. The *Nation* questioned whether Neihardt was well advised to collect his lyrics into one volume: "His poems are of a kind which makes it politic to afford the reader the relief of intervals."[64] Neihardt's regular antagonist Harriet Monroe also reviewed the collection in *Poetry*, expressing a "certain feeling of disappointment": "Some of these poems seemed quite 'advanced' when they first appeared," she wrote, "but the art has gone a long way since then, and many poets have raced past Mr. Neihardt, perhaps because they carry fewer impedimenta."[65] Neihardt could not resist pointing out Monroe's review to Sterling, ridiculing her claim that the art of poetry had progressed in recent years. "That is to say, the art of Aeschylus, Sophocles, Virgil, Goethe, Moliere and Shakespeare (not to mention certain passé individuals!) has made 'great progress,'" Neihardt wrote, "since Miss Monroe established her house of refuge for literary imbeciles!"[66] Sterling, ever in agreement with Neihardt, responded: "If any poets have 'raced past' you, I'd be damned obliged to Miss Monroe for their names! As to her vers libre gang, they are all racing backwards! The poor old hen!"[67]

With Sterling's encouragement—and not without a significant amount of critical support—Neihardt continued to oppose the new movements in poetry. Early in his career he had written poetry along the lines of the *vers libre* crowd—many of those poems were included in *The Quest* and earned him a place in what the *New York Times* called the "new movement" in American poetry—but he had abandoned the new forms entirely for the rhyming pentameter he was using in his poems of the fur trappers. "I'm working steadily, as usual, on *The Song of Three Friends*," he wrote to Sterling in June 1917. "Will complete it in December. It works with much more power than *Hugh Glass*."[68]

9   A MOVE AND A TRIBUTE

John Neihardt did not finish *The Song of Three Friends* in December 1917, as he had hoped. As 1918 began he was further delayed in finishing his new poem by an ever more rigorous schedule of public appearances. For the first time his travels took him to California, where he spoke at both Stanford University and the University of California at Berkeley. (At Berkeley he discovered that he had gone to grade school in Kansas City with the janitor working at the hall where he spoke.)[1] While in California Neihardt visited George Sterling, and the two traveled, in dapper suits and overcoats, to the Muir Woods National Monument, established only ten years earlier. Like countless visitors before and since, Neihardt was enchanted by California. "Lord! What a country! Looks impossible!" he wrote home to his family. "Ripe oranges on the trees, and just yesterday I was in December. Here it is the gentlest kind of June weather. I'm afraid poor old Nebraska may lose its chief literary reason for existence one of these years! Yes & a sculptor & a Grandma & three lovely Wubs too!"[2] Yet despite having "a bully time" in California, as he described it in a letter home to his mother, Neihardt was soon missing Nebraska.[3] "I'll be glad to be home," he wrote only a week later. "Nebraska has charms that this country lacks."[4]

    He had continued to revise the plan for his epic cycle, and at this point he expected to write three more extended poems after *Friends*: two more on the fur trade, *The Song of Jed Smith* and *The Song of the Last Rendezvous*, and then the finale, *The Song of the Sioux Wars*. During his stay in California Neihardt traveled to Monterey to research the poem he planned on Smith, another of the famed Ashley-Henry men. Smith had spent time in Monterey, and Neihardt wanted to see it for himself. On his return trip he stopped in southeastern Montana to see the site of the Battle of the Little Bighorn.

When he returned home Neihardt worked to finish *The Song of Three Friends*, and that September he sent it to the Macmillan Company. The book was published in February 1919 and was dedicated to his newest baby, Hilda. Neihardt relied not only on his research but also on his own experiences when he wrote almost anything, and this was certainly true of *Friends*. One scene, when the men have taken to the river after the spring thaw, was based on an incident from his *River and I* trip in 1908 in which Neihardt and his friends had gone nearly a week without a real meal when they managed to kill a deer. The men were so famished that they stayed up well into the night eating venison. In *Friends*, he has the travelers come upon a large herd of bison.

> So they beached their boats and killed
> Three fatling heifers; sliced the juicy rumps
> For broiling over embers; set the humps
> And loins to roast on willow spits, and threw
> The hearts and livers in a pot to stew
> Against the time of dulling appetites.
> And when the stream ran opalescent lights
> And in a scarlet glow the new moon set,
> The feast began. And some were eating yet,
> And some again in intervals of sleep,
> When upside down above the polar steep
> The Dipper hung.[5]

When he wrote of Fink and Carpenter coming to blows he recalled fights he had seen himself during his earliest years in Bancroft, but the personal experience that he relied on most was his encounter, as a young boy, with the Kansas prairie fire. The fire—its sounds, sights, and smells as well as the fear it caused—loomed large in his memory, but he also questioned Doane Robinson about the specifics of such a fire. "I want a prairie fire—a good big one," he wrote to Robinson. "Can you hypothecate conditions under which a good healthy blaze could oblige an anxious poet in June?"[6] In the book the fire came at night, and for a few minutes Talbeau thought its brightness on the horizon was simply the approaching dawn. Slowly his other senses told him otherwise.

> What sound was that? Perhaps a thunder storm
> Was working up. He coughed; and then it broke
> Upon him how the air was sharp with smoke;
> And, leaping up, he turned and looked and knew
> What birdless dawn, unhallowed by the dew,
> Came raging from the northwest! Half the earth
> And half the heavens were a burning hearth
> Fed fat with grass inflammable as tow![7]

Like *Hugh Glass* before it, *Three Friends* met with a mixed critical response. The *Boston Evening Transcript* called Neihardt's cycle "one of the profoundly notable and one of the few original things in the development of American poetry."[8] The *New Republic*, however, thought Neihardt's use of archaic words and allusions too often worked against him: "The real clarity of thought and sentence-structure which he deliberately achieves is often negated by a reference to Clio or a self-conscious designation of his poem as 'the Song'—in the manner of Milton addressing his muse." Yet the magazine's reviewer thought the book deserved more readers and consideration than it was likely to get. "It has the odds against it, and is not sufficiently rugged to win out over them."[9] The *Nation* understood what Neihardt was trying to do with the rhyme scheme. "The point, of course, is to make the rhyme not a determining factor in verse structure, but a partially muffled—though regularly recurring—note, like a gratuity added to blank verse. Tastes will differ as to the relative effectiveness of this mode in narrative, but it is undeniable that Mr. Neihardt handles it skillfully and with surprising naturalness, almost never permitting a rhyme-word to draw attention to itself for its own sake."[10] Charles Hanson Towne, then editor of *McClure's Magazine*, wrote to tell Neihardt that he could not stop thinking about *Friends*. "How good it is to think of a man living up to his ideals as you are doing! But that shows in your work, and that is the reason I could picture your life on the prairies as I did."[11] The *New York Times*, while arguing that Neihardt deserved readers' gratitude for rescuing the tale from oblivion, believed he had not altogether succeeded with *Friends*. "He is a plodder, not a flier, and a tale of this sort needs the wheeling, swooping vision of the hawk or the eagle for its proper recording."[12]

In 1919 the Poetry Society of America awarded the book its annual prize for the best volume of poetry published by an American. The vote was actually a tie between *The Song of Three Friends* and *Poems* by Gladys Cromwell. Before the winners were announced, however, Cromwell and her twin sister, who had both been working with the Red Cross during the war, committed suicide by jumping from the ship returning them to the United States, and the monetary portion of the prize went entirely to Neihardt.

Only after the award was announced did Harriet Monroe write about *Friends* in her magazine, arguing, as she had done when reviewing *Glass*, that the book was unsound as a work of art. "The reasons are essentially one," she wrote, "the discord between the story and the style." While she praised Neihardt's project of preserving the historic tales, she once again attacked his approach. "Having started, he lacked the native human spirit, the unconscious courage, of his heroes—he couldn't give himself wholeheartedly to his adventure, let his subject carry him, but must needs load it with all the rhetorical and legendary impedimenta of many races, many literatures."[13]

Neihardt always valued the opinions of his friends more than those of critics, and once again his friends were enthusiastic. "Gods! Such a poem is worth thousands of the brief singings of our magazines!" Sterling wrote to Neihardt. "You have builded deep and wide and strong, and these books of yours will be classics for Heaven knows how many years."[14] That was all Neihardt needed to hear. He responded to Sterling, "I'd

rather convince one real he poet than get tons of taffy from the reviewers and have a hundred thousand readers!"[15] Neihardt also made a new
friend with the publication of *Friends*: philosopher John Elof Boodin,
who was then teaching at Carleton College in Northfield, Minnesota.
"As a child I was brought up in the heroic background of ancient story
and saga," Boodin wrote to Neihardt. "I have always felt grateful for this
background. Not only has it given me much enjoyment, but I feel that
it has given me a saner perspective of life. Now you are making it possible [through *Hugh Glass* and *Three Friends*] for the American youth
in beautiful poetry to make real to itself its own heroic background."[16]

The month after he finished writing *The Song of Three Friends* Neihardt
began a new project, taking a different approach to the story of the exploration of the West. Macmillan wanted a book on the subject for young
readers, along the lines of biographies it had already published of Daniel
Boone, Abraham Lincoln, Thomas Edison, and Theodore Roosevelt.
Neihardt agreed, mostly for the extra money. "I'm undertaking a book
on Western exploration for schools," he wrote to Sterling in December
1918, "a prose narrative, strictly historical in its main outlines but flavored
with fiction whenever it can be introduced without distorting the truth."[17]
Neihardt thought such a book would help him build a background—and
a readership—for his poetic cycle by introducing the period to youngsters.
He was able to use material he had gathered for *Hugh Glass* and *Three
Friends* and for other epic narratives still in the planning stages, and he
focused the book on another of the Ashley-Henry men, Jedediah Strong
Smith, a man Doane Robinson had included in his catalogue of heroes
of the fur trade. Neihardt titled the book *The Splendid Wayfaring* and
gave it a lengthy subtitle: "The story of the exploits and adventures of
Jedediah Smith and his comrades, the Ashley-Henry men, discoverers
and explorers of the great Central Route from the Missouri River to the
Pacific Ocean, 1822–1831."

In the preface to the book Neihardt again argued that historians had
concerned themselves too much with governments, "too little with the
activities of the people themselves," and had thereby missed the real

explorers of the western United States. "I have made Jedediah Smith the central figure of my story," he told readers, "for of all explorers of the Great West he was in many ways the most remarkable, though, heretofore, our school children have not even heard his name." Neihardt began his story long before Smith's birth, tracing the western migration across America all the way back to Indo-Europeans living in the valley of the Euphrates. Some of those people eventually headed toward India, but others headed to the west "and so began a journey that should continue for thousands of years and thousands of miles, to reach our own Pacific Coast during the 19th century."[18] Those "westering people" were "our ancestors," he wrote, and they were the people, in this book and in his cycle of long narrative poems, who had come to mean so much to him. He was clearly proud to count his own ancestors among them.

The story—which Neihardt quickly brought to 1822, to the frontier town of Cincinnati, Ohio, where a young Jedediah Smith has just boarded a boat bound for St. Louis—was essentially a biography of Smith. Robinson had argued forcefully for Neihardt to include Smith, and in response, Neihardt wrote to Robinson in 1914, "Jed Smith looks good to me also. How can I get at all of him? I find very little in the books I have—nothing circumstantial."[19] Robinson certainly would have shared with Neihardt his own writing on the subject, his massive *History of South Dakota*.[20] Central to Robinson's telling of Smith's story was a prayer Smith offered on June 2, 1823, after members of the Arikara tribe had attacked a contingent of trappers led by Ashley, killing twenty-three and wounding many others. When Ashley asked for a volunteer to take a message to his partner, Henry, at a camp several hundred miles away on the Yellowstone River, Smith stepped forward. Before he left on his new mission, he knelt and prayed beside a dying young man named John S. Gardner—whom Smith had dragged out of the fight, according to Smith family legend.[21] Hugh Glass sent a letter to Gardner's father: "My painfull duty it is to tell you of the deth of yr son who befell at the hands of the Indians 2d June in the early morning. . . . Mr. Smith a young man of our company made a powerful prayr wh moved us all greatly and I am persuaded John died in peace."[22] Robinson had Glass's letter as part of the historical society's collection, and Neihardt quoted from it in *The Splendid Wayfaring.*

Robinson, a devout Congregationalist devoted to South Dakota, could not resist being attracted to Smith's story. Neihardt's interest in Smith, which sprouted directly from Robinson, came to focus more on Smith as a representative figure. Though Neihardt admired the specifics of Smith's life and achievements, he valued Smith more as being the "type" of man who arose in the time of exploration. Rather than focus on Ashley or Henry, who led the expeditions and owned the company, he focused on Smith, one of a hundred men in their employ. Jed Smith, Neihardt believed, was bound to become "one of the great torch-bearers of the race."[23]

Even as he pushed Neihardt to memorialize Smith, Robinson was trying to build his own monument to the explorer. As a historian and secretary of the South Dakota State Historical Society, he was looking to combine South Dakota's natural scenery with its history to make a popular tourist attraction. In 1911 sculptor Lorado Taft had completed a forty-eight-foot statue called "The Eternal Indian" that stood on the eastern bank of the Rock River near Oregon, Illinois. In late 1923, three years after *The Splendid Wayfaring* was published, Robinson contacted Taft to see if he would be willing to try something similar by carving some of the granite pinnacles near Harney Peak into likenesses of Western heroes. "Having in mind your 'Big Injun,'" Robinson wrote to Taft, "it has occurred to me that some of these pinnacles would lend themselves to massive sculpture. . . . I am thinking of some notable Sioux as Red Cloud, who lived and died in the shadow of these peaks. If one was found practicable, perhaps others would ultimately follow."[24]

Taft was ill and would not consider undertaking such a project, but Robinson continued to promote—and even expand—his idea. "The plan I suggested to you grows upon me as I think of it, and I am sure that an artist of vision and imagination could work out a wonderful scheme," he wrote to Taft. "I can see all the old heroes of the [W]est peering out from them: Lewis and Clark, Fremont, Jed Smith, Bridger, Sa-kaka-wea, Red Cloud, and in an equestrian statue, Cody and the overland mail."[25] Still Taft declined, and Robinson eventually turned instead to another sculptor, Gutzon Borglum, then involved in a colossal sculpture at Stone Mountain, Georgia. Borglum, unlike Taft, was immediately interested, but he wanted to carve national heroes rather than Western ones. In the end the monument that Borglum gave Robinson and South Dakota was Mount Rushmore.

Neihardt complained that Macmillan thought of *The Splendid Wayfaring* only as "a child's book for twelve-year-olds" and promoted it as such.[26] In a short time he dismissed it as "not one of my more important books."[27] Yet some preferred his prose rendition of the period's history to his poetic version. One reviewer complained, "Evidently Mr. Neihardt instead of following the rich vein which he struck in *The Splendid Wayfaring* intends to follow the less profitable one which he explored in his first books, *The Song of Hugh Glass* and *The Song of Three Friends*.... They are as meretricious as *The Splendid Wayfaring* is meritorious."[28]

In Neihardt's mind, winning the Poetry Society of America's prize for *The Song of Three Friends* more than made up for any negative criticism his narrative poems were receiving. Now, at the beginning of the 1920s, Julius T. House, his friend from the Nebraska Normal School in nearby Wayne, strengthened his confidence even further by writing a book-length biography, *John G. Neihardt: Man and Poet*. Since discovering that the author of "The Poet's Town" lived just down the road, House had been teaching English and immersing himself in all things Neihardt. No record remains of the conversations between Neihardt and House that produced *Man and Poet*. But later letters between the two men make it clear that Neihardt was the driving force behind the book. (Five years later, Neihardt asked House to write an article on his growing collection of epic poems, giving him specific points to emphasize.) According to the biography, five incidents were key to his narrative. Given that House was reporting Neihardt's life story as Neihardt wanted it known strongly suggests that these five incidents were key in Neihardt's own mind to his poetry and to his life.

The first was the dream he had had when he was ill in the fall of 1892. The second was the realization, shortly after the dream, that his childhood interest in electricity and mechanics had vanished, leaving in its place a strong desire to write poetry. The third was the sense he frequently had, if ever he felt satisfied with an achievement, that "something seemed to take the joy of it away." The fourth incident was the writing of the poem "The Ghostly Brother," which explored his childhood fever dream and the sense that he was being called away to some larger purpose. And the final and most recent incident was his visit to a medium in Omaha in 1912, in which she reported communicating with a Scottish minister who had been watching over Neihardt. These incidents would remain important to Neihardt's version of his life story. He remained interested in mysticism and psychic phenomena, and he frequently cited instances where poems, or at least lines of poems, came to him as in a dream. On occasion he awoke with a nearly complete poem ready to be written down.

Another small reflection of Neihardt's growing standing was his being asked, that July, to serve as editor-in-chief of *The Poet's Pack*, a collection of selected poems by members of the Order of Bookfellows, an organization of writers and poets run by George and Flora Warren Seymour in Chicago. Working with three associate editors, Neihardt reduced a thousand submissions to one hundred poems representing forty-five mostly midwestern poets, among them Neihardt's good friend George Sterling and Joseph Mills Hanson, who in 1909 had written a biography of Neihardt's Missouri River hero, Grant Marsh.

Neither House's book nor *The Poet's Pack* did much to enhance Neihardt's national reputation, but both were important to Neihardt. Selecting the poems opened him up to a score of new poets, and he proudly wrote to friends and family about the biography. "Dr. House's study of my poetry is out & selling finely," he wrote to his sister Lulu. "A National Neihardt Club has been organized to push my epic cycle all over the country."[29]

During the twenty years that Neihardt had lived in Bancroft, he had often thought of leaving Nebraska. He briefly considered moving to New York, South Dakota, and California—and in 1912 he *had* left for Minneapolis, only to return within a year. In early 1920 he considered moving to Oregon, as soon, he told Sterling, "as I can see some real money." He wanted his son to grow up where there was still a wilderness with good hunting and his daughters to grow up where there were suitable men. "This is hog country," he said of Nebraska, "and the climate has a perfectly vicious disposition. Sometimes I want to slap it for its un-Christian conduct."[30] Late in 1920 he remembered another place he had once hoped to make his home, the Ozarks in southern Missouri. He had first considered it in the spring of 1909, telling friends it was a place where one could live cheaply. "Plenty of woods, springs, fruit trees—peace."[31] Now, though he disliked the idea of leaving the Great Plains and thought he might eventually "wander back," he once again talked of leaving Nebraska.[32] This time he quickly decided to follow through: in October he bought a house and nearly five acres in Branson, Missouri, just twenty-five miles north of the Arkansas border, overlooking the White River.

As soon as Neihardt and his family arrived in Branson, he was certain the move was the right one. "At the present moment," he wrote to a friend, "the grass is as green as a relative's eye, and the butter we make is golden."[33] Mona, who had discovered right after moving that she was pregnant again, also liked Branson. "The children are in love with things here," she wrote to a friend after only a couple of months, and "the people are so kind—our neighbors refined good people." She was also excited by something she had in Branson that she had not had in Bancroft: electric lights. "Now does that sound as good to you as it does to me?"[34] Only John's mother, who was living with her son and his family until she could find her own home in Branson, was unhappy. "The natives are a shiftless set," she said, "drawl out their words and they work the same way."[35]

Almost immediately it became clear that the move had come at an awkward moment for Neihardt. Within a month of moving he learned that the Nebraska Legislature was considering naming him the state's poet laureate. "Now, of course, I see how funny this could be," Neihardt wrote to Sterling, "but there's evidently some affection in it, & I can't feel funny about any expression of affection."[36] The next spring, on April 18, 1921, Nebraska's Senate and House of Representatives passed a resolution naming him "Poet Laureate of Nebraska, in recognition of the American Epic Cycle upon which he has been engaged for eight years." Neihardt had turned forty only four months earlier, meaning he had become a poet laureate at an earlier age than his idol Tennyson, who was forty-one when he became laureate in 1850. Two months later representatives of the state government, along with leaders of the University of Nebraska, held a public ceremony in Lincoln. "No state, it appears, has, by legislative recognition, a poet laureate," said Lucius A. Sherman, a professor and Shakespearean scholar at the university and the acting chancellor at the time, as the ceremony got underway. "No other state, we may fairly say, has such a reason," Sherman said. "Nature has not shaped for us, in this paradise of prairie country, mountains that might become by myth or fancy, the home of gods or muses. There is, there can be, no Olympus, no Parnassus here. But we have that which has given fame to all the sacred groves and mountains and fountains of spiritual history. We have the poet himself in presence with us now."[37]

Addressing the gathering, Neihardt spoke for a few minutes on education, which he described as "fundamentally a spiritual process" and which, he told the crowd, should properly be less concerned with teaching students how to acquire the means of life than with the larger problem "of knowing what to do with life after one is in possession of the means to live."[38] He championed what he continued to call the "higher values"— that collection of "spiritual and mental attitudes that have resulted from man's age-long struggle."[39]

Mostly, though, he devoted his remarks to the writing of poetry, "the supreme form of human expression." Poetry, he said, was necessary at those times when a prose construction of words simply could not get a writer's point across satisfactorily. In those moments, poetry becomes "the universal language . . . bearing something like the same relation to the language of words that perfume bears to the rose."[40] Poetry, he continued, required four principal means to succeed: the use of symbols, the use of rhythm—with or without rhyme, the manipulation of sound, and an appeal to memory.[41] Expanding on the issue of rhythm allowed Neihardt to bring his fight for tradition to a new public.

We have been hearing a great deal about 'free form verse' of late years; but there can be no such thing as free form in the sense intended. Form can not be conceived as free, simply because it is not essentially arbitrary, but is determined in accordance with inexorable law—the same that determines the course of the sun, the roundness of the celestial bodies, the beating of the heart, the ebb and flow of the tide. It was not through whim or chance that poets first chanted in rhythm. Rhythm in poetry is not an artificial device, but a natural phenomenon. It is no less than the artistic manifestation of power's tendency to return upon itself, to make cycles.[42]

The "phenomenon of impressionism" was marring "nearly every field of intellectual and spiritual endeavor," he told his audience, yet he remained optimistic. "Respect for standards, love of order, will return," he said. "The petty personalism, that has long dominated us, will die away. Our poets will achieve the objective view of the world of men and things— and it is out of that view that all great art, as all great life, must grow."[43]

The audience that day represented a new crowd of listeners for Neihardt, and they responded enthusiastically. No one mentioned that Nebraska's new poet laureate actually lived in Missouri until the university officials took Neihardt to catch his train home: Though the state resolution contained no appropriation to pay Neihardt, they wondered if he would return to live in Nebraska if the university could come up with a suitable salary—and no duties. Neihardt returned to Branson without giving the university an answer, and Sterling could not help teasing him about the situation. "I have to grin every time I think of it: as soon as your devoted Nebraskans crown you laureate, *you light out for Missouri!* How in Hell do you explain it to them? I should think they'd lynch you, or revoke the honor!"[44]

The issue of which state would lay claim to Neihardt would not go away. A year later he lectured at Minnesota's Carleton College, and before he left the college offered to pay him to stay on campus. Before he could even consider it, word reached the newspapers in Omaha. The *Omaha Bee*, in an editorial headlined "Keep Neihardt in Nebraska," argued, "Surely if a college in Minnesota appreciates him so much as to consider making a place for him, the great state of Nebraska can do no less than match the offer."[45] The *Bee* quoted F. J. Hirsch, a former Nebraskan then living in Minnesota, who chastised Nebraskans for taking so long to appreciate Neihardt and explained how people at Carleton College had come to embrace the poet. Hirsch recounted the time Neihardt had read some of his poetry at the campus chapel. "With the first line his voice rose through a dead hush," he said. "The audience was entirely his, and as the epic unrolled before our imaginations, the spell of the frontier settled upon us and thrilled us for the better part of two hours. When he had finished we remained spell-bound for a moment, and, then, the clapping of 2,000 hands broke the silence like a crash. The impression that he had left was deep and lasting."[46]

Paul Greer, the managing editor of the *Bee*, pushed hard to bring Neihardt back to Nebraska and to keep him from going to Minnesota. As part of his campaign Greer sent Neihardt a telegram asking for a poem on the subject of Easter. He offered fifty dollars and said he would publish the poem on the front page of his paper on the morning of Easter Sunday. Neihardt was ready to respond immediately that he could not "just turn on the spigot and get a poem on Easter," but Mona persuaded him to wait a day. "Maybe something will happen," he remembered her telling him. Neihardt held off, and that night, as was his habit, he read the lines of the poem he had worked on that day, and then he went to bed and dreamed. "I was in a dark room, and it was black. I could see nothing. But I could hear the voices of men. And those men were good poets. Each one was trying to recite a poem on Easter, and nobody would let anybody finish his poem. They were very impolite to each other and very eager. Very eager. Well, I got up in the morning and I was worn out, as though I'd been working all night. Perhaps my subconscious had been working, I don't know."[47] When Neihardt told Mona about his dream the next morning, she suggested he try to get down on paper the pieces of poetry he remembered. He did not think it would be possible because the segments seemed too disjointed. But he could not clear his head of the fragments, and before long he set to work trying to write a poem from them. In less than twenty minutes he had the pieces in place. "I made up the connections," he said later. "But the poem was there."[48]

Neihardt sent the poem to the *Bee*, which immediately announced its arrival. "A new poem from this master's pen is a literary event of the first magnitude," the *Bee* exclaimed on the front page four days before Easter. "It would be eagerly sought by any of the national magazines. But Nebraska's laureate wishes to give it as his offering to the people of his home state."[49]

In "Easter—1923" Neihardt compared the Biblical Easter story to the rebirth that nature experiences every spring. "Once more the Ancient Wonder / Brings back the goose and crane," he wrote in opening the six-stanza poem. Each subsequent stanza of four lines contained such a comparison: a raging river breaks through a gorge and Christ emerges from the tomb, birds sing of how snow *and* Christ's glory cover the grass. A Congregational pastor from Ithaca, New York—named, all too perfectly, Edward L. Christ—wrote to Neihardt to say the poem was "the loveliest expression of the Easter thought that I know."[50] Years later Neihardt sold the poem to Hallmark for use in an Easter greeting card.[51]

On Easter Sunday, 1923, the poem ran at the top of the front page of the *Bee*, directly above the two-column headline "State and Colleges Make Rival Claims for Neihardt" on an article that brought readers up to date on the ongoing story of the places vying for Neihardt's presence. "Two great colleges are hoping to induce him to accept a resident fellowship at a salary but with no duties, merely to attach himself to the faculty and lend the intellectual influence of his name," the article reported, before adding, a paragraph later, "Meantime Neihardt remains a quiet citizen of Missouri."[52] Within the month, the University of Nebraska offered Neihardt a professorship in poetry that allowed him to continue to work on his cycle of long narrative poems—and to keep living in Missouri—in return for a brief series of lectures.[53]

Neihardt accepted the position, but he apparently did not think it required him to do everything he was asked: when the chancellor asked Neihardt to write a poem for the new football stadium being built on campus, Neihardt declined, saying he was too focused on a poem he was writing. "I am having a good run on the poem now, and must keep at it while I can," Neihardt told the chancellor. Though a football poem seemed an odd subject for Neihardt, who had never written about sports, he tried to convince the chancellor otherwise. "The stadium lyric would be sure to grip me, and as I never let myself do less than my best, the thing would be sure to take a lot of me."[54]

IO A STORY THAT NEEDS NO EMBELLISHMENT

John Neihardt was progressing on the next book in his cycle of epic poems, but his move to Missouri, the hubbub over the poet laureateship, his regular work for the *Minneapolis Journal*, and the ever-increasing amount of time he spent reciting and lecturing interfered with his work. He had first prepared a two-page outline for a poem on the Plains Indian wars five years earlier, in 1918. At that time he had planned to focus exclusively on the Sioux and their fight to hold onto their bison hunting range of the Great Plains. In October of that year, returning from a lecture tour in California, Neihardt had stopped at the Crow Agency in southeastern Montana to visit the Little Bighorn site. Crow Indians had acted as scouts for Custer, and Neihardt interviewed one of them at the agency, an elderly man named Curly, who was then regarded as the first person to report the defeat of the Seventh Cavalry when he located the *Far West*, Grant Marsh's supply boat, at the confluence of the Bighorn and Little Bighorn rivers. Through an interpreter Neihardt spoke with Curly about the battle, and when they were finished the two men exchanged rings, a gesture that Neihardt interpreted as bonding them as brothers and one that took on an almost mystical importance for the poet. "[T]o think that *I* who am to write *The Song of the Sioux Wars* should wear Curly's ring! It looks like spirit influence, & who knows that the ring won't in some way give me influences?"[1]

Neihardt planned to begin his new poem with the Fetterman Fight, a battle during Red Cloud's war in late 1866 in which a small group of Indians, acting as decoys, drew some eighty soldiers into an ambush. All the soldiers were killed. Neihardt also planned to include the Battle of Slim Buttes, ten years later, the first cavalry victory after Custer's loss at the Little Bighorn, the fight that Neihardt saw as his major focus. As he had with the two earlier narrative poems, Neihardt turned to Doane Robinson for advice. "What do you think? Should I begin so far back, or should I begin with the marching of the Seventh [Cavalry] from Fort Abraham Lincoln? . . . I would be grateful for any suggestion from you."[2] A month later he leaned on Robinson again, asking if any of the old Sioux leaders were still alive. "I must know well the fundamental characteristic of each. They must appear as *persons* with their distinct characteristics."[3] Robinson sent Neihardt a copy of his own lecture, "The Last Stand of the Sioux," and advised Neihardt to begin even further back, with the Dakota War of 1862, which resulted in the execution of nearly forty Indians, and to end with the Custer battle. Before long Neihardt expanded the scope of his poem even further. H. R. Lemly, a retired major in the U.S. Army and one of the first officers Neihardt contacted for background for the book, told him that calling his poem *The Song of the Sioux Wars* would unfairly limit him. "[Y]ou can scarcely leave out Dull Knife and Chief Joseph in writing of the Indian wars."[4]

Though Neihardt was eager to work on what he quickly renamed *The Song of the Indian Wars*—"How I wish I could stay at home and work on the *Wars*!" he wrote in December 1923—he needed the money that his lecturing provided to pay for research trips to relevant sites in western Nebraska, Wyoming, and southern South Dakota. On the last day of 1923 he set off on another lecture trip to Texas, California, Oregon, and Washington, not returning to Missouri until the first week of February 1924.[5] Among his stops was the Ebell Club of Los Angeles, where he read from *The Song of Three Friends*. The *Los Angeles Times*, in an article promoting the engagement, said Neihardt "belongs to our boundless, original America," adding, "He is the voice of the prairie, and of the mountain, and of the heroes who passed that way."[6] While in California Neihardt interviewed elderly veterans of the U.S. Army's fight against the Plains Indians, productive meetings that had been arranged by E. A. Brininstool, a historian, journalist, and poet who, Neihardt wrote to his mother from Los Angeles, "has *everything* about the Indian Wars & knows everybody who knows anything."[7] The research Neihardt did in California gave him the materials he needed to finish the long poem, and upon his return to Missouri, he wrote with renewed enthusiasm. When he finished a section, he noted in the margins the date of its completion. He finished the final section, "The Death of Crazy Horse," on August 23. As he wrote to Sterling, "I'm feeling like a kid with his shoes off for the first time in the spring."[8]

In *The Song of the Indian Wars*, though some of Neihardt's fundamental conflict regarding the country's native inhabitants remained, he made an effort to include the Indians' viewpoint and, significantly, did not take sides in the conflicts themselves. He began the story at the end of the Civil War, what he calls in the poem that "four year storm of fratricide." Westward migrants are, Neihardt writes, "the takers of the world." While these Euro-American settlers find "virgin meadow-lands" in the west, Neihardt repeatedly makes clear that others were already living there, people for whom those meadows were "ancestral pastures." Before long the newcomers and the original inhabitants are at war, and Neihardt, in telling the story, shifts his descriptions from side to side, taking care to outline preparations on both sides of the conflict. He introduces Red Cloud, for example, by calling him "serene with conscious might, a king of men," then switches to the seven hundred troops under Brig. Gen. Henry Carrington. Throughout the poem he alternates between the cavalry and the native resistance, writing first of the ambush of Captain William Fetterman and his men, a fight the Indians won, and then the Wagon Box Fight, one they lost.

Neihardt's storytelling in *Indian Wars* was more restrained than it had been in *Hugh Glass* and *Three Friends*. In those earlier books, part of his approach, in seeking to make them *epic*, was to enlarge them beyond

what the evidence allowed, openly fabricating sections of both stories
to expand them to mythical status. With *Indian Wars*, though Neihardt
dramatized selected episodes and used his imagination to round out
characters, his writing held more closely to the truth. Here, Neihardt
seemed to be saying, was a story that did not need embellishment.

The climax of *The Song of the Indian Wars* is the murder of Crazy
Horse at Nebraska's Camp Robinson in 1877. Neihardt based his version on eyewitness accounts, many of them collected by Brininstool, and
including that of Lemly. On September 5, 1877, according to Lemly,
Crazy Horse was being taken to the camp's guardhouse for what he had
been told would be a conversation with Gen. Luther Bradley, who commanded the post. Once inside, Crazy Horse saw a narrow, barred cell, and
he believed the commandant instead intended to imprison him. "Crazy
Horse immediately made a rush for the door!" Lemly wrote. Crazy Horse
was wrestled to the floor by an Indian named Little Big Man, who Lemly
believed was working for the post. "[W]hipping out a long and slender
knife from the folds of his red blanket, Crazy Horse drew its keen edge
across the wrist of his assailant, and cut it to the bone," Lemly wrote.[9]
Crazy Horse managed to get outside, where he was bayonetted by a
guard. Neihardt's version dramatically recreated the moment.

> The stifling, dim
> Interior poured terror over him.
> He blinked about—and saw the iron bars.
>
> O nevermore to neighbor with the stars
> Or know the simple goodness of the sun!
> Did some swift vision of a doom begun
> Reveal the monstrous purpose of a lie—
> The desert island and the alien sky,
> The long and lonely ebbing of a life?
> The glimmer of a whipped-out butcher knife
> Dismayed the shrinking squad, and once again
> Men saw a face that many better men
> Had died to see! Brown arms that once were kind,

A comrade's arms, whipped round him from behind,
Went crimson with a gash and dropped aside.
"Don't touch me! I am Crazy Horse!" he cried,
And, leaping doorward, charged upon the world
To meet the end.[10]

Lemly also reported that Crazy Horse, after lying unconscious for a time and near death, came to and "gave vent to his feelings." Lemly included an English translation of Crazy Horse's last words in his account.

> I was not hostile to the white man. . . . Occasionally my young men would attack a party of the Crows or Arickarees, and take their ponies, but just as often, they were the assailants. We had buffaloes for food, and their hides for clothing, and we preferred the chase to a life of idleness and the bickerings and jealousies, as well as the frequent periods of starvation at the Agencies.
>
> But the Gray Fox (Crook) came out in the snow and bitter cold, and destroyed my village. All of us would have perished of exposure and hunger had we not recaptured our ponies.
>
> Then Long Hair (Custer) came in the same way. They say we massacred him, *but he would have massacred us had we not defended ourselves and fought to the death.* Our first impulse was to escape with our squaws and papooses, but we were so hemmed in that we had to fight. The government would not let me alone.[11]

Neihardt turned Crazy Horse's speech into poetry.

> I had my village and my pony herds
> On Powder where the land was all my own.
> I only wanted to be let alone.
> I did not want to fight. The Gray Fox sent
> His soldiers. We were poorer when they went;
> Our babies died, for many lodges burned
> And it was cold. We hoped again and turned
> Our faces westward. It was just the same
> Out yonder on the Rosebud. Gray Fox came.

The dust his soldiers made was high and long.
I fought him and I whipped him. Was it wrong
To drive him back? That country was my own.
I only wanted to be let alone.
I did not want to see my people die.
They say I murdered Long Hair and they lie.
His soldiers came to kill us and they died.[12]

In January 1925, after Neihardt had delivered the *Indian Wars* manuscript to Macmillan but before it had been published, he had the opportunity to read a section of the poem to an audience that included a former soldier who played a small part in the events the poem chronicled. Central High School in Omaha organized a special midyear commencement program around Neihardt's new poem that began with the high school's orchestra playing what were billed as "three genuine Indian melodies." Then Neihardt, just back from a ten-day lecture trip, read from the "The Wagon Boxes," the section of the poem that commemorates a battle between the U.S. Army and Lakota warriors near Fort Phil Kearny, along the Bozeman Trail in Wyoming, during what was known as Red Cloud's War. In July 1867 fewer than three dozen soldiers held off a much larger force of Lakota—estimates run from three hundred to more than a thousand—by laying wooden wagon boxes end-to-end in a circle.

Neihardt had worked the names of some of the soldiers into the poem. In one grim section he described their preparations as they waited for the Indians to attack.

And Littman yonder, grunting in the lull,
Arranged a keg of salt to fight behind;
While Condon, having other things in mind
Than dying, wrestled with a barrel of beans.
And others planned escape by grimmer means.
Old Robertson, with nothing in his face,
Unlaced a boot and noosed the leather lace
To reach between a trigger and a toe.
He did not tell, and no one asked to know

The meaning of it. Everybody knew.
John Grady and McQuarie did it too,
And Haggirty and Gibson did the same,
And many others.[13]

The Gibson mentioned in the poem was Samuel Gibson, and he had been a private when the battle occurred nearly sixty years earlier. As Neihardt read that night in Omaha, Gibson, now a white-haired Omaha resident, sat in the audience near the stage. If Gibson's reaction was muted—reports said he nodded his approval as Neihardt read—the audience's was not: the *Omaha World-Herald* reported that those in attendance responded with such a "deafening" applause "that it was apparent the author was taken unawares." Neihardt motioned audience members to be quiet, then asked if they wanted to hear him read of another fight from his poem, this one at Beecher's Island in Colorado. "A roar of handclaps was the answer," the newspaper reported, and Neihardt read for another forty-five minutes.[14]

When *The Song of the Indian Wars* was published in the spring of 1925, the book earned Neihardt his best reviews so far. One reviewer declared it "an almost unparalleled achievement—a successful long historical poem," calling the Wagon Box Fight section "without a doubt the best story of any Indian fight in American poetry."[15] Arthur Guiterman, a cofounder of the Poetry Society of America and at that time its president, reviewed the book for the *Outlook*, praising its "warm sympathy and fiery vigor." He observed: "Mr. Neihardt's Red Cloud, Man Afraid, Spotted Tail, Sitting Bull, and Crazy Horse are no cigar-store Indians, savage fiends, or noble bronze statues, but men revealed as men in peace and war, men whose lives you can relive, whose hearts you can enter and share. Their motives are made plain, their speeches in council are natural, trenchant, and convincing."[16]

Even his long-time antagonists at *Poetry* reluctantly praised it. Though the magazine criticized Neihardt's continued use of poetic diction—the *'twas* and *'twere*, the *alas* and *aye*—it praised his knowledge of America's

West. And though still critical of the rhymed pentameters, the magazine's reviewer, the poet Berenice Van Slyke, found that "the vividness of the terrific combats, the spectacular endurances and courage of the white men battling against the Indians" caused her to forget the poem's shortcomings.[17] Guiterman, in his *Outlook* review, said he hoped *Indian Wars* would win Neihardt the Pulitzer Prize for poetry, and though the idea certainly appealed to Neihardt, he pretended not to care about gaining the accolade.

The book also earned Neihardt entry into an organization he was proud to join. Lemly notified Neihardt that he had been elected an honorary member of the Order of Indian Wars.[18] "There are not only living heroes—my own heroes—in that Order," he wrote to a friend. "There are ghostly heroes, and Custer is one of them."[19]

Neihardt dedicated *The Song of the Indian Wars* to his newest child, Alice, born in Branson in 1921. In "To Alice, Three Years Old," he chronicled the time it had taken him to write the book: "When I began the gift I bear / It seemed you weren't anywhere." The book had taken him seven years to write, and in that time he had left his home in Nebraska and become the state's poet laureate. By the end of the twenty-line poetic dedication, *Indian Wars* is finished, and little Alice has grown: "And now that we are wise and three, / And I love you and you love me / We know the whole conspiracy!"[20]

Just as he was finishing *The Song of the Indian Wars*, Neihardt returned home from another month-long lecture trip to find a contract for another collected edition of his poetry.[21] The idea of gathering up his life's work, so far, set Neihardt to thinking back over his career. He wrote to Robert Davis, the magazine editor who had earlier published so many of his short stories, that he thought appreciation of his long, narrative poems was "spreading all over the country."[22] To his old friend George Sterling, Neihardt wrote more personally. "Sometimes I wonder if I feel a little old at 43. Perhaps I shall feel younger later on. God knows I don't think feeling old is a good sign. But won't it be bully to die and FIND OUT?"[23]

For months Neihardt continued to think about his place in the world, trying to balance his literary ambitions with the simple living of his life. "Though I have spent all my years since boyhood on the art of poetry—and at a cost that was sometimes hard to pay—I have not fallen into the belief that even the greatest poetry is important in itself. Life itself is everything."[24] Still, he could not stop wanting to expand his reach. "There are, undoubtedly, a great many people who would be strong for my stuff if they knew it," he wrote to Julius House. "I am too human not to care about reaching people. I care greatly. And I'd like to live long enough to see something of what I know will be the good fortune of the stuff in the future."[25] The current period, Neihardt believed, was "raw, dishonest, ignorant, four-flushing, sex-mad, obsessed with the desire to be smart."[26] Time was "the only authoritative critic," he thought, and he was certain there was a future "that will love me a little at least."[27]

Even before *Collected Poems* was published, in the fall of 1926, critics too seemed to be taking the time to assess Neihardt and his work. Jim Tully, five years younger than Neihardt, had been a hobo and a fighter before becoming a writer. He wrote poetry, novels, and several volumes of autobiography that recorded in simple, masculine prose his impoverished childhood and his rough and tumble life on the road—Neihardt once praised one of Tully's books as exhibiting "much strong writing of the popular goddam school."[28] After Tully moved to California, he began to report on Hollywood, and he is believed by some to have been the first to do so regularly. Tully also wrote about the literary world, and he had long been a fan of Neihardt's poetry. In October 1924 Tully wrote a lengthy essay for the *Literary Digest International Book Review* in which he praised the man he called "the epic poet of the pioneer West": "A man like Neihardt," Tully wrote, "is born with more soul than others, and by a mighty chance of destiny he manages somehow to save it." Tully, writing from the West, was critical of the power of the East in the book publishing industry, and he blamed it in part for Neihardt's lack of fame. "Had Neihardt been born in the shadow of Park Row he would be the most famous poet in America. But, had he been born there, we should not have had Neihardt."[29]

A few months later the *Christian Science Monitor* weighed in with an article headlined "Has America Found an Epic Voice?" It described

Neihardt as "one who has embodied his belief and his vision into living forms of art"; he was "a poet-seer who has envisaged the stirring pageant of the winning of a continent and has wrought the story into the first American epic verse." The *Monitor* believed that epic poetry was dead until *The Song of Hugh Glass* had appeared "almost without warning." Then came *The Song of Three Friends*, "more lurid, more tense" than *Hugh Glass* but also "more complex, a colorful pageant of those forces of human nature which found tumultuous expression in those early western days." The newspaper ended up answering its own question with a qualified yes. "Perhaps in Neihardt himself we have an American Homer, or, at least, the epic pioneer who may point out the path to one that shall follow."[30]

Neihardt responded within the year when he was interviewed for a lengthy profile in one of the Nebraska newspapers that continued to champion him and his work. "It does not please me to be called a Homer or Walter Scott," he told the *Omaha World-Herald*. "I want to be known and remembered as Neihardt or nobody." The *World-Herald* went on to declare that even at forty-five, Neihardt still gave "the impression of youthfulness." "There is no scantiness or gray visible in his bushy head of hair," it said in its front-page story. "His face is ruddy and unlined, reflecting abounding energy."[31]

Neihardt's boyhood home of Wayne, Nebraska, chose to recognize him as well, dedicating a bust of its poet in the city park. "The world is not hopeless when a little town, much given to money-chasing, can do what Wayne is doing," Neihardt said.[32] His mother, whom he sent in his place to unveil the monument, told an audience that included the state's governor and the University of Nebraska chancellor that she now realized her son was not only in her heart but in the hearts of many people. "My dreams," she said, "have been realized."[33] Neihardt was glad he had asked his mother to participate in the unveiling. "Such poetic justice," he said, "seldom comes to mothers."[34]

During the winter of 1924–25 Neihardt worked on the lectures required as part of his University of Nebraska professorship. "I began to get drunk with ideas two days ago," he wrote to his mother. "Night before last I was so exalted with thinking about the job that I couldn't sleep and had to get up and smoke."[35] Neihardt originally planned to give three lectures, and though he started writing a third, in the end he gave only two. His appearances on campus were front-page news in the student newspaper, but Neihardt later joked that "the two given seemed about all a general university audience could stand."[36] The Macmillan Company, without seeing the finished lectures, had offered to publish them, and the published version, *Poetic Values: Their Reality and Our Need of Them*, contained only the two: "Common Sense" and "The Creative Dream."[37]

Though Neihardt, his supporters, and his critics never regarded *Poetic Values* as among his most important books, its topic is key to understanding him. In these lectures, as in his laureate address, many book reviews, and early morning conversations with Mona, Neihardt focused on his "higher values." His attachment to them, to the very idea of them, is perhaps the most consistent element of his character, showing up at every stage of his life, in nearly everything he said or did. "My whole purpose is to insist that men are finer than they think they are," he told House when *Poetic Values* was published, "that the dreadful limitation they accept under the present social illusion is a part of the illusion. I try to show why poetic values are real values like any other values we know, and I give no sentimental reasons. We are trying to live in the kitchen of a wonderful palace."[38] His concentration on these values was not simply a focus of his writing. Daughter Hilda recalled sneaking downstairs early in the morning to eavesdrop on her parents' breakfast conversations. "They spoke of art, poetry, the beauty and sorrows of life, and—above all—their unswerving belief that the pursuit of what they called 'the higher values' was worth all the desperate effort it might demand."[39] His original title for the book, *How Shall We Be Human*, offers a clue to his message.

The lectures, and the subsequent book, also allowed him the opportunity to explore further his ideas about the Hindu religion, an abiding interest since his days as a teenager in Wayne working on *The Divine Enchantment*. *Poetic Values* represented the best look, up to that time, at the philosophy of expanded consciousness that motivated Neihardt.

"I undertook to show how science and mysticism merge in one flowing circle of human reality."[40] Years later he told a biographer that he presented the lectures to show that a person's worldview could be both Aristotelian and Platonic, "to show that there is *no gap between the two,* that our scale of values is continuous." As he elaborated, "All our values, from 'lowest' to 'highest'—from common sense through science and on through the esthetic, the ethical, the religious values *are obviously* creations in consciousness from selected data of our experience. It is commonly assumed, without examination of the assumption, that our *sense values* are 'objective,' and therefore 'real.' But they are created in consciousness too. Surely, nothing in the 'sense world' is essentially as we conceive it."[41] As he put it in an introductory note to *Poetic Values,* "I have undertaken to suggest for the common-sense man, who sometimes doubts the wisdom of the prevailing view of life, a means by which he might come to think of poetic values as real, and necessarily integral in the scale of practical values."[42]

The book, of course, was written as two long lectures—he delivered one on a Wednesday morning and the other the next evening in late October 1925—and it is easy to imagine him pausing for audience applause or laughter. One also senses that he is sometimes reacting defensively to comments made or imagined about him and his choice of poetry as his life's work. "Now what . . . may poetry be?" he asks rhetorically early in the first lecture. "Simply 'hokum' set to rhyme; a thing to which one may descend in occasional sentimental moods, but always with one's fingers figuratively crossed, and with the distinct understanding that of course one knows better and that it is 'no fair' to tag an otherwise practical man caught in the act."[43] Though the point of the lectures can be difficult to find, it is there: Neihardt does not deny the day-to-day necessities of life and people's need to feel respected by others, but he demands a higher set of values by which to live. "Only by the general widening of the conscious field in which men act can we hope to live down our animal ancestry and set up standards of value that are human," he writes at the end of the second lecture, in the final pages of *Poetic Values.* "Only by the systematic stimulation of the art consciousness in men and its application to the problems of society can we hope to be saved from ourselves. We have within us the means of our salvation."[44]

When *Poetic Values* was published, the *New York Times* praised its approach and its succinctness. "In a volume of less than 150 sparsely printed pages," it said in January 1926, "John G. Neihardt has presented a more comprehensive and far-seeing survey of poetic principles than many authors have been able to offer in thick and laborious tomes." The best thing about the first lecture, the *Times* argued, was that it prepared the way for the second, "The Creative Dream," which it saw as attempting—and accomplishing—far more. This creative dream, wrote the *Times* reviewer, "is at once the only index to a wider reality of sense, and the key to the full enjoyment of life and its full usefulness."[45] When Edmund Wilson reviewed the book for the *New Republic*, he found the lectures "very earnest and well informed," but he thought it was clear that Neihardt imagined his initial audience, University of Nebraska students, as having "100 percent practical views" rather than a full "life of the imagination."[46] The *Dial* praised Neihardt as "ardent, intelligent, and honest" in trying to teach students that "poetry is deeper than science," but tired of "his popular Chautauqua manner."[47] William Rose Benét, in the *Yale Review*, called the book "one of the most individual utterances concerning the nature of poetry that we have had in recent years."[48]

Neihardt would have made himself even clearer had he finished the third lecture and included it in the book. "[A]s a mass, we live in the lower consciousness"—he wrote in a draft of what he called "The Mood of the Moment"—"obsessed with curious and pitiful notions as to getting for self, not greatly different from those revealed at the troughs of a sty." He argues that if people must hate something, they must be careful what they choose. "It is for the evil dream that grips us as a social body that we should reserve our hateful names, and not for individuals or for any class, though it is often hard to act upon that view. So long as brute values are generally regarded as the only real ones, the exploited will be potential exploiters yearning for the chance."[49]

Neihardt hoped that *Poetic Values* would "get hold of the people." If it did, he confessed to his mother, he was going to push his publisher to bring out a second similar volume called *The Modern Mood*, which he thought he could have ready in sixty days and which would build off the uncompleted third lecture. "I *do* hope I may be compelled to do this second book."[50] *Poetic Values* proved a hard sell, though, and Neihardt, without expressing any regrets, never finished the third lecture or a second volume.

By the time Neihardt moved to Missouri in 1920 he had been writing for the *Minneapolis Journal* for more than eight years, the first year as a resident of Minneapolis and the other years mailing in his articles from Bancroft. Each week the *Journal* would ship him a box of books, and he would spend his Mondays, Tuesdays, and Wednesdays reading and writing his books column, leaving the rest of his time for his more literary pursuits.[51] When he had a lecture tour scheduled, he would work to get weeks ahead on his columns so that he would not have to review books while traveling.

In those years Neihardt had reviewed hundreds of books of prose and poetry, strongly disliking some of them—he panned Amy Lowell's collection *A Dome of Many-Colored Glass*, and Edgar Lee Masters' *Domesday Book*, which Neihardt argued would have worked better as a novel—but liking many more.[52] He thought John Jay Chapman "one of the most illuminating and least known" of American essayists; judged Edgar Allen Poe to have been America's greatest poet, followed closely by Ralph Waldo Emerson; and remained conflicted about Jack London: "At his best, he is the equal of any fiction writer of our time," he wrote. "At his worst, he is a little disgusting."[53] Not surprisingly, Neihardt reviewed volumes and volumes of poetry collections. He liked books by two of his friends, George Sterling and Louis Ledoux, as well as the work of George Edward Woodberry, Edwin Arlington Robinson, John Masefield, Sara Teasdale, whom he declared "a genuine artist," and Robert Frost, whom he thought "may indeed go far."[54]

No matter what book he was reviewing, Neihardt often took the opportunity to comment, as he had in *Poetic Values*, on two topics important to him: poetry and contemporary American culture. On both he could become quite gloomy. "This is the age and America is the country of the catch-phrase. It is the time of predigested foods and ready-to-wear culture," he wrote in 1912. "Conversation hardly exists."[55] Business and the quest for riches seemed to Neihardt to have taken over the country, to have made America a "nation of vulgar shop-keepers."[56] Too many of his countrymen, as he saw it, were hustlers and schemers. "We do not cherish the passing moment," he wrote, but instead, "we gamble on tomorrows," mistakenly believing that material success will bring happiness.[57] He briefly—and unsuccessfully—tried to move from the books page to the opinion page at the *Journal*, writing an editorial that questioned "the inevitable righteousness of Big Business," only to find himself soundly chewed out by his boss and told, as he recalled it, "business is sacred."[58]

Neihardt often found that poets trying to create in such a time were misguided. "One might well sum up the condition of art today by saying that the Vandals have broken into the Temple," he wrote.[59] Genuine writers of any kind, but perhaps especially poets, should not concern themselves with the market. Neihardt believed that the "body of lovers of poetry has never been large."[60] Because the audience was small, he feared, artists of all types, including poets, were trying to change their art to appeal to more and more people, coarsening and degrading it because the "uninstructed" public was likely to exhibit taste that was "naturally vulgar or vicious."[61] "Since the mass could not climb up to Art," he declared, "Art has very obligingly come down to the mass."[62]

Yet despite his opinion of the country's culture and its poetry, Neihardt remained optimistic about both, believing the country to be ripe for advancement. The nation, "composed largely of the flotsam and jetsam of foreign immigration," was ready to experience explosive growth, he believed.[63] Neihardt was certain that the nation's politics were controlled by "a corrupt few," that government was in the pocket of big business, but he believed Americans of all stripes agreed that something was wrong.[64] All it would take to set things right, in Neihardt's opinion, was a return to tradition. "What this Country needs is not roaring prophets and pretentious rhetoricians," he argued. "Our supreme need, economically, politically, ethically, is clear thinking, sound thinking, creative thinking."[65]

Neihardt felt much the same way about the state of American poetry. The crass craving for riches that he saw everywhere around him diminished the desire for genuine art, including poetry. Art simply was not practical enough to matter in the modern world. "The present time and rising generation are not much touched by poetry," he wrote, because they both ask, "What's its use?" Neihardt offered his own answer: "It is for its own sake. It is beauty, it is consolation."[66] Poetry, he firmly believed, would persevere because like religion, it was required by "the unchanging spiritual hunger of Man."[67] Genuine poetry, a purely aesthetic force in the world, offered "a glimpse of the heaven to come which the human spirit craves," and it could not be created simply by a public demanding it.[68] The reading public needed to prepare itself so that when a genuine poet did arrive, it would be ready. For that to happen, poetry—just like America—required clear thinking; in the case of poetry and literature, Neihardt believed this meant quality criticism, which he defined as being "utterly divorced from the publishing houses and their commercial exigencies and unaffected by the journalistic function of reciting the news of new books."[69] Neihardt was so certain this would happen that he offered a prediction: literature textbooks by the early twenty-first century would record a poetic renaissance in the first two decades of the twentieth.[70]

During the years he wrote for the *Minneapolis Journal* Neihardt had a few run-ins with the editor, whom he found to be overly committed to business and Christianity. Faced with the demands on his time of reviewing, lecturing, and writing poetry, he finally decided to reduce his commitments, and in 1921, not long after moving to Missouri, he resigned his position with the *Journal.* He soon discovered that he missed the soap box—and, even more, the income—and regretted giving up his newspaper job. He briefly considered editing a books page for his friends at the *Omaha Bee,* but in the end he accepted an offer to review books for the *Kansas City Journal-Post,* a daily newspaper that traced its history to 1854. The newspaper announced his hiring with a note of surprise that he could find the time to read so many new books. "He reads them with the eyes of a middle western man," it offered. "He sees their beauty with the eyes of a poet."[71]

Neihardt's inaugural offering in the *Journal-Post* was an eighteen-hundred-word article on "The New Reading Public" on March 7, 1926. In it he argued, perhaps oddly for a poet and author, that too many books were being published. More precisely, he believed too many bad books were being published—"quantity production involves quantity consumption," he said—and as he had done in the *Minneapolis Journal*, he pushed for stronger criticism to help the expanding reading public find the good ones. "Can we hope to find our way through the wilderness of contemporary literature unless we find some means of orientation other than our personal likes and dislikes?" he asked. He promised readers that he would try, in his *Journal-Post* columns, not only to help them judge contemporary literature but also, repeating his argument from *Poetic Values*, to help them in "the far more important business of living well": "Literary values are values in living or they are not values at all."[72]

Neihardt did his best to keep his promise. Perhaps he felt more welcome at the *Journal-Post*, or had more talented editors, or perhaps, after years of experience on the Minneapolis newspaper, he was simply better at it, but it was clear from the beginning that his journalism had improved. His articles were longer—he usually wrote four or five pieces totaling as much as five thousand words each week—and more developed. He stayed with the same subjects—the power of literature, America's declining culture, the universal language of poetry, and the higher values—but he was less folksy, more philosophical. "The saying that art is unmoral is easy to defend," he wrote. "But always genuine art is ethical; that is to say, it is somehow concerned with the abiding, as opposed to the accidental and transient. It is the facts that may be accidental and transient. It is the truth about their relations that abides; and the harmonies to be felt in those unchanging relations are what we love as beauty."[73]

II AN OFFER DECLINED
AND ANOTHER MOVE

John Neihardt had first encountered John Macy in early 1913 when he had thoroughly panned Macy's book *The Spirit of American Literature.* Macy was an important literary critic who had worked for the *Youth's Companion* and helped edit Helen Keller's autobiography, eventually marrying Keller's teacher Anne Sullivan. In the book, a survey of the "emergent" American novelists and poets of the time, Macy proclaimed that the "American spirit in literature" was a myth, in the same way that "American valor" was a myth: the valor of Americans, Macy argued, was no different than that of the Italians or the Japanese.[1] He focused on sixteen men working in what he called the American branch of English literature. Neihardt, a true believer in American literature, was not happy with Macy's opinions—his suggestion that James Whitcomb Riley was one of two poets "who have made literature," Neihardt thought, was a "Philistine judgment"—but what bothered him most was what he saw as Macy's "imperial manner." In the end Neihardt concluded that Macy must have been "living in a trunk for the last ten years."[2]

A little more than a decade later, in the spring of 1926, Neihardt read a new Macy book, *The Story of the World's Literature,* at about the same time Macy was reading Neihardt's *Song of the Indian Wars.* This time, both liked what they read: Neihardt gave Macy's book a glowing review in the *Kansas City Journal-Post*, calling it "a glorious trip, worth any amount of intellectual shoe leather and a deal of honest panting," and Macy thought enough of *Indian Wars* to ask Neihardt to write a book for his new boss, William Morrow.[3] Morrow, who had been working in New York publishing for two decades, had just organized his own company, and he wanted a book that explored the American Indians' relations with the white population. Macy told Morrow that Neihardt was the man to do it and set about persuading Neihardt to write the book. "Your interest is poetic, and most of your expression is, I believe, in the form of verse," Macy wrote to Neihardt. "But would you not be interested to put your experiences into the form of straight prose narrative and exposition of the nature of the Indian, and perhaps go into the history of the breeds that you do not know by personal contact?"[4]

Neihardt, though flattered, wanted to get to work on his next long narrative poem, one he was envisioning as a continuation of *The Song of the Indian Wars*, and he had no interest in taking on another prose book. Still, like writers everywhere, Neihardt was occasionally dissatisfied with his regular publisher, and he used Macy's offer to poke gently at the Macmillan Company: he asked H. S. Latham, Macmillan's vice president, what he should do about the offer. "I think this letter of Macy's is a very clever approach in the hope that Morrow may sooner or later publish something for you," Latham responded, "and I want you to regard Macmillan as your publisher, and not to pass us up for anything." Latham also reminded Neihardt that Macmillan was planning to bring out another collection of Neihardt's short stories, to be called *Indian Tales and Others*, and that "to publish another book of prose about Indians would be to dissipate the public's interest, with the result that neither book would get its maximum sale."[5]

Latham promised Neihardt that if *Indian Tales* did well, he would gladly look at another Indian book later. Though Macy and Morrow continued to try to get Neihardt to write a prose Indian history, he politely declined.

Throughout 1926 Neihardt wrote for the *Kansas City Journal-Post*, and it remained clear from the beginning—to himself and others—that he was attempting more serious pieces of criticism than he had written for the *Minneapolis Journal*. "It is only through the process of reading that men can hope to come in contact with the larger environment that alone can humanize," he wrote in March.[6] He also continued to expound on his theory of the higher human values, the "poetic values" he had addressed in his laureate speech and in his university lectures. It was the prime function of education to make people social beings, "to make them . . . citizens of all time and of all countries; to give them the widest possible comprehension of a man's relation to other men and to his physical environment; to substitute sympathy for prejudice in the list of human motives. . . . It must be made possible," he argues, "for the one to live vicariously the life of the many from the beginning."[7]

And he continued to write about American Indians, taking at one point what must have been an unpopular position on a major military defeat. Writing in June 1926, about the fiftieth anniversary of the Battle of the Little Bighorn, Neihardt wrote:

> We were not only outnumbered; we were inferior both in strategy and tactics to our uncivilized foe; and morally, we were in the wrong. Our foes were fighting in defense of "inalienable rights" such as our Fourth of July orators proclaim every year in thousands of village parks. They were defending their women and children and the land that was their home against the invasion of a powerful and arrogant race. Not only was the country for which they fought their own by natural right; it was theirs by solemn treaty with our government. But more powerful foes than the integrity of a great Christian nation were at work. The land hungry white race was crowding westward, and social necessity on so large a scale is always above all moral considerations.[8]

Even the language used to recall such events was suspect, he wrote. "When our forces attacked Indians and slaughtered them, that was a battle. When our forces attacked Indians and got slaughtered, that was a massacre. So much depends upon whose bull is gored."[9]

Neihardt firmly believed that the "modern tendencies" in culture—which he defined as "salacious fiction, cheap movies, free verse, flappers, bootlegging, the Charleston state of mind and leg"—were an abomination. He had long been clear in his correspondence and in his lectures regarding how he felt about such tendencies, and he used his weekly books page now to make his position public.[10] At least one reader of the *Journal-Post* liked what Neihardt was offering. Thomas Hinkle, an author of horse and dog stories for young people, including *Tawny, a Dog of the Old West*, wrote to the newspaper from the Kansas suburbs: "Every review on the page is a classic essay on literature. . . . If you should put them out in book form later I want one."[11]

By June, as Neihardt read proofs on two new volumes, *Indian Tales and Others* and *Collected Poems*, and continued to lecture—he had six engagements in Texas before spending three days at the University of Nebraska—he was also exploring the idea of syndicating a weekly books column. As part of his attempt to gauge interest, he met with George Sibley Johns, editor of the *St. Louis Post-Dispatch*. Before the end of their meeting Johns raised another alternative: why didn't Neihardt just come to work for the *Post-Dispatch* instead? Neihardt, always trying to arrange for as much income with as little drain on his time for writing poetry as possible, was pleased that Johns mentioned a salary of one hundred dollars a week to produce only two columns. At the time he was also considering an offer from the University of Nebraska to teach both fall and spring semesters, one class on values and criticism of current books and another on poetic content and form, all for $2,250 dollars a year and requiring a great deal of his time.[12] Finally, in early October, after only thirty-four weeks and before he could even get his family moved from Branson to Kansas City, Neihardt was through at the *Journal-Post*.

In November he moved his family to the St. Louis suburb of Kirkwood, with dreams of creating "the only distinguished book section west of the Mississippi."[13] *Indian Tales and Others* was out, *Collected Poems* was expected any day, and Macmillan was considering collecting his *Journal-Post* columns into a book.

For twelve years Neihardt and George Sterling, his friend and supporter in California, had exchanged letters, praising one another's work and making fun of many of the more modern poets. But by the mid-1920s their letter writing was slowing. In a letter to Neihardt in May 1926, Sterling wrote of their "aversion to correspondence": "It falls on all men who have to write much more than letters," he told his friend. "Oh! well! you must *not* write to me unless you feel a strong impulse. I'll know I am in your friendly thoughts."[14] It was the last letter Neihardt received from him. Sterling had long carried with him a vial of cyanide, and on November 17, 1926, two weeks before his fifty-seventh birthday, a depressed Sterling used it.

Neihardt was in his office at the *Post-Dispatch* when he first heard. "[I]t cut deep into my bowels," he wrote to House. "That was a dismal day."[15] The news of Sterling's death, Neihardt wrote in an appreciation published in the *Post-Dispatch* on November 27, was "too bitter to be true," and he lamented that none of the many people who had loved Sterling could have been with him in his "blind moment of agony." But no matter how sad Neihardt was for the loss of "the lesser Sterling," he refused to mourn Sterling the poet, instead taking the opportunity to praise the timelessness of his work. "Nothing that was great in Sterling had gone away," he wrote, "for nothing of his characteristic values were of the moment." Neihardt chose to partner with Sterling one final time in their stand for "enduring values" and against many of the newer approaches. "His characteristic values were not those that are essential to a revolting generation, though his sympathies, as a man, were with the insurgent group," Neihardt wrote. "He was neither old-fashioned nor 'modern' as an artist. He was Sterling."[16]

On May 20, 1927, twenty-five-year-old aviator Charles Lindbergh took off from Long Island, New York, in a single-seat, single-engine monoplane called the *Spirit of St. Louis*. Less than thirty-four hours and 3,600 miles later, he landed on the other side of the Atlantic Ocean in Paris, and America had a new hero. The American public had followed Lindbergh's story closely, and his flight had been supported in part by the

Post-Dispatch's rival, the *St. Louis Globe-Democrat*. The *Post-Dispatch* wanted some piece of the story, and the editor of the editorial page, on orders from "J.P."—publisher Joseph Pulitzer II, the son of the original Joseph Pulitzer—decided that having Neihardt on staff provided a unique opportunity. Neihardt was given three days to come up with a poem that suitably reflected on Lindbergh's accomplishment.

Neihardt struggled to write the poem. He was conflicted about current American life and culture, believing that Americans had become too materialistic, too enchanted with the current moment rather than the enduring values he saw as fundamental to humanity. Yet for more than two decades Neihardt had argued that America's advances in technology forecast an unprecedented era of progress. "Having conquered the sea, we coveted the lordship of the air," he wrote in the *Minneapolis Journal* in 1912. "We make day by pressing a button. We talk casually over leagues and leagues of wire. We hurl messages across the sea in the twinkling of an eye, very much as a small boy throws a stone over a frog pond."[17] He worked to put those ideas into a poem.

On June 19, below an editorial cartoon showing a tiny *Spirit of St. Louis* flying toward a magnificent sunrise, the paper published "The Lyric Deed," a poem of seven four-line stanzas. In it Neihardt, identified as "Epic Poet of the *Post-Dispatch*," sets the stage: Americans are living in a world that worships money and has lost its "high purpose." But even if no one listens to "the bard" any longer, all is not lost. In modern times, Neihardt makes clear in the poem, the country will be more welcoming to a pilot than to a poet. "The dreaming doer is the master poet— / And lo, the perfect lyric in a deed!" Lindbergh—"Winged with the old divinity of beauty"—was saving the human spirit. Ever since he was a boy Neihardt had admired heroes, and here was a real one. "Lindbergh," Neihardt wrote, "rides with God!"[18]

Neihardt told friends that his colleagues at the *Post-Dispatch* had liked the poem and that there had been "some favorable comment."[19] A literary journal reprinted it the next year, but Neihardt never included it in any collection.

Just before he was assigned to write the Lindbergh poem, Neihardt had had a chance meeting with Joseph Pulitzer II and took the opportunity to complain that his work for the *Post-Dispatch* left him too little time to work on his poetry. Pulitzer, who liked Neihardt's column and did not want to lose it, told Neihardt to propose a schedule that would free up more writing time.[20]

Before he could formulate any such plan, Neihardt found a way to take even more time away from his poetry. He and Percy Werner Jr., a former newspaperman and the son of a prominent St. Louis attorney, put together a plan for a "transcontinental travel camp"—the All-America Movement—a school that would be housed on a train that would tour the United States. Open to young men who were in college or who had at least graduated from high school, the program, with the slogan "Understand America," would last forty-two days. The plan was to start the tour in Chicago in the summer of 1928, traveling first to the Northwest, then down the Pacific Coast to Los Angeles. From there the train would travel across the country to Washington DC and north to Boston, before returning to Chicago through Canada. Throughout the tour local experts would explore the history of each region of the United States and its contribution to the American way of life.

Neihardt was the face of the organization, and he fashioned an advisory board of David Starr Jordan, retired president of Stanford University; Katherine Lee Bates, the poet who wrote the lyrics to the anthem "America the Beautiful"; poets Carl Sandburg and Richard Burton; and sculptor Lorado Taft. Werner supplied the business brains and put together an arrangement with the American Express Company to handle logistics. Neihardt spent a great deal of time in the fall of 1927 writing letters and submitting to interviews to promote the tour. "Judging by the summer traffic on our highways, it seems that the great portion of our population is bent upon 'seeing America first,'" he told the *Christian Science Monitor* in February 1928. "But seeing America first is not the same thing as understanding it at last. What we need is the integrating sympathy that can grow only out of some intelligent and concerted effort to appreciate the various human values that each section of the country is best able to contribute."[21]

The project, which would showcase Neihardt's loyalty to his American heroes, seemed to be building steam, but just as suddenly, it crashed when Werner was found dead at his father's home in St. Louis. Neihardt still believed in the plan—"It is a winner and will make big money for someone."[22] But the program had lost its businessman and momentum. Without Werner it went no further.

Neihardt continued to chafe under the demands of his job at the *Post-Dispatch*. His newspaper work took too much of his time, but he believed he could not afford to give it up. "The fact is, I am worn thin all the time and never get any relief from the tension of my job," he wrote to House midway through 1928. "And there is no relief in sight. It is either over-work or over-worry for me."[23] Generally things were good—he had begun, in a small way, to invest in the stock market, and his investments were growing; Wayne State College, the current incarnation of his old Nebraska Normal School, built a new women's dormitory and named it Neihardt Hall; and Creighton University in Omaha awarded him an honorary doctorate. Yet in other ways it was a dark time for him. "It is a curious and saddening time we are living in," he wrote to House that fall. "*All* things are becoming a matter of mob-action controlled by low-minded demagogues."[24]

He continued to travel extensively to lecture and recite his poetry, and Macmillan continued to push him for a collection of his newspaper prose, planning to call it *Straws in the Wind*. With the help of his daughter Enid, now seventeen and acting as her father's secretary, Neihardt delivered a manuscript before the end of the year. What he was not doing was working on the next installment of his book-length poems. Near the end of 1928 he wrote to his mother from Massachusetts, where he was speaking at Wellesley College. "I want to live in Branson again & finish my *Cycle* & several other books. . . . The strenuous life in civilization isn't worth what it costs."[25] Costs were definitely on his mind. He and Mona and their children were living in Kirkwood, but they also still had their home in Branson, where his mother remained. And he knew his worries were putting him in a bad frame of mind much of the time. When he wrote to his mother at Christmas, he seemed apologetic. "I *am* sincerely glad that I have all of you and am able to treat you all pretty decently," he wrote. "It *is* a pleasure that I feel pretty steadily now, though sometimes when I'm off feed or perhaps more than ordinarily sick of 'litrachoor' I can't see so well. But I am, deep down, delighted to be able to do this and to have you all to do it for."[26]

Neihardt had remained interested in parapsychology and still occasionally consulted psychics. In December 1928 he visited one, and he reported her insights to his mother: He would soon be called away from Missouri for a visit to "the New York World." Neihardt agreed with the medium's assessment that this probably meant that New York *was* the world as far as publishing was concerned. "The peculiar thing is," Neihardt wrote, "that I don't in the least believe the N.Y. World will want me, and I don't want it either."[27]

When the invitation actually came, he quickly changed his mind. The Poetry Society of America invited Neihardt to come to New York as one of its guests for the group's annual meeting at the end of January 1929. "This looks as though the most powerful literary gang in America wants to let me inside," Neihardt wrote to House.[28] He left for New York on January 25 and, while there, chronicled his week in letters to his mother. During his visit Neihardt met more poets and people important to poetry than ever before, and he recited his own poetry before most of them. He read at a benefit at the Waldorf Astoria along with six other poets, among them Edwin Markham, best known for his 1898 poem "The Man With the Hoe," and he met Corrine Roosevelt Robinson, sister of Theodore Roosevelt, who told Neihardt that her brother had once used in a speech a line from *The Song of Hugh Glass*—"Men, fit to live, were not afraid to die!"[29] Poet Leonora Speyer hosted a reception for Neihardt at her Washington Square home at which he read "The Death of Crazy Horse." "My god, what a company of distinguished men and women!" Neihardt reported to House. "It was bully, too. I have never been so honored, I think—I mean, never with so much brilliance."[30]

Despite his reception, Neihardt remained unsure of the value of his

East Coast visit. "The New York experience doesn't mean that 'the crowd' down there has definitely fallen for me," he wrote to House. "I did not touch all by any means." He did believe, however, that he had weakened whatever resistance might have existed to his poetry—"if indeed there is any serious resistance left."[31]

Though the trip to New York was a welcome pleasure for Neihardt, it was not enough to counteract completely a period of darkness. He looked externally for a reason for his blue moods and, as usual, easily found one. "I am pretty well fed up on this scurvy civilization," he wrote to House shortly after returning from New York. "Culture turned over to the women, the men more and more enslaved to their females, life allowed no meaning but the grubbing for more and more cash that one may spend more and more!"[32] That spring he wrote to House again to explain why he had not been writing many letters. "The fact is, comrade, that my swimming in this sewer of the modern consciousness sometimes nearly kills me with disgust." His openness with House about his moods offers a glimpse into the conflicted feelings that Neihardt often experienced. "I know the world is not lost," he continued, "and I know that even now I am victor, in the long run, through my work."[33]

Neihardt's outlook seeped into his thoughts about his publisher, who he often believed was doing too little to promote his books, and about his employer, who continued to take too much of his time and energy. "If I can't get something more than flattery out of Macmillans, I'll bolt," he wrote to House that spring.[34] He took his complaints directly to George Brett, head of the company. "It seems that my turn ought to be coming along one of these days, and I am wondering if I can not have some assurance that more will be done in the promotion of my work than has been done thus far." A "great deal more" needed to be done, Neihardt told Brett, and it needed to be done "fairly soon."[35] Brett assured Neihardt that Macmillan remained interested in his books, though he also pointed out that the books were not generally profitable for the publisher. "In these days of very high advertising costs, the chances of making any money out of the publication of a work of poetry are not very good unless the public responds much more readily than has been the case with your books so far."[36] As for his position at the *Post-Dispatch*, Neihardt knew that every hour he put into newspaper work was an hour he was not working on his *Cycle*, but he also appreciated the certainty of a steady paycheck and the platform his journalism afforded him.

As the year ended, Neihardt's mood was improved by an unexpected compliment from the *New York Times*. In an editorial praising the poetic parodies of Nebraska's U.S. senator, George Norris, the newspaper mentioned that Nebraska held an honorable place in "pure poetry." "The name of Mr. John G. Neihardt is alone enough to give her high distinction."[37]

Neihardt loved the spring—he wrote a number of poems about either the end of March or the beginning of April—and it always improved his spirits. The spring of 1930 was no exception. He was still critical of his countrymen's "spiritual blindness," but the arrival of spring meant "there is nothing wrong with the earth and the sky and the trees and the rivers etc."[38] For the time being he decided to stick with Macmillan and the *Post-Dispatch*. One thing that made it easier for Neihardt to tolerate both was that his mind was now racing with thoughts of a trip he was planning for the summer. He wanted to focus the next book in his *Cycle* on a period known as the ghost dance or messiah movement. "I plan to flivver through the Sioux country, dreaming back the Messiah days and talking to old Indians," he wrote to House. Authorities at the Pine Ridge agency promised to put him in touch with Indians who knew something of the messiah movement. "Believe me, they'll tell me a lot too," he wrote. "I want all this, of course, only by way of becoming saturated with the true mood of the whole affair."[39] He had begun counting on the trip to provide him with the heart of his next poem.

12 A PILGRIMAGE TO PINE RIDGE

During a solar eclipse, most likely on January 1, 1889, a Northern Paiute Indian named Wovoka in southwestern Nevada had a vision. In it Wovoka, then in his mid-thirties, visited God and saw all the people who had ever died "all happy and forever young." When he awoke from the vision, he reported that God, after showing him around heaven, had given him some instructions, a mission to carry out. Three years later, on New Year's Day, 1892, James Mooney, a self-trained anthropologist employed by the Smithsonian Institution's Bureau of Ethnology, interviewed this Indian prophet to learn firsthand what those instructions were. "God told him he must go back and tell his people they must be good and love one another, have no quarreling, and live in peace with the whites," Mooney reported, "that they must work, and not lie or steal; that they must put away all the old practices that savored of war; that if they faithfully obeyed his instructions they would at last be reunited with their friends in this other world, where there would be no more death or sickness or old age."[1] God also gave Wovoka a dance—the ghost dance—to bring back to his tribe. If the people danced it, Wovoka told Mooney, they would be assured of a timely reunion with their dead friends and relatives.

In the three years between Wovoka's vision and his reporting its details to Mooney, Wovoka told many other Indians about God's instructions and the accompanying dance, and as word spread throughout the western United States, his prophecy propelled what became known as the ghost dance or messiah movement. Though Wovoka never claimed to be a messiah, he was widely proclaimed to be one. Mooney spent more than three years researching the movement, talking not only to members of the Paiute tribe but also to Arapaho, Cheyenne, Kiowa, Comanche, Apache, Caddo, Wichita, Omaha, Winnebago, and Sioux. He concluded that many tribes eventually incorporated the movement's beliefs into their religions, which he saw as positive, believing that the doctrine, attractive to a culture in crisis, was founded on "a hope common to all humanity."[2]

Mooney's opinion, however, was not shared by most white settlers, Christian missionaries, or the U.S. Army. To them these ideas and more specifically this dance, both clearly exciting to growing numbers of Indians west of the Mississippi River, signified immorality and, most likely, the reigniting of native resistance and warfare. Together these groups set out to stop the ghost dance. Two years after Wovoka's vision, on December 15, 1890, on the Standing Rock reservation in South Dakota, Hunkpapa leader Sitting Bull was killed as Indian agency police tried to arrest him to keep him from supporting the movement. Fearing they, too, might be killed, more than three hundred Hunkpapa and Miniconjou fled with a Miniconjou leader named Big Foot. On December 28, the U.S. Army's Seventh Cavalry intercepted them and brought them to the Pine Ridge agency, also in South Dakota, and held them at a spot near Wounded Knee Creek. The next morning, as the Indians were being disarmed, a gun went off, and the soldiers opened fire, using Hotchkiss guns, which Mooney determined had "poured in two-pound explosive shells at the rate of nearly fifty per minute, mowing down everything alive."[3] When it was over, somewhere between 150 and 300 Indians, most of them women and children, lay dead in the December snow. The incident, which became known as the Wounded Knee Massacre, brought an end to open adherence to the ghost dance doctrine and effectively ended Indian resistance on the Great Plains.

John Neihardt had first heard of the massacre as a boy in Kansas City when his father read to him from newspaper accounts. He had known about the ghost dance movement since at least the early 1900s and mentioned elements of it in two of his early short stories, "The Ancient Memory" in 1907 and "The Epic-Minded Scot" in 1908. With *Indian Wars* published, Neihardt was eager to start on his next long narrative poem, a continuation of *Wars* that would focus on the movement. He called it *The Song of the Messiah*. "It will be beautiful and somehow true," he told House.[4] In the fall of 1925, after yet another lecture tour—"another spell of torture"—Neihardt had begun writing *Messiah*.[5] As always, he thought his current book would be "my top rung," the reason being that "the theme is exactly right for the stage of life I seem to have entered."[6] Neihardt explained the theme in slightly different ways during the years he worked on the poem. Sometimes it was "the triumph of spirit through apparent defeat."[7] At other times it was "the highest wins only through defeat."[8] However he described it, what he was after was the idea that like Jesus Christ in the Christian Bible, the Plains Indians would achieve their destiny only through their own destruction. That, to Neihardt, was the story he was now seeking to tell.

The move to Kirkwood and the *Post-Dispatch* and final work on *Indian Tales and Others* and his *Collected Poems* had interfered with Neihardt's progress on his new poem, and this frustrated him. "In all these years, I have done just five hundred lines on it," he told a newspaper reporter in 1930. "It has been like dying itself to see the work there to be done, with no time to do it in."[9] Neihardt resented the time his *Post-Dispatch* work required, but he never relaxed his reviewing, maintaining a punishing schedule of reading fiction, nonfiction, drama, and poetry. He regularly insulted most literary critics, whom he found generally to be more interested in commercialism than literature. "The fault with most of what passes for literary criticism is that books are dealt with as things in themselves, just as oranges or hams are."[10] And he continued to offer his opinions on his fellow poets, challenging free verse enthusiasts and targeting "the obstreperously modern and the unintelligibly futuristic."[11]

Eventually, in mid-July 1930, accompanied by his son Sigurd, now seventeen, driving a used Ford Model T sedan, and carrying letters of introduction from the Board of Indian Commissioners and his reliable friend Doane Robinson, Neihardt made what he called "our pilgrimage" to the Pine Ridge agency in southwestern South Dakota, home to what was then generally known as the Oglala Sioux tribe.[12] Once there he hoped to find Sioux who had firsthand knowledge of the ghost dance movement.

The Board of Indian Commissioners, Neihardt had been assured, had instructed Pine Ridge's field agent to find "the Indians I want," someone who could give him the background he needed for *Messiah*.[13] The agent suggested an elderly man named Nicholas Black Elk, born in the 1860s and a witness to many of the interactions between his tribe and the U.S. Army, including the Battle of the Little Bighorn. He had been recognized as a medicine man in 1881, the year Neihardt was born. In the brief time between Wovoka's vision and the Wounded Knee Massacre, to which he was also a witness, Black Elk had promoted the ghost dance movement. What really sold Neihardt on Black Elk, however, was that he was a second cousin to Crazy Horse, the focus of the climax to Neihardt's *Song of the Indian Wars*.

Neihardt and his son, accompanied by an interpreter named Flying Hawk, drove to Black Elk's home. The agent warned Neihardt that other writers had approached Black Elk before and been rebuffed. "I went to see him, expecting no more than the satisfaction of exchanging a few words," Neihardt wrote later.[14] Instead, the two hit it off from the very beginning. Neihardt, who had had years of practice talking with tribal elders of the Omaha from his years in Bancroft, always believed that understanding another culture meant first understanding that culture's religion, and he was drawn immediately to Black Elk's accounts of his spiritual encounters. Black Elk, for his part, had had experience with white storytellers, having traveled and performed when much younger with Buffalo Bill's Wild West show in New York and Europe, a trip that had allowed him to seek answers to his own questions about white culture.

The two men ended up talking all afternoon. If Neihardt took any notes that hot August afternoon, he did not keep them. No record exists of their conversations that day, but Black Elk certainly talked about his life and that of his tribe. Among the stories Black Elk related to Neihardt was at least a glimpse of the prophetic visions he had had as a boy, mystical encounters that had come to direct his life. That Native Americans had—and believed in—such visions would not have surprised Neihardt. He had heard of similar occurrences from his Omaha sources, and his early short stories had included characters whose lives were often directed by their dreams and visions, but he was not prepared for what he heard that day from Nicholas Black Elk. "Although my acquaintance with the Indian consciousness had been fairly intimate for more than thirty years," Neihardt said, "the inner world of Black Elk, imperfectly revealed as by flashes that day, was both strange and wonderful to me."[15]

With his experiences with the Omaha, his years of study of Plains Indians, and his close reading of popular books about Indians, Neihardt knew he was hearing something special. "I heard things that afternoon that astounded me," he wrote later, "and I decided that I must get on the inside of Black Elk's world."[16] Neihardt left Pine Ridge that day believing that through Black Elk, he could tell the story of the Sioux "in the good old times as well as in the tragic and heroic years of their final defeat and degradation," and he thought he knew a publisher who would be interested.[17] John Macy and William Morrow had never given up trying to get Neihardt to write an Indian book for them, and after returning to Missouri, Neihardt wrote to Morrow, telling him about his encounter with Black Elk. By the end of October he had a contract. "They want me to do a book on the Sioux Indians built around the life of Black Elk," he wrote to House, "and they offer me one thousand dollars cash advance and better royalty than I have been receiving if I will undertake the job. They seem surprisingly eager."[18]

In early November Neihardt wrote to Black Elk. "I feel that the whole story of your life ought to be written truthfully by somebody with the right feeling and understanding of your people and of their great history. . . . I would want to tell the story of your life beginning at the beginning and going straight through to Wounded Knee. . . . So, you see, this book would be not only the story of your life, but the story of the life of your people."[19] By the end of the month Neihardt and Black Elk were planning to meet again the next spring. Standing Bear, a friend of Black Elk's reputed to be a talented pictograph painter, set about creating illustrations for the book. "Black Elk," Neihardt reported, "is a fine wise spirit and he is entering into the plans with enthusiasm."[20]

Neihardt decided to take his two oldest daughters, Enid and Hilda, on his second trip to Pine Ridge. Enid, nearly twenty, would be his secretary and stenographer during the interviews, and he would take Hilda, turning fourteen, just "for the good she will get from the experience."[21] Sigurd was in school in St. Louis and would not be out until July, too late to make the return trip to Pine Ridge, and Alice, his youngest, was just nine and too young to go along. Neihardt traveled often and, between his responsibilities at the *Post-Dispatch* and his writing on *Messiah*, was often working, and he reveled in the opportunity to spend time with his children. "I'm a bit astonished at all of them," he said at the time, "each with an individual equipment of virtues and powers." His wife remained his confidant and adviser, the glue that held the family together. As he told House, "Mona is still Mona."[22]

In January 1931 Neihardt celebrated his fiftieth birthday. "I have more power—or rather have access to greater sources of power—than ever before," he said, "and care less to use it than ever." As he aged, Neihardt's "higher values" remained important to him, and what he saw as the modern materialism continued to annoy him. "We are now living in a vast kindergarten without a teacher," he wrote. He, for one, was ready "to try the first grade."[23] Each week he received one or two reminders that people cared about his books: requests for autographs, expressions of appreciation, passing references to his work, "and always the plane of regard seems high."[24] Enid, in her role as his secretary, had recently sent letters to universities and colleges promoting her father's lectures and readings, and the response was encouraging. "About thirty replies in a week—all favorable thus far."[25] Neihardt knew that he was on his own, that he belonged to no school or group of writers. "The joy of partisanship is not in me," he said. "I wish it were."[26]

He still wanted to complete his *Cycle of the West*, especially *The Song of the Messiah*. "[T]o tell the greatest of all human stories again with a new emphasis, with a whole new race on the cross—that might be worth doing!"[27] Other work continued to stand in his way, however. He was in his fifth year at the *Post-Dispatch*—though Pulitzer had allowed him to work from Branson for a year after he returned from his first visit to Black Elk—and he continued to read and critique books every week. Though he often resented the time the newspaper took away from his poetry, he enjoyed having the voice it gave him. Macmillan had eventually passed on his collection of what he considered the best of his literary criticism, the manuscript he called *Straws in the Wind*, and he tried unsuccessfully for years to place it with a different publisher. "For obvious reasons," he wrote to House, "such a book of criticism can not be handled in the East. No publisher would care to risk offending his supporting cliques."[28] He and House also tried unsuccessfully to get a revised edition of House's Neihardt biography published.[29]

Plans for the Black Elk book also were already taking his time and energy. "Can hardly wait until spring—want to go now," he wrote to House. "It will be a wonderful experience, for I can feel that everything is shaping up just as I would have it."[30]

On the first of May 1931, Ray Lyman Wilbur, U.S. secretary of the interior, wrote to Neihardt, granting him permission to go once again onto the Pine Ridge reservation to interview Nicholas Black Elk. All that he asked in return was "a short report of your meetings with these Indians."[31] B. G. Courtright, the Pine Ridge agent, had been somewhat reluctant to let Neihardt meet again with Black Elk and his friends, but Malcolm McDowell, secretary of the Board of Indian Commissioners, wrote to Courtright on Neihardt's behalf: "Mr. Neihardt is not an investigator, an uplifter nor anything of that kind and while I thoroughly appreciate the fact that it would be unwise for you to grant wide open permission to strangers to hold meetings in your jurisdiction, I think you need have no fear whatever about helping Mr. Neihardt to get in touch with some of the old fellows up there."[32]

Neihardt may not have known he had been approved until he arrived at Pine Ridge because on May 1 he had taken off for South Dakota, crammed into the narrow front seat of the family's Gardner automobile with Enid and Hilda, staying with friends and relatives along the way when they could and camping when necessary. Neihardt, for all the types of writing he tried, never kept a journal, and throughout most of his life the best guide to his thoughts and whereabouts was his regular correspondence. But on this trip he had brought along a stenographer, daughter Enid, who in addition to being his official note taker, kept a diary in which she recorded the doings of "Daddy," "Hilda Grace," and "yours truly, Enid Volnia." On May 2 the three stopped in Lincoln, Nebraska, and stayed with Neihardt's aunt and uncle, Martha and Charles Culler. Neihardt spoke to the local Writers Guild that evening at the Hotel Lincoln, and his daughters, who rarely had the opportunity to hear their father speak or recite his poetry publicly, attended. "Daddy read beautifully!" Enid recorded.[33]

After a week spent visiting some of Neihardt's old Nebraska haunts—including an opportunity in Omaha for Enid and Hilda to visit a movie theater and see a revival of D. W. Griffith's "Birth of a Nation"—the Neihardts pulled into Manderson, South Dakota, on May 9. Hilda later wrote that they stopped at the bottom of a low hill to take in the scene. "Black Elk's cabin was partway up the rather barren hillside, and the grass surrounding it was still brown." To the right of Black Elk's house stood a pine shade that his family had built.[34] "When we got to the Black Elks' place, he had made many arrangements for us," Enid recorded, "and apparently he considered this as one of the great things in his life!"[35] Black Elk had arranged for a tepee for the Neihardts, set atop a knoll near his house and adorned with symbols: a pipe, an antelope, a buffalo, and an eagle.[36] "[W]e will all live together in the ancient way—no white people but Enid, Hilda & myself," Neihardt wrote to House. "Horses ready for riding, they assure us."[37]

Neihardt had conducted research for his writing many times before. He had traveled to libraries and battle sites, read books and letters, questioned those who had knowledge of the people and events about which he was writing. But he had never taken on a project quite like this one, in which he had set aside three weeks to interview one man intensely, with some assistance from his friends, about a thirty-year period that had ended some forty years earlier. Work began early on Saturday, May 10, with Neihardt passing around cigarettes to Black Elk and his friends. As the men smoked, Neihardt briefly outlined what he hoped to get from the conversations. Enid recorded in her diary simply, "We started out with the book today," offering no hint of the cumbersome and complicated process that the collaboration required. Black Elk and his friends spoke Lakota. Black Elk's son Ben then translated what they said into English. Neihardt then rephrased Ben's translations, smoothing and tightening while working to make sure he had understood everything completely. Ben would then translate Neihardt's version back to Lakota and Black Elk and the others would offer elaborations or corrections. This continued until both Black Elk and Neihardt were satisfied with the wording and the meaning. At that point Enid wrote it all down in shorthand in her stenographer's notebook.

Hilda, when older, remembered her father, as he sat down to interview Black Elk, as being "very strong, very intense, with wavy blond hair that had darkened to a sandy brown and bright blue eyes that revealed his enthusiasm for the job he had undertaken."[38] Accompanying Black Elk that first day were Fire Thunder, Iron Hawk, Chase-in-the-Morning, Holy Black Tail Deer, and Black Elk's oldest friend, Standing Bear. Enid recorded in her diary that they were "nice-looking and interesting Indians and ready to give us their best." Hilda recalled that all the men were dressed in white men's clothing, and that several wore cowboy hats. "Fire Thunder was the oldest," she remembered, "but he was still slim and strongly built, as was deep-chested Iron Hawk, and I thought how powerful they must have been as young warriors. Standing Bear was one of the most memorable for me. In him the stereotype of the dignified Indian became real. Tall and straight in spite of his seventy-two years and the hard work he had done, Standing Bear was kingly. When he walked into a group—even when we sat out on the prairie—Standing Bear had the imposing bearing of a monarch."[39] One of Black Elk's granddaughters, Ben's daughter Esther, waited on the men. "I'd take the coffee and pour it out very slow, just to listen to them," she remembered years later. She was fascinated by the way her grandfather spoke. "It just had a rhythm, the way he talked. And then the way my dad brought it out in English, it rhymed now and then. The language sounded like a rhythm."[40]

That first day of work went slowly, with the participants struggling to understand one another enough to make progress. Enid recorded the men's names—both their "Sioux name" and their "white name"—and their ages. Then Black Elk gave a brief recitation of his family history, including his father's role in a battle Neihardt had already written about. "I was three years old when my father was in battle of the Fetterman fight—he got his right leg broken," Black Elk told Neihardt, referring to the battle on December 21, 1866, between the U.S. cavalry and warriors of the Lakota, Cheyenne, and Arapaho in northern Wyoming.[41] Fire Thunder offered context by telling more about the campaign under Red Cloud that included the Fetterman fight, explaining about tactics and positions, sometimes making it sound routine and at other times telling of death-defying attacks on army soldiers. "When we came closer someone hollered: 'Let's go. This is a good day to die,'" Fire Thunder said. "I killed five or six of these soldiers myself—three with my six-shooter and three with arrows."

Standing Bear and Holy Black Tail Deer also spoke that first day, answering a question Neihardt asked about the impact of the whites' arrival. "The way I felt about this question," Standing Bear said, "is that I felt that the white men would just simply wipe us out and there would be no Indian nation. I felt this when I was a mere child." Holy Black Tail Deer remembered thinking, as a young boy, that he would have to do his part in the fight against the whites. "We roamed the country freely, and this country belonged to us in the first place," he told Neihardt. "But since the white man came, we were fighting all the time. . . . At the age of ten or eleven, I had a six-shooter and a quiver full of arrows to defend my nation." Fire Thunder added that he had first gone to war when he was sixteen. "I remember that the white men were coming and that they were going to fight us to the finish and take away our land, and I thought it was not right. We are humans too, and God created us all alike, and I was going to do the best I could to defend my nation."

Black Elk also gave a brief outline of an event that had occurred when he was only five years old. His father had made him a child's bow and arrows, and he had gone into the woods to try to shoot a bird. As he did, a thunderstorm blew up, and he heard a voice. "This was not a dream," Black Elk said. "It actually happened." Black Elk saw two men coming toward him out of a cloud in the northern sky and heard them singing a sacred song: "Behold him, a sacred voice is calling you. All over the sky a sacred voice is calling you." A kingbird sitting nearby told Black Elk to listen to the men and repeated the message that a sacred voice was calling the boy. As he watched the men, they turned into geese and headed west. "This vision lasted about twenty minutes," Black Elk said.

The next day, a Sunday, the Neihardts drove eighty miles southwest to Chadron, Nebraska, where Neihardt had arranged to speak at the normal school. They returned late on Wednesday, slept for the first time in their tepee, and the next morning resumed the interviews, continuing the discussion of Black Elk's visions. But little progress was made that day—or the next. Neihardt had purchased a Holstein bull, and the men butchered it for what Enid called in her diary "the Great Feast." The ceremony began early the next afternoon when a drummer, surrounded by a group of six singers, took his place in a small circle of pine trees. Holy Black Tail Deer and Black Elk made kill-talks, and then Hilda, Enid, and Neihardt were made members of the tribe and given tribal names: Daybreak Star Woman for Hilda, She Walks With Her Holy Stick for Enid, and Flaming Rainbow for Neihardt.[42] They were the only white people in attendance besides a reporter from a newspaper in Lincoln, Nebraska, sent to cover the latest adventure of the state's poet laureate.

Saturday was devoted mostly to recuperation. Finally, on Sunday, May 17, Neihardt and Black Elk and the others began three long days of work on what had truly brought Neihardt back to Pine Ridge: Black Elk's life-changing vision at age nine, which Neihardt came to call the "Great Vision." After Black Elk's first vision at age five, he had heard voices from time to time over the next few years. When he was nine he and his family and their band were moving toward the Rocky Mountains when one evening, after they had stopped for the day, a man named Man

Hip had invited Black Elk for supper. While eating the boy had once again heard a voice. "I heard someone say, 'It is time, now they are calling you,'" Black Elk told Neihardt and the others. "I knew then that I was called upon by the spirits, so I thought I'd just go where they wanted me to." When he got up to leave, though, his thighs ached painfully. By midway through the next morning he was unable to walk, and the illness, whatever it was, was spreading. "Both my legs and my arms were swollen badly and even my face. This all came suddenly."

Soon Black Elk lay ill in his family's tepee, and as he did, he realized he could see through the tepee walls. He saw coming toward him, from the clouds above, the same two men he had seen in his first vision four years earlier. "They came and stood off a ways from me and stopped, saying, 'Hurry up, your grandfather is calling you,'" Black Elk said. He got up and followed the men, and when they headed up into the clouds, a small cloud came down to the ground for him. He stepped onto it and was taken into the air, quickly reaching a height from which he looked down to see his parents looking up at him. "I felt sorry that I was leaving them." But leave them he did, following the two men higher into the clouds. There the men introduced Black Elk to a bay horse that spoke to him: "Behold me, my life history you shall see." A mystical allegory then unfolded in front of young Black Elk, a performance of horses, with the bay as a guide—a dozen each of black ones, wearing necklaces of buffalo hoofs; white ones, wearing necklaces of elk's teeth; and sorrels and buckskins, each group representing one of the four directions.

The bay then told Black Elk, "Your grandfathers are having a council, these shall take you, so take courage," and the boy looked up to see "a sky full of horses." The bay took Black Elk to a place on a cloud under "a rainbow gate," and sitting there were six grandfathers. The first grandfather, representing the west, gave the boy a wooden cup filled with water and a bow and arrows. The second, representing the north, offered an herb and told the boy "you shall create a nation," which Black Elk told Neihardt meant he would eventually cure illnesses and bring children back to life. The third, representing the east, gave him a peace pipe with a spotted eagle outstretched on its handle and told Black Elk he was to make whoever was sick well again. The fourth, from the south, gave him a flowering stick containing singing birds, and outlined for him two roads available on the earth, a good red one, running north to south, which would give him the power to do good, and a fearful black road, running east to west, from which Black Elk would derive powers necessary to vanquish his enemies. The fifth grandfather, representing the Great Spirit above, told him the things in the skies—which Black Elk interpreted as meaning the stars—would be like his relatives. "Your grandfathers shall attack an enemy and be unable to destroy him, but you will have the power to destroy," he told the boy. The sixth—the last—grandfather was "a very old man with very white hair." He carried a spear and told Black Elk that his nation would suffer great difficulties. Looking at him, at first Black Elk was frightened. "[T]hen as I looked at him longer I knew it was myself as a young man," Black Elk said. "At the first I was an old man, but I got younger and younger until I was a little boy nine years old."

Then, in the vision, Black Elk was astride the bay, and as he turned west, all the forty-eight horses—the white, black, sorrels, and buckskins—lined up behind him, going through the four directions again and repeating what Black Elk was to do with the gifts he had received from the grandfathers. Black Elk said he realized then that the horses were following him. "I was the leader." They all headed east from Colorado's Pike's Peak. "As we went along I noticed that everything on the earth was trembling with fear," he said. He believed, riding along, that he was "the chief of all the heavens."

Late in the vision, Black Elk's attention was drawn to a man, who then turned into a gopher and then into an herb. "This was the most powerful herb of all that I had gotten," he said. "It could be used in war and could destroy a nation." Black Elk told Neihardt that he called the herb "soldier weed," and that one touch of it would kill a man immediately. He was told, in the vision, that he might need the herb to defend his people. "I was not old enough when I was supposed to use this herb, or else I could have used it and killed many enemies," Black Elk said. "It was too terrible to use, and I was glad that I did not get to use it." Black Elk told Neihardt that had he used the soldier weed, he might have become a tribal leader. "[B]ut I am satisfied that I didn't become a chief."

Eventually Black Elk's vision returned him to the six grandfathers, and they cheered for him as he came back, telling him he had triumphed. They told him to return to his people, who were struggling. He could see all his people in his dream, and all of them but one were happy. "I took good notice, and it was myself and I had been sick twelve days. This was probably the twelfth day when I was just going back to my body." Soon he saw his family's tepee, saw himself lying there, and then heard someone say, "The boy is feeling better now. You had better give him some water." Black Elk could see that his parents were bending down over him. "They were giving me some medicine, but it was not that that cured me," he told Neihardt. "It was my vision that cured me."

Relating, understanding, and transcribing the vision, with all its complicated imagery, was difficult and time-consuming, and the men—as well as Enid—worked hard to record it correctly. "We did nothing much but work on the Vision on these days," Enid recorded in her diary. Generally Black Elk stayed focused on relating the dream, but occasionally he broke from the telling to comment on the dream itself. At one point in the vision, a number of animals turned into a band of poor humans. "It was a sight," Black Elk said.

As a child, Black Elk had been frightened by the dream, but by the time he told Neihardt and the others about it in 1931, he had had a lifetime to think about it, to shape it, to interpret it. Though much of the imagery in the vision was common to nineteenth-century Lakota, some of Black Elk's language—the repetition of the word for "behold" and the frequent use of the word for "shall"—suggests his familiarity with the Christian Bible, which would have come years after he had experienced the vision. In the early 1900s Black Elk had converted to Catholicism, eventually becoming a lay preacher on Pine Ridge and elsewhere.

Black Elk made it clear that the vision had often been on his mind throughout his life. Sometimes, he told Neihardt, when he saw clouds forming in the sky, he thought his guides might be returning to take him again. "I think about this dream often," he said. "And many times I feel bad about it, and other times I feel good about it." Black Elk believed the vision was the source of his power and his spirituality. "It was a power dream," he told Neihardt, "and it will never be forgotten until I die."

Over the next week Neihardt continued to interview Black Elk and his friends, always with the help of Ben and Enid. Standing Bear shared his memories of Black Elk's twelve days of unconsciousness. "Everybody in the whole village was excited over it, but they could not tell what sickness it was Black Elk had," observed Standing Bear, who had been about thirteen years old at the time. He remembered Black Elk's father visiting his family's tepee and telling them about the illness and relating how since recovering, Black Elk had not been the same. "It's strange the way he acts," Standing Bear recalled the father saying. "It seems that he doesn't think of his home very much." Seeing Black Elk soon afterward, Standing Bear found him to be more like a man than a boy, even though still only nine years old.

The men also moved beyond Black Elk's personal story and talked a great deal about day-to-day tribal life, about going to the Black Hills to cut poles to be used in constructing tepees, about attending gatherings where treaties were worked out, and about joining Crazy Horse's band on the Tongue River. Black Elk told of his first time on the warpath when, as one of the two youngest there, he joined an attack on a wagon train of white immigrants on a trail to the Black Hills. He fired a six-shooter that his sister had given him, peering out from under his horse's neck, and noticed that though the settlers were firing back, none of the bullets were hitting the warriors or their horses. "It probably was my power that kept us from being hurt," Black Elk said.

Neihardt also heard about fighting between the Lakota and the cavalry, well-known battles that he would have known from white sources, such as the Battle of the Rosebud on June 17, 1876, and the most famous of all, the Battle of the Little Bighorn, a week later on June 25 and 26, 1876. But now he had the opportunity to learn what these battles felt like from the other side. Standing Bear and Iron Hawk offered their views, and Black Elk told of watching, with his mother, through "the dust and the buzzing of the bullets and shots," the fight with Custer's Seventh Cavalry. So many Indians were fighting, Black Elk said, that it seemed "as though the Indians could have just trampled them down even if we had not had weapons." Later Black Elk and other adolescent boys walked through the battle site. "Before we got there, the whites were all wiped out," he told Neihardt. "When we got there some of them were still alive, kicking. Then many more boys came. And we got our arrows out and put arrows into the men and pushed some of the arrows that were sticking out in further." Black Elk took a pocket watch from one soldier, not knowing at the time what it was and wearing it for a time as a necklace, and he scalped another soldier. "Then I got tired of looking around here. I could smell nothing but blood and gunpowder, so I got sick of it pretty soon." Sick, but not sad. Black Elk said he knew before the battle that the soldiers would "get wiped out." And "I wasn't a bit sorry."

The group also visited the site of the Wounded Knee Massacre, and Black Elk walked them through the events of December 29, 1890, including how he had arrived after hearing the shooting that day. "[H]e showed us a scratch he had received from a bullet and the way it had gone right through his guts and did not kill him," Enid noted in her diary. As Neihardt later summed it up for House, "I got a great amount of material on the everyday living for many years and some startling accounts of battles from the Fetterman Massacre . . . up to the Wounded Knee fight in 1890. . . . It's all out of the Indian consciousness."[43]

As interesting as the conversations were, and as much information as Neihardt was able to glean from them, still they paled when compared to Black Elk's relating of his visions. "Black Elk is not nearly so good at remembering his history as he is in telling things about himself," Enid recorded in her diary. "When he talks about his Vision, he is marvelous."

During breaks in the discussions, Black Elk and Neihardt also talked about the poet's own life. Upon hearing about Neihardt's childhood fever dream, Black Elk assured him that he, like Black Elk, had not merely been ill. "This was a power vision that you had," Black Elk told him. He told Neihardt that describing the land along Hugh Glass's crawl in *The*

Song of Hugh Glass without having ever seen it proved Neihardt was "a sacred man thinker." "It was your Brother Ghost who had the power to describe that land that you did not see and had been helping to do all these other things." The same was true with Neihardt's arrival at Pine Ridge, he said. Black Elk told him he had long wanted to tell the world about his vision. "It seems that your Ghostly Brother has sent you here to do this for me," Black Elk told Neihardt. "You are here for the vision just the way I wanted."

Naturally, these interpretations thrilled Neihardt. "A strange thing happened often while I was talking with Black Elk," Neihardt wrote to House soon after the trip. "Over and over he seemed to be quoting from my poems, and sometimes I quoted some of my stuff to him, which when translated into Sioux could not retain much of their literary character, but the old man immediately recognized the ideas as his own," Neihardt wrote. "There was often an uncanny merging of consciousness between the old fellow and myself and he seemed to have remembered it."[44]

On May 29, three weeks after arriving at Pine Ridge, the Neihardts, followed by Nicholas and Ben Black Elk, drove to Harney Peak, the highest point in the Black Hills and South Dakota as well as in the United States east of the Rocky Mountains There they rented cabins. Black Elk believed he had been taken to Harney Peak in his vision, and early the next morning the group climbed to the top, where to commemorate the relating of his vision to others, Black Elk prayed, stripping down to a breechcloth worn over a red union suit of long underwear and reciting a lengthy plea to the Great Spirit and to the six grandfathers that they do what he could not: make the tree bloom again. "Hear me," he pleaded, "that my people will live, and find a way that my people will prosper."

The group returned to their cabins, and after a dinner of roast beef sandwiches, the Neihardts left for Deadwood, South Dakota, where they spent the night. They planned to visit the Custer battlefield in Montana, but they got lost and then their car broke down. Once their car was repaired, John, Enid, and Hilda headed for home. Any disappointment

Neihardt experienced at not being able to show his daughters the battle-field was outweighed by what they all had enjoyed with Black Elk. "We talked sixteen days with Black Elk and his old friends and sometimes far into the night," he wrote to his aunt and uncle. "The material I got was far beyond even my expectations and some that has never been given to a white man before."[45]

8. Baby Alice and older siblings (left to right) Enid, Hilda, and Sigurd with their father at their home in Branson, Missouri. Neihardt Center

9. Neihardt with Black Elk after giving a speech at the Lakota's victory dance in September 1945. Neihardt Center

10. Mona Neihardt with one of the busts she created of her husband. Neihardt Center

11. Mona and John Neihardt looking content, probably around 1956. WHMC

12. Neihardt speaking at the unveiling of his bust in the Nebraska State Capitol in 1961. Neihardt Center

13. Neihardt teaching on a particularly cold morning at the University of
Missouri in November 1963. WHMC

14. Neihardt with fellow author Mari Sandoz, who had suggested *Black Elk Speaks* as one of the first Bison Books. Neihardt Center

13 A WISE AND GOOD BOOK

The 1930s were a time of expanded literary interest in America's original inhabitants. In the 1920s the *New York Times*, in its weekly literary section, reviewed fewer than forty books about American Indians, slightly more than it had in the previous ten years. But in the decade of the '30s that number jumped to nearly ninety. In the opening years of the decade, white writers of all kinds were discovering the country's various tribes. Anthropologist Margaret Mead spent several months in the summer of 1930 on a Great Plains reservation—though she disguised the tribe in her book as "Antlers," she was actually with the Omaha in northeastern Nebraska—researching a book that became *The Changing Culture of an Indian Tribe*.[1] Frank Linderman, a Montana writer, politician, and amateur ethnographer, began writing the life stories of Indians he knew, including two Crow Indians, Plenty-coups and Pretty-shield.[2] Nebraska author Mari Sandoz and her friend Eleanor Hinman devoted three weeks one summer to traveling through North and South Dakota, Wyoming, and Montana, collecting information that would eventually make its way into a biography of Crazy Horse.[3]

Into that literary environment John Neihardt returned, a changed man after his time with Black Elk. Neihardt had connected with tribal elders before, but his conversations with Black Elk and the power of Black Elk's vision touched him deeply. For twenty years Neihardt had explained away the western expansion of the United States by comparing it to a flooding river. Just as one cannot blame a river for the damage it causes when it overflows its banks—it is, after all, merely doing what water does—one cannot blame men and women when they explore and exploit new territory as part of a mass movement. The individuals were but drops in the flood of western settlement, part of something too large to stop. Now, however, he had experienced an awakening, learning from a fellow mystical thinker about what had happened to the individuals and their communities when that exploration had overrun them. More than two decades earlier Neihardt had argued that a writer hoping to portray Indians accurately would need to undergo a "soul-change" in order to get at the Indians' religious consciousness. Through his conversations with Black Elk, Neihardt had experienced this "soul-change": he realized now that the "otherness" he had sought for so long, the spiritual element that his culture—the dominant white culture—considered separate from this life, a reward to be waited for, was an everyday part of Black Elk's life. Insights that Black Elk gained from his vision were just as valuable, just as meaningful, as any information he gathered from the living world, perhaps more so. This caused Neihardt to question deeply for the first time the treatment of the continent's native inhabitants, and as soon as he arrived back home to Branson he forcefully stated his newfound beliefs in a letter to Ray Lyman Wilbur, U.S. secretary of the interior under President Herbert Hoover. The letter, which Neihardt had promised Wilbur in return for permission to go onto Pine Ridge and interview Black Elk and the others, began with a brief summary of the work he had completed there. "The meetings, which were practically continuous during the entire period save for the time when we were either sleeping or feasting, were very successful indeed, and I was able to procure some very valuable material that has never before been given to white men." Then Neihardt took up his primary point.

As you, of course, already know, the Ogalalas are hardly a happy or a prosperous people and those who fancy that they could be made so through political reforms and by measly 'practical' measures, do not understand the Indian consciousness. I did not go there in a criticizing spirit nor did I come away in any such mood. While I was among the old men and feeling deeply the profound spirituality of which they are capable, funny as this may seem to one who does not know Indians well, I had a dream of what might be done for these Ogalalas if the effort could be made. The simple fact about them is that they cannot be turned into white men and as a people they cannot be supervised successfully after our fashion. They are visionary, lively, and improvident for very good reasons. One feels that they as a people have lost their self-respect and that the only way they could be made really happy and prosperous would be through some revival of their own courageousness and their own religion. Incidentally, they had the courageousness and the spirit both and in the course of this study they are indeed seen to be admirable. There were times when I felt very humble before these old men, and especially when Black Elk, who is in spirit a great poet, was describing the great vision upon which his whole life has been based. What a pity it seems that these people, who are living now in what amounts to a social vacuum, could not be encouraged to revive and cherish their ancient culture to the end that they might develop a proud self-consciousness as a people."

Neihardt knew, of course, that such steps would not be taken. "I know this is a dream for the reason that the modern world would not allow it," he wrote, "but it is not so foolish as it may sound."[4] No evidence exists that Wilbur ever responded.

To others Neihardt was, if anything, even more emphatic. After spending time with Black Elk and his friends, after learning about Black Elk's "marvelous" and "vast" vision, "full of profound significance and perfectly formed," Neihardt struggled to find his place again in "the rottenness of our white civilization." Reviewing a book by Russian writer and poet Dmitry Merezhkovsky shortly after his return to Branson, Neihardt referred to his time with Black Elk and the others, telling readers he had been able to "feel with extraordinary intensity the profound and perhaps fatal truth about our civilization in its dominant aspects."[5] As he wrote to

House at the time, "I wasn't quite sure that I cared to return to civilization, and the girls felt practically the same."[6] Neihardt knew he had forged a profound connection with Black Elk, a "merging of consciousness," during their conversations, and he was excited to use that connection to craft a different kind of book. The only thing weighing on Neihardt was that Black Elk, in the aftermath of their visit and the sharing of his vision, seemed melancholy. Neihardt wrote to him to try to cheer him up. "The finest things in your life are going to be saved for other men," Neihardt told him. "This ought to make you happy."[7] Neihardt argued to Black Elk that though other white writers had tried to get Black Elk's story before, Neihardt was uniquely qualified to do something special with the material. "We are going to do something real with this book about the tree that never bloomed and I am sure that you are going to be a good deal happier because of this book," Neihardt wrote to him. "Keep a good heart and be patient until next spring when the book appears. I have to work hard on the book and be patient too, and I can do both with a strong heart because I know that the book is wise and good and that thousands of people will find good in it."[8]

The *Post-Dispatch* granted Neihardt a six-month leave of absence to write the book, and throughout the late summer and early fall, he worked from typewritten transcripts of Enid's notes, fashioning a narrative of Black Elk's—and the tribe's—life.[9] Neihardt, through the give-and-take with Black Elk and his son during the interviews, had already played a part in the wording that Enid captured in her shorthand notes and later her transcripts. Now he further worked her notes into Black Elk's story, sometimes using them nearly verbatim, sometimes not.[10] Neihardt remained confident as he wrote the book, because of the bond he believed he had forged with Black Elk, that when he ventured off his daughter's transcripts, he did so as Black Elk himself would have done if he had had a better understanding of the English language and American literature. The poetic and archaic allusions that had often drawn criticism from reviewers of Neihardt's earlier books had diminished in *The Song of the Indian Wars*, and they disappeared entirely in this new book. The language, building on Black Elk's direct recountings, remained simple and powerfully descriptive.[11]

As he had planned, Neihardt began the book, after a brief introductory chapter, with Black Elk's birth in 1863 and ended it with the massacre at Wounded Knee in 1890. In between he wrote of Black Elk's life and that of his band and tribe, of hunting buffalo and living in Canada, of fighting "Three Stars"—General George Crook—and "rubbing out" Custer, of performing his first cure, and of enduring the death of Crazy Horse. But Neihardt had been most taken, during the Pine Ridge interviews, with Black Elk's vision, and he crafted it as the centerpiece of the book and worked hard to bring it to life on the page. Neihardt wrote the book in the first person, making it seem that Black Elk was writing the story, and he believed throughout that he was remaining "absolutely true to Black Elk's spirit and meaning," truer, in fact, than Black Elk himself might be able to be. As he told House, "If you could spend a day with Enid's stenographic report, out of which the book is mined, the whole thing would be made clear."[12]

He gently rewrote Black Elk's words—already sifted through the layered interview process—tightening and focusing his story and, in the process, trying to make it more understandable to white readers. For example, Enid had written in her notes: "Just before we got to Greasy Grass Creek, we camped again for the night. There was a man by the name of Man Hip who invited me for supper. While eating I heard a voice. I heard someone say, 'It is time, now they are calling you.'" In Neihardt's manuscript, this passage became: "We camped one evening in a valley beside a little creek just before it ran into the Greasy Grass, and there was a man by the name of Man Hip who liked me and asked me to eat with him in his tepee. While I was eating, a voice came and said: 'It is time; now they are calling you.'"[13] Throughout the book, Neihardt worked similarly, compressing and brightening Black Elk's words. He used occasional footnotes to explain Sioux terminology, identifying such landmarks as "their iron road" as the Union Pacific Railway, the Greasy Grass as the Little Bighorn River, and "the Soldiers' Town" as Nebraska's Fort Robinson, and translating such terms as *aguiapi* as bread, *paezhuta sapa* as coffee, and *chahumpi ska* as sugar.

Only in three places did Neihardt vary significantly from Enid's transcripts of what Black Elk and his friends had said: he chose to focus on the vision's bestowal on Black Elk the power to create life, omitting most mentions of the complementary power to destroy, and he fashioned, based on nothing more than his sense of Black Elk, both an opening and an ending to the book that were presented as Black Elk's words. In the ending especially, two powerfully written paragraphs, Neihardt made Black Elk's disappointment at his inability to bring his vision to fruition—to make the tree bloom again—the central theme of his long life. Though the ending comes immediately after the Wounded Knee massacre, Neihardt constructs the ending so that Black Elk is looking back at that moment from old age, making the massacre a metaphor for the destruction of an entire nation.

> I did not know then how much was ended. When I look back now from this high hill of my old age, I can still see the butchered women and children lying heaped and scattered all along the crooked gulch as plain as when I saw them with eyes still young. And I can see that something else died there in the bloody mud, and was buried in the blizzard. A people's dream died there. It was a beautiful dream.
>
> And I, to whom so great a vision was given in my youth,—you see me now a pitiful old man who has done nothing, for the nation's hoop is broken and scattered. There is no center any longer, and the sacred tree is dead.[14]

As Neihardt later told an interviewer, "If you do not understand *Black Elk*, you do not understand me."[15]

While writing the book, Neihardt as usual issued frequent updates to friends and family. "The book is going on in great shape," he told House, "and physically and mentally I am in good condition."[16] Neihardt, of course, was optimistic about the book, which he believed was "likely to be a wow according to present indications." He finished the manuscript on October 21 and before the end of the month eagerly sent it to William Morrow. On November 11, however, Morrow died, at age fifty-eight, after a brief illness, never having had the chance to read the manuscript he had long wanted, and depriving Neihardt of his strongest supporter in the publisher's office. "He was waiting to get well enough to read the book in bed, when he died," Neihardt wrote. "There was something between that man & me, & had been for ten years."[17]

Macmillan, Neihardt's regular publisher, by this time had heard that Neihardt had been granted a leave of absence from the newspaper to finish a new book, and H. S. Latham wrote to him wondering what it was and expressing eagerness to have an opportunity to publish it.[18] For two months Latham continued unsuccessfully to hound Neihardt, who enjoyed Macmillan's anxiety. When after repeated pleas Neihardt finally explained the deal he had with Morrow, Latham gave up and offered instead a contract for *The Song of the Messiah*, stipulating that *Messiah* would be the next book after the Morrow book and that Macmillan would also publish the book Neihardt wrote after *Messiah*.

Meanwhile, Neihardt had grown genuinely excited about the prospects for what he had hoped would be called *The Tree That Never Flowered* but was now being called *Black Elk Speaks*. The book had been scheduled to be published in April 1932, but in mid-January the publisher decided to hurry the book out by February 18 in order to beat out another Indian book, Frank Linderman's *Red Mother*, on the Crow woman Pretty-shield, expected in March. Neihardt believed his book was a winner. "I doubt . . . if the Indian religious consciousness has ever been so clearly revealed before," he wrote to House. "It is *essential* religion, pretty close to the source."[19]

Reviews from Los Angeles to Boston were generally positive. "It is about as near as you can get to seeing life and death, war and religion, through an Indian's eyes," a review in *Outlook* offered.[20] The *Chicago Tribune* noted the book's "simple and forceful" language but wished Neihardt had injected "the colorfulness and the vivid imagery as well as the charming and quaint idiom that characterize much of the better done translations of Indian life and lore."[21] *Time* magazine praised the way Neihardt had "superbly set down" Black Elk's story, and the *New York Times* praised Neihardt's value as "an amanuensis," calling the book "one of the saddest and noblest that has ever been told." "Battle accounts are not in terms of ammunition used nor of numbers slain," the *Times* reviewer wrote, "they are, rather, in terms of very human and tragic miscellany."[22]

The *Philadelphia Inquirer* thought Neihardt had turned Black Elk's story into an epic. "This comes nearer to being a real Indian book than any that we have yet had. There is in it the playfulness and humor, tragedy and pathos, dignity and simplicity that belong to the old warrior himself."[23] The *St. Louis Globe Democrat*, the *Post-Dispatch*'s local rival, dismissed Neihardt's claim that he was only the interpreter of Black Elk's story. "[O]nly a fine writer could present it so simply and effectively, and only a poet could have preserved that beauty and imaginative sweep of the Indian's conception of nature."[24] The *Los Angeles Times* found Neihardt to be well-fitted to write the book. "For he understands the Indian and his point of view, sympathizes with him without becoming sentimental, and falls easily into the rhythm and spirit of his story."[25] The *New Republic* called attention to the book's "modern tone," saying the "description of the fight with Custer might almost have been written by Ernest Hemingway, and that is a great tribute indeed to Mr. Hemingway."[26]

As happy as the reviews made Neihardt—"I'm surprised at the good words, very much surprised," he wrote to House—he once again found most valuable not the published opinions of critics but the privately delivered words of a person in a position to understand what he was trying to do.[27] Ella Cara Deloria, who had been born on the Yankton Indian Reservation in South Dakota of Dakota, English, French, and German ancestry and was now working in the Department of Anthropology at Columbia University in New York, wrote to Neihardt as soon as she finished reading *Black Elk Speaks*. "I want you to know that it makes me happy and sad all at once—sad for the days that are gone, and glad that a white man really lives who can enter into a right understanding of a Dakota's vision, and can translate it into so poetic a form." She told Neihardt that her grandfather had been a medicine man among the Yankton, and that her father, like Black Elk, had converted to Christianity "after 'the end of the dream' when it was apparent to him that he could do nothing under the old regime for his people and he thought he must try to train himself to lead them under the new conditions." She wrote that in her work at Columbia, in which she been recording stories and ethnographic material from Lakota and Dakota elders throughout South Dakota and Minnesota, she had accumulated many examples of other visions. "I find them very inspiring—but I never knew until now how their meaning could be expressed in such a way as to be understandable to people of such a material civilization as this."[28] Two months later she wrote again, assuring him that "I am not only happy, but passionately eager, to say everything I can in favor of your *Black Elk Speaks*."[29]

Despite the good reviews, the book sold poorly. Neihardt blamed Morrow's death, followed in August 1932 by John Macy's fatal heart attack, for robbing him of his two supporters in the publisher's office.

That October Neihardt appeared on Broadway through one of his early poems. Actor and playwright Barton MacLane, in one month that summer, had written a three-act play originally called "The Master Melody" but produced as "Rendezvous." He sold it to a producer with the understanding that he would star in it. MacLane's character, Private Oakley, has managed to survive the war in France, and he returns to an unspecified American city and puts a gang of his stock character army buddies to work as beer-runners. They are competing with the entrenched thugs of Tony Rossalino, and Oakley decides his gang must kill three politicians controlled by his rival. Oakley remembers that to keep their spirits up in the trenches of France, one of his buddies used to recite Neihardt's poem "Let Me Live Out My Years," which ends with the lines "O let me be a tune-swept fiddlestring / That feels the Master Melody—*and snaps!*" Now Oakley launches his scheme in a different kind of fight and, in the words of theater critic Brooks Atkinson, then still fairly new at the *New York Times*, "intoxicated by a defiant poem of Neihardt's." Though two of the politicians are killed, Oakley's plan fails, and he is caught and eventually sentenced to the electric chair, where, in the play's final scene, he once again recites Neihardt's poem to steady his nerves. Atkinson called it "a play of high impulses," written "in a glow of youthful exaltation," but he found that the script needed "coordination, variety and movement": "Only a whole volley of shooting blows this performance out of the doldrums."[30] After preparatory engagements in New Haven and Hartford, Connecticut, "Rendezvous" played only twenty-one performances at New York's Broadhurst Theatre, but MacLane was impressive enough to land a lucrative contract with Warner Brothers. If Neihardt knew about the play, no record exists of his having commented on it. "Let Me Live Out My Years" remained forever one of his favorites of his own poems, and he would have enjoyed the fact that Atkinson needed only to identify him by last name for New York readers to recognize him. But in all the letters he wrote that fall, even to House, he made no mention of it.

Neihardt had resumed work on *The Song of the Messiah* soon after he shipped *Black Elk Speaks* to the publisher. Getting back to it was "as usual, rather punishing," but it left him feeling "nearly happy," he reported to Julius House. "Mona & Enid say the lines I have written so far are real," he said. "Mona said: 'It's the sort of thing nobody else does.' She meant that something gets through me that doesn't get through most other holes. Maybe it's so."[31] At first progress was slow, but by fall Neihardt believed the poem was "developing steadily," adding, "[S]urely whatever it is that has helped me in the past is more than ever on the job."[32]

One reason he was able to focus so clearly on the new poem for much of the year was that he was no longer having to churn out reviews for the newspaper. Neihardt had expected to return to the *Post-Dispatch* in January 1932, but the continuing decline in the economy had led the newspaper to hold off resuming his column until that November. The Neihardt family, like a great many people across the country, worked to avoid being crushed by the advancing depression. Enid and Sigurd struggled to find jobs, but for the most part the Neihardts kept their heads above water. "I can see a year ahead easily without lowering our standard of living," Neihardt said that fall.[33] In an exchange with his former teacher U. S. Conn, Neihardt talked about the meaning of the current situation. "You and I are not exactly the same age, but we are of the same world which appears to be dead, and we know something about need that it might be well for our younger generation to know," he wrote. "It seems a pity that so many excellent people should be punished by way of getting this lesson across."[34] Neihardt, as long as he could continue to support his family, was happy to hold off resuming work at the *Post-Dispatch*. "I do not want to return to a steady job of literary criticism. I want to finish the *Cycle* which is my major reason for living, beyond the needs of my family."[35] He continued to travel extensively, speaking and reciting his poetry, often now in partnership with Sigurd, a skilled pianist. Neihardt would lecture on "the race-mood of courage" west of the Missouri in the nineteenth century and read some of his lyrics, and Sigurd would perform such pieces as Leopold Godowsky's "Humoresque," Frederic Chopin's "Nocturne in F-sharp Major," Felix Mendelssohn's "Spinning Song," or one of José Iturbi's "Spanish Dance" compositions.[36]

Neihardt returned to the *Post-Dispatch* late that year, writing a once-a-week column called "Of Making Many Books," which usually included reviews of at least four books. He still tried to spend as much time as possible on *Messiah*. "I am just approaching a very impressive climax . . . which involves the aging Red Cloud," he wrote that winter. "Once he would have been advising war. Now he advises his people to live on the hope that the spirit world is coming. It is a simple and pitiful scene."[37] By the summer of 1934 Neihardt wanted some time away from Missouri. Packing up Hilda and his youngest daughter Alice, he returned to South Dakota, setting up camp outside Black Elk's home in Manderson: "Wonderful place to work." He mailed in his *Post-Dispatch* work and continued pushing ahead with *Messiah*. "Sitting Bull is dying now. A few more days, & I'll be working on the final & relatively short section—'Wounded Knee.' That will be like eating dessert after a meal of many courses."[38] The three drove to Wounded Knee Creek, and while the girls explored, Neihardt wrote in the quiet of his car. The three returned to Branson in late August, and he continued to divide his time between reviewing and work on the long poem that fall and the next spring. With the summer came the finishing touches, and in July 1935 he finally sent off the manuscript to Macmillan in New York. By the end of October copies were being shipped to bookstores.

Neihardt had spent more time on *Messiah* than on any of his other books. Newspaper work, speaking engagements, family responsibilities, *Black Elk Speaks*, and even a wild turkey season or two had interrupted him during the ten years he worked on it, crowding the work he most wanted to do. He had set it aside for weeks, even months at a time, but feeling unhurried, he had never lost faith in it or in his larger *Cycle of the West*. He believed, as he told friends, that "there will be a whirlwind of strange glory toward the end of the poem" and that writing it was worth whatever time it took.[39] Originally he had envisioned *Messiah* as part of *Indian Wars*, but even broken into two volumes he never thought of them as "merely an 'Indian epic,'" as he put it. "It is essentially the human story," he explained to House, "utilizing the compact history of a race peculiarly well placed in time, as a medium for representing the whole trajectory of the human spirit through this world."[40]

Neihardt chose two epigraphs for the title page of *Messiah* to underscore his point. One from the book of Acts in the Christian Bible recounted how "your young men shall see visions, and your old men shall dream dreams." The second was from the preface of a book published just before he finished the manuscript: "Is it not, indeed, the core of man's mystery, that in his greatest follies his last wisdom lies enfurled?" The book was *Leaders, Dreamers, and Rebels: An Account of the Great Mass Movements of History and the Wish-Dreams That Inspired Them*, by Austrian cultural historian, writer, and journalist René Fülöp-Miller, and it appealed to Neihardt's belief in universal truths and that dreamers—and their failures—were age-old stories. As a reviewer in the *Brooklyn Daily Eagle* had argued, Fülöp-Miller's message "amounts simply to the theory that there is nothing new under the sun."[41]

The Song of the Messiah is set in western South Dakota, south of the Black Hills, and opens in the spring of 1887. Like the early 1930s, when Neihardt wrote much of it, the years leading up to 1890 were dry. "The Earth was dying slowly, being old," he wrote to set the scene.[42] Rivers—the Cheyenne, White, Niobrara, Grand, Moreau—barely contain any water, and cornstalks are "drooping in the bitter dust."[43] The people, too, are diminished, dreaming back the days of buffalo and plenty, when they were known as fearless fighters, not fearful farmers. Their leaders have grown old and, too often, timid. "[I]t was hope that perished."[44] It is into this bleak and desperate time that, out of the West, a rumor arrives.

> And many strove to say what someone said
> That someone said, who had it from the Crows,
> To whom the Cheyennes or else Arapahoes
> Had brought it from the Snakes.[45]

Though Neihardt never mentions Wovoka by name, he lays out the Paiute's message in four simple lines:

> *The man had died, and yet he had not died,*
> *And he had talked with God, and all the dead*
> *Were coming with the whirlwind at their head,*
> *And there would be new earth and heaven!*[46]

By the spring of 1889 the rumor had taken hold among the Sioux, who decided to send a team of their own, five men, to hear straight from the source. When they returned, "awe upon their faces," people got their hopes up. "And suddenly the prairie took the hue / Of faith again."[47] The five, one by one, recount what they have learned, including the ghost dance. Soon, men and women, among them a young man named Black Elk, are dancing the dance. Neihardt includes some of Black Elk's vision, though his portrayal of it in *Messiah* initially sounds almost more like his own childhood fever dream.

> He clove the empty spaces, swift and prone.
> Alone he seemed, and terribly alone,
> For there was nothing anywhere to heed
> The helpless, headlong terror of the speed.[48]

He goes on to explain the "good Red Road" and the "hard Black Road" and includes Black Elk's instructions to the people to make "holy shirts."[49]

When the Indian agent orders the people to stop dancing, calling it "superstitious doings in a day / Of Christian light and progress," the stage is set for the violent final act. Sitting Bull is killed, and Sitanka, also known as Spotted Eagle but called Big Foot by U.S. soldiers, takes flight with his band. As he did with *Black Elk Speaks*, Neihardt chose to close *Messiah*, in its seventh chapter, with Wounded Knee. Taken by cavalry soldiers to Wounded Knee Creek, Sitanka and his people spend the night. In the morning he awakens "to the prison of his bed," and watches it all happen:

> In a gasp of time
> He saw—like some infernal pantomime
> A freeze of horror rendered motionless
> Forever—horses rearing in a press
> Of faces tortured into soundless yells,
> Amid the gloaming of the Hotchkiss shells
> That blossomed in a horizontal flaw
> Of bloody rain that fell not.[50]

When *Messiah* was published in October 1935, reviewers generally were supportive, and in 1936 it earned for Neihardt the gold scroll medal of honor as the "foremost poet of the nation" by the National Poetry Center in New York. John Holmes, a critic and poet writing in the *Boston Evening Transcript*, wondered, after reading the book, "Why haven't the drum-beaters and star-spanglers made of John G. Neihardt a dozen times over what they have made of lesser poets?" He praised the poem's "great vision . . . epic sweep and power," and suggested that if Neihardt's *Cycle of the West*, when completed, did not win the Pulitzer prize, then the committee might as well disband: "the prize was created for such work."[51] Marquis Childs, in the *New Republic*, called attention to Neihardt's "passionate, vigorous couplets" and praised *Messiah* for having "a truly epic quality, a breadth and a daring that assure its recognition after a troubled, transitory age has passed."[52] As was often the case with Neihardt, the reviews that meant most to him were not those in newspapers and magazines but those from individuals who wrote personally to him. In this case, it was his old friend and lifeline of history, Doane Robinson. "I am certain that old Homer would be burned up with jealousy if he could rise up long enough to read the cycle. I see you have addressed the *Messiah* to Mona. It was coming to her."[53]

14 A TIME OF CRISIS

John Neihardt believed that all important questions were questions of values, and the two values that outranked all others were courage and spirituality. "I believe that the inclusive virtue is courage," he told Julius House for his early biography, a sentiment that he repeated over and over throughout his life.[1] His focus on courage was why he never really focused, when writing about battles during the Plains Indian wars, on who won or lost. "The human side of high courage is what mostly matters."[2] Ranking right behind courage was his devotion to what he considered essential religion. Religious dogma might change—in fact, he believed history proved conclusively that it did—but the essence of religion did not.[3] "Religion is not a fantastic story to be accepted," he wrote. "It is an illuminating experience to live by," and for him, the essence of religion was mystical experience.[4] Throughout his writing life, Neihardt strove to focus on one or the other of these values. Whenever possible, he wrote about both.

Now, after more than ten years of being focused primarily on spirituality, with the writing of *Black Elk Speaks* and *The Song of the Messiah*, Neihardt was ready to devote some time to courage. He had a subject in mind, a lawman of the American West by the name of Jefferson Davis Milton. Neihardt had researched enough of Milton's life story to know that he wanted to be the writer to tell it. The day after sending off his

Messiah manuscript in the summer of 1935 he wrote to Milton, then seventy-four years old, asking him to let Neihardt write his biography. Milton was reluctant. "He is an honest-to-God man and not eager to show off to the world," Neihardt said at the time. "That only makes me eager to tell his stories."[5]

It is easy to understand why Neihardt would have been attracted to Milton. Born in 1861 in Marianna, Florida, and named for Jefferson Davis, president of the Confederacy, Milton was the son of John Milton, the fifth governor of Florida and an ardent Confederate. When it became clear that the South would lose the Civil War, Milton's father shot and killed himself, leaving his wife and ten children. It must have been especially tantalizing to Neihardt that Jeff Milton, the youngest of those children, was also a descendant of John Milton, the seventeenth-century English epic poet, author of the blank-verse poem *Paradise Lost*. At age sixteen Jeff Milton left Florida for Texas, where, lying about his age, he became a Texas Ranger. Eventually he made his way to Tombstone, Arizona, where he worked for many years as a lawman of the Wild West, capturing and sometimes killing outlaws—and occasionally being shot by them.[6]

Despite Neihardt's entreaties, supported by Milton's wife, Milton continued to resist. Within a month of Neihardt's initial contact with Milton, Macmillan was sure enough that the book was going to happen that Neihardt was offered a contract and a small advance.[7] "I am waiting, in the hope that old Jeff D. Milton may be able to shake loose from his modesty and agree to let me do his story."[8] Despite Neihardt's regular attempts to persuade him, by mid-September it was clear that Milton was never going to agree, and Neihardt reluctantly gave up. Neihardt was disappointed, but Mona was not. "She thinks that sort of book is not for me," he wrote to an old friend. "Anyway, I have plenty to do."[9]

Neihardt then considered writing a biography of yet another character of the American West, one with whom he was considerably more familiar, a continuation of his work on the ghost dance movement. "There is the bare chance that, as an alternative, I might arrange to do the life of Wovoka."[10] Wovoka had died in the fall of 1932, between the publication of *Black Elk Speaks* and that of *Song of the Messiah*, so Neihardt had no need to persuade him to cooperate, but within four months Neihardt gave up this idea, too. "I am sorry that the Wovoka project is off entirely," wrote H. S. Latham at Macmillan to Neihardt in December, "but I shall be glad to hear about something else for you to tackle."[11]

Neihardt had one more subject in mind: the final volume in his *Cycle of the West*, a book-length poem he had long planned on another fur trapper and explorer, Jedediah Strong Smith. Smith was one of the two men—the other being Hugh Glass—that Doane Robinson had suggested to Neihardt in 1907 as the men who had contributed most to white exploration of the old Northwest. In 1918 Neihardt had taken his first trip to California and visited Monterey, explaining to his California host, George Sterling, that "one of my heroes goes there & mixes with the Spanish authorities."[12] Three years later, during a lecture trip to the Pacific Northwest, Neihardt had visited the Columbia River. "It was good for me to see the Columbia River, as it was so important in the old heroic days of the fur trade," he wrote to Mona. "Jed Smith passed up that way on his return from California."[13]

In Smith, Neihardt had a subject that would allow him to address both of his most sacred values: Smith was congenitally courageous, regularly traveling alone or as the leader of men into difficult, dangerous, and, for white men, unknown territory, and one of the reasons Robinson was so enamored of him was that he credited Smith with conducting the first Christian religious service in what became South Dakota. Smith, who was born northeast of Binghamton, New York, was said to have arrived in St. Louis as a young man carrying two books, the Bible and an account of Lewis and Clark's expeditions. Smith had been the hero of Neihardt's early history *The Splendid Wayfaring*, and Neihardt had always argued in his lectures and book reviews that Smith—and not better-known men such as John C. Fremont—was the country's chief explorer. "If we must decide upon a 'greatest' in the field of western exploration, certainly Jedediah Smith is that one, though his name has not yet found its way into our orthodox school texts and the general public has never heard of him."[14]

Neihardt had thought about Jed Smith for nearly three decades, and he had almost started the book several times. Each time, Mona had stopped him. "I would say to Mona, 'Well, I believe I'll begin on *The Song of Jed Smith*,'" Neihardt told a friend much later. "'No, you're not ready yet, don't do it, you're not ready yet.'" When Neihardt wrote, he wrote alone, usually closed off in a study at home, the door kept shut to keep out any daily disturbances. But he always trusted Mona's judgment. With the other books of the *Cycle* now complete—he had decided against an additional book on the Mormons—he once again thought he was ready to tackle Jed Smith. This time, "She agreed I was."[15] That fall, as Neihardt and daughter Enid headed west on a research trip financed by an advance from Macmillan that had arrived, with a contract, as soon as the firm had received the *Messiah* manuscript, he discovered another reason it had been wise to wait.[16] As he crossed the Continental Divide, Neihardt realized that the center of gravity of his life interest had changed. Up to this point, his work has been situated on the Great Plains, but with the completion of *The Song of the Messiah*, that phase had ended. Now, with his mind on Jed Smith, he was feeling drawn to the Far West. For nearly two years, as Neihardt continued to write for the *Post-Dispatch* and to lecture and recite his poetry, he researched Smith, traveling throughout the West whenever he could.

In the fall of 1937 he put pencil to paper and began to write *The Song of Jed Smith*. Instead of writing the poem as a straight biography, Neihardt chose to focus only on the highlights of Smith's life. He created a scenario in which three mountain men meet by chance at the mouth of Henry's Fork of the Green River. Two of them, Art Black and Bob Evans, had really been trappers, and the third man, identified only as Squire, is a Neihardt creation. Around a campfire the three swap stories of Smith's exploits and their time with him. "Quite a neat device for hitting only the high spots of Jed's career!" Neihardt bragged to a friend.[17] During the writing of *Jed Smith*, as usual, Neihardt issued periodic updates to family and friends. "I've just finished a really beautiful thing," he wrote to Mona from the road in early 1939, "and now I do feel 'Jeddy' again."[18] Enid had married *Post-Dispatch* journalist Oliver Fink, and Neihardt regularly wrote to them—and sometimes to just his new son-in-law—with *Jed* updates. "More real stuff came through this morning, and I didn't seem to make it," he wrote to Fink in September 1940. "It's glorious to feel it coming through with the precision and clarity of something that always was."[19]

As the poem opens the year is 1838, and two of the men are staring into a campfire in the Southwest, not far from the adobe houses of Taos. The older of the two drifts off, momentarily imagining that it is 1825 again. "'This valley came alive with fires, alive / With men and horses!'"[20] Soon a third man stumbles onto their campsite, with a jug freshly filled at Taos, and he is invited to spend the night. The men quickly discover they have a friend in common: Jedediah Smith, "the man that never sinned."[21] As they reminisce they offer their view—which was also Neihardt's—that men like Smith were a special lot. "What a bunch of men!" one says. "This valley will not see their like again."[22] To make perfectly clear who he is talking about, Neihardt has one of the men run through a list:

"Fitzpatrick, Ashley, Jackson, and Sublette!
Jim Bridger, newly bearded, half a boy
For all his doings! Hanna and McCoy,
LaPlant, Reubasco, Harry Rogers, Ranne,
Luzano, Gobel, Gaither—man by man,
I see them laughing yonder, soon to die,
The men who followed Smith—and you and I
Return alone, Bob, out of thirty-two!"[23]

Spread throughout the poem are Neihardt's descriptions of Smith: his "wide-set" eyes and how they turned into "slits of blue" when he thought hard; his brown hair that "grew in waves that broke like surf around his ears"; his jaw and its "flint-hard setting"; and his "long-range hawk-gaze" that had a way of penetrating through a man.[24]

The poem, through the men's remembering, offers highlights of Smith's explorations—discovery of the South Pass; the crossing of the Sierra Nevada, the Great Basin, and the Mojave Desert; and the overland trip to Oregon Country—and of his final work along the Santa Fe Trail that led to his death, likely at the hands of the Comanche along the Cimarron River in what is now southwest Kansas. The poem also offered Neihardt the opportunity to explore his own mystical view of life, the belief that everything is connected, that things are happening just outside our reach that we cannot understand. Mystics understood this, and Smith, in Neihardt's view, was one of those mystics. In *Jed Smith*, the men discuss the feeling they used to get around him:

> "A feel of something you could never know,
> Except that it was big and still and dim
> And had a secret."[25]

Smith had a way of looking at things, they agreed, as though they had been waiting "a million winters and a million springs" just to be seen. "'Twas the other side of things— / Another world!'"[26] Smith also carried that more obvious symbol of his religious leanings, a Christian Bible, and the men recall him referring to it and reading from it, "'Some verses from the Scripture where it said / The whole earth was the Lord's.'"[27]

While he was working on *Jed Smith*, Neihardt made one of his occasional visits to a medium, a woman named Leona Boyles. He had first met her in 1923, and they had become friends, visiting each other's homes and getting to know each other's families. On this particular visit he had not come for her psychic advice but rather just to talk. They had been discussing their children when she surprised him by saying she knew something about the man he was writing about. "He didn't die down there in that dry river," she told Neihardt. Smith was alone when he died, and the few people who cared about what had happened to him believed he had been ambushed along a dry patch of the Cimarron River by the Comanche. Boyles told Neihardt that as a girl she had taken a train that had crossed the Cimarron and that she had envisioned a spot upstream where a tree had fallen across a gorge. Below that point, she said, a sandstone ledge jutted over the dry riverbed, and on that point was a boulder. She said Smith was digging beneath that ledge, trying to find water, when the Comanches surprised him. She said he was struck in the back with a knife, then hit many times by arrows. Eventually, she told Neihardt, the Comanche had rolled the boulder on top of Smith.[28] Neihardt chose to use Boyles's version of Smith's death to end his poem. In it Evans tells of a vision he had had of Smith's final moments, of Smith clawing in the sand for water, of his horse standing nearby, when he is hit by a thrown knife, then arrows, turning him into a "bloody, feathered huddle," left for dead. He crawls up the bank to try to get to his horse, but the Comanche come back:

> The band returning for the horse and gun
> To find him there, still moaning, in his tomb
> And roll the bowlder [sic] on him.[29]

With Jed Smith's death scene completed, in April 1941, Neihardt had finished the poem and, more important, his life's work. Since Mona had first encouraged him, in 1913, to save the story of Hugh Glass for posterity, the fur trappers and explorers, the warriors and the medicine men had filled Neihardt's imagination, and he had spent countless hours over the years creating the poetic celebration of the mood of courage that he found expressed in the Great Plains. Neihardt felt grateful for the years he had been able to devote to "the great task," but he admitted later that he also felt "a backlash of sadness" in completing it.[30] He had been, as one journalist called him, a perfectionist and a zealot, "the sort of man who could give his life to one project."[31] Although he assured those who asked that he had not set out to become an epic poet, his correspondence often sounded as though that had been precisely his goal. "I knew and loved my country and its traditions, and I wished to preserve in an art form the heroic mood that was developed there in the early years."[32]

When *The Song of Jed Smith* was published in September 1941, most reviewers recognized that Neihardt had not only finished another long poem but had also completed a series he had started nearly thirty years earlier. The *Post-Dispatch*'s rival, the *Globe-Democrat*, praised the completed *Cycle* as an "enduring memorial," called Neihardt an "authentic poet," and drew attention to the dialogue in *Jed Smith*. "To invent a speech like that, so faithful in spirit, so inclusive in depiction, so imaginative in implication, is mental achievement no less great than an Edison's invention of a mechanism that sound may be recorded."[33] A month later his own newspaper added its praise of Neihardt's use of "the vernacular" in the campfire conversations. "It is a feat of versatility that Mr. Neihardt has been able to avoid both banality and bathos," the *Post-Dispatch* said. "If poetic imagery suffers to some extent from his device, there is a gain in homely color and realism."[34] Not every review, however, was so positive. The *New York Times* liked Neihardt's descriptions of the Western country but criticized him for jumping back and forth between "philosophizing and the singing of an epos" in the poem. "The poet has to shift back at intervals to his storyteller, who makes innocuous intrusions by passing the whisky jug each time to hold his unity in the poem."[35] Harriet Monroe had died in 1936, but *Poetry* magazine remained critical of Neihardt, arguing that in *Jed Smith* "there is considerable disparity between the breadth of the conception and the execution."[36]

As usual, however, Neihardt found comfort and confidence in the reactions he received from friends. Irving Dillard, the *Post-Dispatch*'s editorial page editor, wrote to congratulate him:

> Do you know that Taft was president when you went to work on the cycle, that the Lusitania went down the year *Hugh Glass* came out; that the Peace Conference was on when you issued *The Song of Three Friends*; that Coolidge was in Harding's chair the year of the *Indian Wars*; that Hitler had come to power and was taking citizenship away from the Jews when you gave us *The Song of the Messiah*? Now *Jed Smith*—peace, war, peace and war again! How magnificently you set your star and how unswervingly you have stayed to it.[37]

Latham at the Macmillan Company also was happy to see the *Cycle* complete. "It is a most distinguished contribution to American literature and I am hoping that we can impress that fact upon people and secure for it the recognition it deserves."[38]

Within days of finishing *Jed Smith* Neihardt was telling friends that a collected volume of the five songs would likely be published within a year or two.[39] When the Macmillan Company failed to announce such an edition, Neihardt began years of complaint. "You were enthusiastic about the completed *Cycle*," he wrote to Latham at the end of 1941, less than a month after Japan's attack on Pearl Harbor, "and I can't believe that you are indifferent now."[40] America's entry into the war complicated Macmillan's publishing plans. "Times are not propitious for the issue of a work of this sort," Latham told Neihardt.[41] Neihardt believed that the war could just as well be used as a reason *to* publish the *Cycle*. "The Trans-Missouri country *is* a great and important part of our America," he wrote to Latham, "and if there ever was justification for invoking Americanism in support of a literary work, you have it in this case."[42]

Neihardt kept pushing Latham to collect the five poems, and almost a year later Macmillan gave in and offered him a contract on the *Cycle* with the thin hope of publishing it by the fall of 1943.[43] When it quickly became clear that this would not happen, a disappointed Neihardt again began to complain. Latham saw a bright spot in the company's delay in publishing the *Cycle*. "The *Cycle* is not an ephemeral work, but is just as important one year as another, and frankly I suspect that it will do better when the world conditions are somewhat calmer than it will now."[44] The next year Latham assured Neihardt that the Macmillan Company still planned to publish the *Cycle*. "The only thing that hasn't been settled is *when*."[45] Neihardt, never giving up, eventually complained, "I do wonder if publication must be postponed until after the last shot has been fired in this war."[46]

Neihardt certainly had artistic reasons for wanting his five songs published in a single volume, but he also hoped that such a collection would sell. "And, who knows?" he wrote to Mona from the road during a lecture trip. "Maybe we will not *need* supplementary incomes after the *Cycle* is completed & published as a whole!"[47]

Alice Neihardt, John's mother, had believed in him his entire life, believed that he always knew best. She had many friends in Bancroft during the two decades she lived there, but when Neihardt decided to move to Missouri, she happily packed up and accompanied him. "I want to be with John," she told a magazine writer at the time.[48] In Branson, as she had in Bancroft, she lived next door to John and Mona. When Hilda came home from college at Christmas in 1935, Alice told her she would not be there by spring. Hilda did not believe her, but it was true. In February 1936

Alice Neihardt died at the age of seventy-eight. Though Neihardt had written in an early short story that "mothers can never really understand the ways of men," he had been devoted to her, the only parent he had had for more than forty years.[49]

That fall John and Mona returned to live in St. Louis to make Neihardt's job at the *Post-Dispatch* more convenient, but after only a couple of years they moved once again to Branson. During the 250-mile drive the moving van crashed, destroying most of their furniture and many of Neihardt's files, including correspondence with such other poets as Ezra Pound and Edwin Arlington Robinson. Also lost was the petition, signed by members of the Order of the Indian Wars, that urged an amendment to the organization's bylaws so that a civilian—specifically John Neihardt—could join.

In addition to this setback, the economic devastation of the 1930s finally began to squeeze the Neihardts: in 1938 the *Post-Dispatch* eliminated his position at the paper. For a time he and Sigurd continued to travel with their program of lectures, lyrics, and music—including an April 1939 standing-room-only performance at the Temple Theatre in Lincoln, Nebraska—and he took the extra time available to keep writing on *Jed Smith*. In January 1940 monthly benefits under the federal government's old-age and survivor's insurance first became available, and Neihardt, now fifty-nine years old, began drawing a regular payment.

In letters to her children, all now grown and gone, Mona painted a picture of a couple relearning how to be alone with each other. Sigurd and his wife, Maxine, were busy building their own lives, and Enid and Oliver were doing the same. In August 1942 Hilda married Albert Petri in a wedding that included a Sioux purification ceremony and a cake topped with the statuettes of the bride and groom sculpted by Mona, and Alice moved to the West Coast to become a dancer. The Neihardts, after more than three decades of raising a family, were once again just two. "Cutting grass, washing clothes, transplanting geraniums, etc., house cleaning, changing furniture to suit the new needs," Mona wrote to Enid and Oliver. "Cleaning out the shed, *Daddy and I* together." Mona planned to can tomatoes and apples, do a little painting inside their house, and then set aside time for what she really wanted to do: "sculp Daddy for the last and best time."[50]

John and Mona drove to Colorado for a dinner with the Colorado Poetry Fellowship and a luncheon with the Colorado Author's League in the fall of 1940, and on the way out they drove through northwestern Kansas to see Neihardt's grandparents' homestead outside Stockton. On the return trip they drove across Nebraska, stopping in Wayne and in Bancroft, Mona's first return in twenty years to the small town she had first entered as a new bride in 1908. When they stopped at their old house, Mona got out and touched "the little front porch Daddy made." "The place is going to pieces, but it is *very dear* and lovely to me," she wrote to her daughter. The trees and the grape vines had grown since she last saw them, and Mona entertained thoughts of returning. "The ground is so rich and I'd just love to go to work and fix it up and Daddy and I live there again for a while!" They also drove by his mother's former house, which was in better shape. Mona wanted John to dig up some of his mother's peonies to take back to Missouri, but he was afraid people would be upset. "So we drove away."[51] As the Christmas season approached, they realized that for the first time in a very long time, they had no obligations. "[W]e are planning nothing—and will stay here quietly," Mona wrote, "grateful that our darling children are so fine, and that we have each other and our work and our home. So many blessings in a world like this one."[52]

Neihardt was not so sanguine about this period in their lives. After he finished *Jed Smith*, he scrambled to find employment. He learned during lunch with a group of his former *Post-Dispatch* colleagues that businessman Marshall Field was starting a new newspaper, the *Chicago Sun*, and he applied—in vain—to be its literary editor.[53] He wrote letters to everyone he could think of, trying to find work. He wrote to Archibald MacLeish, who had just become the ninth librarian of Congress in Washington DC, and Representative Dewey Short, his Missouri congressman. When he heard that Addison Sheldon, the secretary of the Nebraska State Historical Society, was thinking about retiring, he wrote to Sheldon immediately. "I realize that you have set a high standard for anyone to maintain, but at least my heart would be in the task, and I would be free to devote all my energy to it, now that my chief life-work, *A Cycle of the West,* is completed."[54] Sheldon responded that rumors of his retirement were unfounded. The war had dried up Neihardt's lecture business—as it had the chances of publishing a single-volume *Cycle of the West*—and his job hunt became more frantic. Even as he complained to Latham about delays in publishing the *Cycle,* he also asked for help in finding a job in New York. Latham promised to "keep my ears to the ground," but as with all of Neihardt's other inquiries, no job was forthcoming.[55]

The Chicago Poetry Circle had feted Neihardt in mid-1940, and at the dinner he had met, among others, George Steele Seymour and his wife Flora Warren Seymour, both authors. As Neihardt continued his job search, Seymour offered to approach the *Chicago Tribune* on his behalf. Neihardt was appreciative but told Seymour he did not think he would be what they were seeking. "What they need is young reporters and, occasionally, desk men."[56] Neihardt knew from the other entreaties he had made that newspapers were not looking to add to their literary staffs. He had thought for some time about moving to Chicago to look for work and, after a brief correspondence with Seymour, decided in May 1943 that it would be best for him and Mona to relocate there, at least temporarily. With very little money, he walked the streets applying for jobs. He found one at the Iron Fireman Manufacturing Company—with so many men having now gone to the war, plants were hurting—but it was not a job for which Neihardt was well suited, and he lasted only a month. "What I knew about stokers wouldn't make an encyclopedia," he said later.[57] He briefly read manuscripts part-time for *Esquire* magazine.

Neihardt then took a job as a counselor at Camp Duncan in Round Lake, Illinois, less than fifty miles northwest of Chicago. At the day camp, which was run by the Joseph S. Duncan YMCA in Chicago and attended by some two hundred boys over the summer, Neihardt, now sixty-two, had charge of a cabin full of boys ages eight to twelve, "dear, ornery little cusses." One day he realized that the camp circle, at which they conducted their meetings, reminded him of Black Elk's hoop of the universe. Neihardt led the campers in Black Elk's prayer, praying to the south, then to the west, then to the north, then to the east, and finally to the center, where he offered a prayer to Wakantanka and Mother Earth. Some of the boys' parents were present as well, and Neihardt got a charge out of hearing them all repeat after him the prayer. "Well, that ceremony suggested to me that I could put on Black Elk's great horse dance, using boys for the horses," Neihardt said. "This was just the sort of thing the YMCA wanted." He got sixteen of the biggest boys in the camp, and they practiced for two weeks before a Sunday afternoon show. Before the boys came forward, Neihardt explained what the people were about to see. "It went off wonderfully well."[58]

John and Mona lived at the Hotel Metropole at Michigan Avenue and 23rd Street, Mona cooking on a one-burner hot plate, and in John's memory, "We had swell meals and we were happy there."[59] But Neihardt wanted better work, and he needed a bigger paycheck. During the war the federal Bureau of Indian Affairs relocated its offices to Chicago. Mona, who had found work as a proofreader for *Time* and *Life* magazines, had been urging Neihardt to contact John Collier, the commissioner, since they had arrived in the city. Neihardt finally did so in early 1944 and was immediately hired. On February 28 he began work as director of the bureau's Division of Information. For the first time in his life, he had a staff, four women, and he found being a supervisor challenging. "I have had to learn how to assign work to others without feeling mean."[60] His office issued press releases about the Bureau, and Collier assigned him to write a "social history" of the Sioux. As part of that project, in November and December 1944 Neihardt and daughter Hilda returned to Pine Ridge, where he interviewed Nicholas Black Elk again, as well as two other elderly Lakota, Eagle Elk and Andrew Knife. But most of Neihardt's time went to editing a publication called *Indians at Work*. Published every two months, the magazine during the war consisted mostly of brief biographies of Indians who were serving in the U.S. armed forces. "Of course I have plenty to keep me busy all the time; but I'm not driven in any way."[61] He continued to mine his Black Elk experience, reprinting Black Elk's prayer on the inside cover of one issue of the magazine and in another running "High Horse's Courting," a chapter from *Black Elk Speaks*, as a short story. He also wrote a new short story, "Red Hail and the Two Suitors," based on stories Black Elk and Andrew Knife had told him.

In early 1945 John Collier resigned after twelve years as commissioner. Neihardt stayed on, working for Roosevelt's new commissioner, William Brophy, but because of a paper shortage and other wartime difficulties in producing the magazine, *Indians at Work* was published less often. That September, after Japan's surrender, Neihardt returned to Pine Ridge yet again, this time to speak in Brophy's place at a Lakota victory dance celebrating the end of the war. Neihardt's speech, "The New Day and the Good Road," addressed the Lakota's heroic past and challenging present.[62] Black Elk attended and told Neihardt the crowd had been pleased. "The Sioux sure liked the way you gave that speech at that celebration," Black Elk wrote to Neihardt. "They sure feel lot of encouragement by you & wish you could help them more in future."[63]

With the war's end the Bureau of Indian Affairs moved back to Washington DC. Neihardt briefly became a field representative for the bureau, on call for special assignments, and in 1946, he returned again to Pine Ridge on behalf of the bureau, but the assignments soon ran out, and Neihardt once again found himself back in Branson, Missouri, out of work. He returned to lecturing and reminded the Macmillan Company of its earlier promise, now years in the past, to publish a single-volume edition of *A Cycle of the West*. To go out on the road "with my poetry out of print" would severely handicap him, he argued. But when he hit the road early in 1947 on a tour of the eastern United States, he did so without the *Cycle* or a current collection of his earlier lyrics.[64] "This is most embarrassing, and will be ruinous for me if it continues much longer. I cannot allow the matter to drift indefinitely beyond 1948."[65]

His frustration with the Macmillan Company was also fed by his disappointment in the publisher's response to his latest book pitch. When Collier resigned from the Bureau of Indian Affairs, his plan for a history of the Sioux was discarded. Neihardt decided to take the new material he had collected, "a rich vein of Indian short stories," and turn it into a new collection of short fiction. Latham was not enthusiastic. "The difficulty is not lack of interest in the material, but in the fact that you are going to use that material in short story form," he responded. "For some strange reason, short stories rarely get by."[66] Instead Neihardt outlined a way to add the material to an idea that had been percolating in his mind for years, a novel—he had been thinking of calling it *An Old Man Remembers*—that would tell the life story of a Plains Indian who "saw a white man for the first time when he was six years old, went through the stirring period of the Plains wars, achieved distinction as a holy man, went with Buffalo Bill to Europe in the late '80s during the 'evil days' of hunger and sickness and despair, fell in love with a French girl in Paris, returned home during the tragic years of the Ghost Dance and was reunited with his Indian sweetheart during the Wounded Knee massacre." As Neihardt told Latham, "It all happened; and just the simple facts are romantic enough, but the creative possibilities are great."[67] Latham declined to commission the book, but he agreed to take a look at it as soon as it was finished.[68]

As he neared his mid-sixties, even without the demands of his weekly newspaper column, Neihardt showed few signs of slowing down. He continued to work on the new book, to travel and lecture, to enjoy the life of a writer. He let a Montana English teacher use excerpts from *Hugh Glass* and *Three Friends* in a high school radio play; he was elected to the National Institute of Arts and Letters; he helped found the Westerners, a group promoting the study of history of the American West; he was named chairman of the advisory board of the Order of Bookfellows; and he joined a hundred other writers and artists who signed a letter protesting the persecution of Chilean poet Pablo Neruda by his country's government.[69]

Then in 1948, as he continued writing the novel, came an offer much like two he had turned down twenty years earlier. In the mid-1920s Carleton College in Northfield, Minnesota, and later the University of Nebraska in Lincoln had offered Neihardt teaching positions. At the time, he had feared that taking such a post would put him in the "too tame . . . 'academic backwaters'"—"I wanted to be out where the tides of the world were flowing strong."[70] Over the years he had also criticized the teaching of creative writing, arguing that any cultured person should be able to write correct English and that any such ability had little to do with being a successful writer anyway. "Art is creative," he wrote in the *Kansas City Journal-Post*. "There never was anyone who could teach anyone to be an original. What makes an artist is simply creative vision."[71] Now, at age sixty-seven, with the *Cycle* finished and his children grown and on their own, he saw it differently. When the University of Missouri, which had awarded him an honorary doctorate the year before, invited him to join the faculty as poet in residence and lecturer in English, he accepted. "My creative period in writing was over, and I entered the new world of education with great enthusiasm."[72]

That next spring, in April 1949, eight years after *Jed Smith* was completed, the Macmillan Company finally published *A Cycle of the West*. The unified publication allowed reviewers an opportunity to look back at the *Songs*, of which the earliest, *The Song of Hugh Glass*, had been published thirty-five years before, and to critique what was essentially Neihardt's life's work. Even the best reviews were of two minds: the stories were gripping, but the poetic technique seemed even more old-fashioned now than it had when the individual books had been published. The *New York Herald Tribune*, though it called the stories memorable, found the verse occasionally a bit thinner than "the deeds chronicled." The reviewer did concede: "It is always good news when a poet sets out upon a large and noble work and lives to bring it to honorable completion."[73] Although some of the regional reviewers were kinder, most of the larger newspapers responded much as did poet and playwright Harvey Breit, writing in the *New York Times Book Review*. He found some aspects he liked and some he did not. "He is an unfinished and unpolished writer and, worst of all, falls into dreadful archaisms," Breit wrote. "But he is a writer of immense vitality, who, at the same time, has a quite precise feeling about the frontier and the frontiersmen he considers and records."[74]

Although Neihardt said little to friends at the time, he was deeply disappointed at the critical reception of *A Cycle of the West*. Once again the reactions he received from people he knew served to bolster his morale. Poet Robert Hillyer, one of Neihardt's compatriots in the battle against modern poetry, wrote as soon as he had gotten a copy. "The publication of your epic songs in one volume is a literary event the importance of which will be more and more recognized as time goes on," he wrote that May. "As the oily tide of Pound and Eliot and their vulgar aestheticism subsides, the American people will make the happy discovery of many fine works which have not been sufficiently recognized. Among these, your *Cycle of the West* will stand in monumental beauty."[75] Neihardt's old boss in Chicago, John Collier, also wrote, admitting that he had known Neihardt's poetry "only somewhat vaguely" before. "What a joy, then, at this time of desolation, to find the very bloom of magic shining out from every page, often many times in a single page."[76]

The general response, however, still represented a "time of crisis" in Neihardt's life, leaving him with a sense that he had died "without the comfort of a funeral." Knowing that his life's work was finished and that it was so little appreciated, he told a friend years later, made it feel like "a voice that had fallen echoless upon empty air," leaving "nothing to fill the emptiness it had left."[77] Still Neihardt was never one to feel bad for long. When he wrote to Latham at Macmillan to tell him he felt sorry for Breit after reading his review in the *Times*, he quickly changed the subject from the recently published *Cycle* to the class he was teaching at Missouri that was based on it. "I wish you could know something of the enthusiasm that my courses at the University have aroused," he wrote to Latham.[78] For Neihardt, the opportunity to teach, to do something different, was saving. The depth of his despair over the reception to the collected *Cycle* indicated the extent to which he had constructed a wall of self-confidence in his art, necessary for the creation of it but dangerous when it came to judging it. As he wrote years later about this moment in his life, "Apparently there was only one of two things I could do—honestly acknowledge my virtual decease, or begin a new life."[79]

That spring John and Mona had bought an acreage—Skyrim Farm—seven miles north of Columbia, Missouri, and he began teaching two courses: Epic America, a large class in which he recited from his *Cycle* and lectured, and The Writing of Poetry, intended as a workshop for six to twelve students at a time. As the chairman of the English department saw it, "There is nothing quite like this combination anywhere."[80] For both

John and Mona it represented a chance to start over, and both of them relished the opportunity. "I am so glad Daddy and I are here together," Mona wrote to Enid that spring, "and I am looking forward to living and achieving here."[81] As for Neihardt, in the semesters that followed, he alternated between the poetry course and another called The Critical Essay, also designed for a small class, and using his *Poetic Values* as a basic text. Epic America, in which he wandered through western history, geography, folklore, anthropology, and of course his own personal philosophy, was offered every semester, regularly attracting more than one hundred students at a time and once, after he had been teaching it for several years, drawing 185 students.

Though some students made light of the tiny man with the long white hair and his reputation as an easy grader, others found themselves engaged, and getting into his classes was considered a scheduling coup. "[To] me, he was an excellent and absorbing teacher," one student said years later, "and fueled in me an intense love for the West."[82] Students reported that "Dr. Neihardt" sometimes stood facing the class with his arms up and his head looking skyward as he sang Indian songs, "mostly in a raspy and sometimes falsetto voice . . . without any embarrassment."[83] One student remembered watching him as he stopped reading from the book and instead recited from memory, "with his eyes locked into a vision only he could see."[84] If he was not standing he was sitting, not behind his desk but on top of it, either cross-legged or with his short legs dangling over the front. The *Columbia Missourian*, a city newspaper staffed by university students and faculty, once published a photograph of Neihardt in class, sitting atop his desk, holding a book in his right hand while gesturing with his left. One student recalled asking Neihardt to sign her copy of *A Cycle of the West* one day at the end of a class meeting in which he had read from it. "He did so with a shaky hand and apologized, explaining he still often becomes so much a part of the story he is telling, it leaves him trembling."[85]

Neihardt usually wore the same outfit to campus—a blue serge suit, a white broadcloth shirt, and a black tie—and between classes he was often found sitting cross-legged on the grass in front of the classroom building, facing the sun, eyes closed, hands in his lap.[86] Neihardt's years of practice at reciting his poetry and in talking about it paid off in front of the undergraduates. "He could make the most mundane thoughts and statements into something beautiful and wonderful," one student recalled years later.[87] No matter which course Neihardt was teaching, he often opened the first class of the semester with the challenge to his students "to regard it as an adventure we're sharing."[88] For many of them Neihardt was the teacher who taught them to appreciate the Great Plains and its history. "He put the Niobrara River forever on 'my geographic mind,'" one student recalled. "Who was Jedediah Smith? I know. . . . Who was Roman Nose? I know. . . . Who was Black Elk? I know."[89]

Students learned about things other than the American West in his classes. One student, Jack Germond, who went on to a long career as a political reporter, remembered Neihardt as "a wonderful old man," who "taught all his students what it was for a man to grow old totally comfortable with himself and what he had done with his life."[90] One of Germond's fellow journalism students was George C. Scott, who went on to a distinguished acting career. In a 1963 interview with the *Kansas City Star*, Scott mentioned two professors who had influenced him: an instructor who directed him in campus plays, and Neihardt. "He was short and when he sat on his desk his legs dangled," Scott told the interviewer. "His hair was bushy and stood up as if electrified. He was a man of great charm and a marvelous teacher."[91] Another student remembered that Neihardt "convinced me that my own brief life could have the same exciting meaning and value for me as his life did for him." The only difference, the student discovered, was that Neihardt "had elevated his life's meaning and value into art, and I had not."[92]

Although Macmillan had not committed to publishing the novel Neihardt was working on, he kept the firm updated on his progress. As he finished his second semester of teaching, just before Christmas 1949, Neihardt wrote to Latham, "I am having a bully time with the story I'm writing, and that it should be completed in the spring." Even with his teaching load, Neihardt devoted five mornings a week to his writing. "I go into my study with a feeling of happy expectancy, as though the yarn were being told to me."[93] He missed his spring target, but by the end of October 1950 he had sent Macmillan the manuscript—which he now called *When the Tree Flowered*—and by the next fall the book was in stores.

Neihardt created the book from the stories he had gathered primarily during his interviews with Eagle Elk, though supplemented with material he had gathered from Nicholas Black Elk and Andrew Knife. Though the tales still read rather like discrete short stories, Neihardt added just enough connective tissue to hold them together like chapters of a novel. He attributed them all to the fictional character of Eagle Voice—calling him Eagle Elk, Neihardt worried, might confuse him with Black Elk. Writing the book as fiction rather than as a true as-told-to autobiography of Eagle Elk allowed Neihardt more room in crafting the stories and let him incorporate stories from the other men as well. Some reviewers had wondered how much of *Black Elk Speaks* was Black Elk and how much of it was John Neihardt. With *When the Tree Flowered*, Neihardt was clearly the author, though he relied on the same philosophy of translation as he had in the earlier book. As he has Eagle Voice say early on, "The story that I have will make me young again a little while, and you shall put it down there in your tongue as I could say it if your tongue were mine."[94] Neihardt himself, or an anonymous stand-in, plays a role, since he wrote the book as a series of framed stories in which Eagle Voice and occasionally his friends No Water and Moves Walking tell their tales to an attentive white "grandson," who provides logs for the fire and coffee for the storytellers over the course of the days they spend talking. The unnamed narrator occasionally asks questions but mostly serves as a catalyst who pulls the old men from their reveries and keeps them focused on the stories. Most of the stories detail events in Eagle Voice's life, but some recount Lakota legends and even one Lakota fairy tale. Connecting them is the central romantic story of Eagle Voice and Tashina Wan-blee, or Her Eagle Robe, the love of his life whom he first met when they were children and who, for much of his life, remained the one who got away.

Covering roughly the same years as *Black Elk Speaks*, *The Song of the Indian Wars*, and *The Song of the Messiah*, the new book allowed

Neihardt to revisit some of his favorite people, places, and events of the nineteenth-century Great Plains without the limitations of adhering to poetic form or remaining entirely true to the facts. His favorite hero of that time, Crazy Horse, appears, and Neihardt once again takes pains to describe him. "He was not a big man . . . and he was not a little man either," Eagle Voice says. "He was slender and very strong; and his face was lean too. It looked sharpened like an arrowhead. . . . His hair was not so dark as most other Lakotas' hair, but was a little brown; and his skin was not so dark either." He returns to the Wagon Box fight, the Battle of the Little Bighorn, and the massacre at Wounded Knee, and explores the messiah—here called the Wanekia—movement not from the perspective of an active participant, as he had in *Black Elk Speaks*, but from that of a skeptical bystander. "My step-father and my mother and my grandparents believed," Eagle Voice says, "but I was not so sure." Eagle Voice had traveled to Europe, personally experiencing the vast size of the world and the seemingly unending stream of white people. "It was so big and there were so many, many Wasichus. I wondered how one Wanekia could rub them all out and make the world new."[95]

Though Neihardt cautioned his publisher not to think of the book as "an interesting contribution to anthropology," he included, as he had in many of his Omaha short stories written half a century earlier, explanations and descriptions, almost ethnographic in their detail, of Lakota dances, government, and ceremonies, including how to set up a sun dance and build a sweat lodge.[96]

As a young man Neihardt had believed he would not live to old age. Now, as he approached seventy, age was on his mind. Not long after the book was published he told a feature writer for a campus magazine that "only a blink of an eye" existed between him and his one-year-old granddaughter, though he admitted that he had grown "a little tired."[97] In the book the men—Eagle Voice, No Water, and Moves Walking—are all elderly, and age flows as a constant undercurrent in the book. "I am very old, and I have learned so many things that I do not know much any more," Eagle Voice says as he begins one story.[98] Throughout the book one character or another, usually before attempting a dangerous, perhaps life-threatening feat, announces, "It is not good to grow old." Resiliency is also a theme—characters are continually hearing someone say, "Hold fast. There is more." But the old men also seem content with the lives they have led, unafraid that the end of this life is growing near. Where *Black Elk Speaks* ended darkly, the dream of an entire people lying dead in the Dakota snow, *When the Tree Flowered* ends more warmly and more personally, assessing the lives not of an entire tribe but of one couple. Eagle Voice and Tashina Wan-blee, their original spouses now gone, finally find one another and build a life together. "It was a good road that we walked together, Grandson," Eagle Voice says. "Sometimes we were hungry, but it was a good road. . . . It was a good road."[99]

Reviews for the book were Neihardt's strongest in years. The *New York Times* called him "probably the most successful" white writer on Indians and found *When the Tree Flowered* to be "anthropologically sound." It pronounced the Indians "deeply felt characters in their own right, projected against the vivid backdrop of their lives." Neihardt's Indians, the review continued, are never examined "through alien eyes."[100] *North Dakota History* thought better accounts of the sun dance might be found elsewhere, but they would not match Neihardt as he dramatized "the inner emotional and mental states of an individual undergoing the actual fulfillment of his vow."[101] James Whittaker, manager of the British publisher Andrew Melrose Ltd., which published the book as *Eagle Voice* in Great Britain, wrote to Neihardt to say he had been moved "almost to tears" by the book, which he called "a most haunting and terrifyingly sad tragedy" and "a minor classic."[102]

With the publication of *When the Tree Flowered* in 1951, for the first time in his adult life Neihardt had no new books in mind. He considered rewriting the fairy tale from *When the Tree Flowered*, the story of Falling Star, as a children's story, but he and the Macmillan Company eventually lost interest in the idea. As he began his eighth decade he focused on teaching his courses at the University of Missouri. Neihardt liked his students—"a fine generation of young people"—and generally they liked him.[103] Throughout the 1950s and 1960s, he carried on a regular correspondence with scores of students as they kept him apprised of their jobs and marriages, their reading and writing of prose and poetry. They sent him newspaper clippings of reports about him or of things they thought would interest him. All spoke highly of his Epic America class. One young couple, both former students, proudly reported that they had given each other different Neihardt books for Christmas. Another former student wrote to say she had been entertained as well as educated in his class. "Had we been discussing even the most obscure government reports, I feel that I would have enjoyed hearing you read them."[104] Neihardt often invited his students out to Skyrim, his farm, occasionally celebrating a semester's end with a picnic. One student recalled going to Skyrim with a group of students from many different countries. "At one point during the visit a young man from India turned to those of us behind him and with a voice husky with awe said, 'In our country he would be a Holy Man.'"[105]

15 THE LOSS OF A COMRADE

John and Mona Neihardt's love affair had begun with letters handwritten in the first decade of the twentieth century, and for years Mona had kept them in a box in their home. Daughter Hilda remembered seeing them at a time when she was too young to read them, but her older brother Sigurd occasionally would look at them, giggling at their romantic passages. Somewhere along the way—Hilda believed it was after a spat—Mona had burned them all. "They would have been wonderful letters," Hilda said.[1] John and Mona had weathered that rough spot and others and now, nearly fifty years after first meeting each other at the train station in Omaha, they were as happy as ever. As Mona once told a writer, "having the same fundamental belief in *what is good* in Art as well as living together, we *could* work it out."[2] In a photograph taken in the late 1950s they appear comfortable together, Mona looking relaxed and pleasant and John, a slight wry smile on his face, still focused and determined. Hilda remembered her father telling her at about this time, "When we are alone, there's perfect understanding."[3]

Neihardt had relied on his wife throughout his career, trusting her judgment as he trusted no one else's about his poetry and prose, about the very subjects that he tackled. "[M]y relation to Mona was no matter of weak dependence—*leaning*," he said. Rather, it was "an untroubled comradeship."[4] He called her his "ideal hearer," and throughout his writing career he read to her from whatever he was working on. "[I]f the light came into her face, I knew," he told a friend. His *Cycle*, as he frequently told people—his life's work—would never have happened without her.[5] He never forgot the courage it had taken for her to get on a train in New York City and head to Omaha, prepared to marry a man she knew only through letters and a photograph or two. Now, as they both approached eighty, life was good. John and Mona had converted the basement of their white frame house at Skyrim into a modest art studio, and Mona, in addition to hosting children, grandchildren—she was Nanny, he was Gaki, they were the Wubs—and her husband's students, had been sculpting again, working on a bust of a local girl. Though she never regretted giving up her sculpting for so long, she also said, "I do feel I should be allowed a place in John's biography as a sculptress as well as a woman."[6] If she wasn't sculpting or baking bread, she was playing, or occasionally teaching, violin. John, too, was teaching, enjoying his college classes and his students. As he to wrote his uncle and aunt, "Things go well here."[7]

In February 1958 Neihardt had been thinking back over his long life, in part because he had received a letter from one of his oldest friends, John Chaffee, to whom he had read his earliest poems when they were boys together in Wayne, Nebraska. "You were the best pal I ever had, and I still feel the old affection," Neihardt wrote to Chaffee, now living in Oregon. "Our years together make a story as good as Tom Sawyer's and Huckleberry Finn's."[8] Reconnecting with his childhood friend stirred early memories and induced Neihardt to think about everything he and Mona had accomplished in their lives. He was not sorry to be old because he believed every age was good. "It is just like a stairway," he told an interviewer in Columbia, Missouri. "What good are the bottom steps if the top ones aren't all right? And beyond the top ones are ones we can't even see."[9] He talked of "graduating" from this life. "Who wants to stay young forever in this sense-bound life? It's only a fragment of life, certainly; and how wonderful it will be to experience a broader existence!" He and Mona, he told them, "are pretty well convinced that there often *is* communication between the living and those who are called 'dead.' . . .

If I go before Mona, I'll do my best to let her know I'm alive, and she will do the same for me if she goes first."[10] As he wrote to Chaffee, "[T]his life is only a beginning. It goes on."[11]

That spring, Neihardt sadly had the opportunity to test his beliefs. On April 2, 1958, the Neihardts drove through downtown Columbia, John behind the wheel. Hilda worked downtown and happened to step out of her office as her parents drove by. She waved, they waved back, and she watched their car go to the next corner and turn onto South Ninth Street. There a truck was double-parked, and Neihardt slowly went around it on the left. Coming toward them was a car carrying two university students. Though neither car was going very fast, they collided head-on, the impact pushing the students' car back into the one behind it. Someone called Hilda, and she came running. "Mother got out of the car," Hilda remembered, "and she said she was fine." She had hit her head on the frame of the windshield and, despite her protests, was taken, along with the female passenger in the other car, to Boone County Hospital, treated for minor injuries, and released. Neihardt, who was charged with careless and imprudent driving and causing an accident, and the young man driving the other car were uninjured.[12] Over the next two weeks a bump appeared on Mona's head, and Hilda and Alice, who was now living in Columbia too, took her to see a doctor several times. Eventually she was admitted to University Hospital in Columbia. Hilda arranged for her mother to be examined by another doctor, who in turn arranged for a brain surgeon to come by. "We went over to the hospital," Hilda remembered, "and we were so happy." Relieved that their mother was going to get the proper care, Hilda and her sister Alice took their father home. "She was going to be all right." But when they returned the next morning, April 17, they learned that Mona had died earlier that morning. "My father," Hilda recalled, "looked as if somebody had hit him in the head with a hammer." Neihardt never drove again, blaming himself for Mona's death.[13]

John and Mona's children had already been working on plans for a fiftieth anniversary celebration that fall. Now, instead, they put together a funeral that followed—for the most part—plans Mona had left. Sigurd played a Bach prelude, Hilda sang, and a friend played violin. Amid masses of flowers—though Mona had given Neihardt strict instructions that there be none—Neihardt read three poems she had requested, his "When I Have Gone Weird Ways," "Easter," and "L'Envoi," which opens with the line, "Seek not for me within a tomb." "I know she heard," Neihardt later reported to a friend.[14] The funeral was on a Sunday afternoon, and the following Tuesday, though his granddaughter Coralie remembered him being a shell of himself for a long time, Neihardt returned to his classes at the university, telling his students he had lost his best friend. "I've handled my classes with a curious new feel of power," he said at the time, by imagining Mona sitting among his students, looking up toward him at the front of the classroom "with a shining face."[15]

Neihardt was no stranger to death, and he had always made a point of not fearing it. He had lost many friends by this time, several to suicide, and he had always been able to approach their disappearance philosophically. Living had always been his focus, not dying, and he had counseled friends to concentrate not on what had left but rather on what remained. But this was different. This was Mona, and no matter what came next, life would not be the same.

As the 1950s drew to a close Neihardt survived by busying himself with the afterglow of his writing life. He enjoyed teaching his classes, which continued to draw large numbers of students. One of his students, the daughter of a circuit court judge who knew former President Harry Truman, arranged for Neihardt to visit Truman at his library in Independence, Missouri, where he had retired in 1953. "It was a happy 15-minute conversation," Neihardt wrote to a friend.[16] He took advantage of being in Independence, adjacent to Kansas City, to be driven past the homes where he had lived as a boy. "The places are all living, except the one at Howard & Olive where I last saw my father."[17]

Neihardt was paired with artist Thomas Hart Benton, another Missourian, for a public conversation on fine arts one evening as part of homecoming festivities at Christian College in Columbia. The two had met once nearly thirty years earlier. "I'm glad they've given me someone my size to fight," a smiling Benton said this time as they met before the program, and Neihardt responded, "I'm not going to take you on."[18] James Michener, the Pulitzer Prize-winning author of *Tales of the South Pacific* and *Hawaii*, stopped by campus one day and was surprised to meet Neihardt. In the early 1930s Michener had taught English at the Hill School, then an all-boys school in Pottstown, Pennsylvania, and among the books he taught was *The Song of Hugh Glass*. "The lilting cadences of your poem and the sweep of the epic portions have always delighted me," Michener wrote to Neihardt after returning home. "You are a man who has been quite important in my life and it was a treat to meet you in person."[19]

Neihardt continued to travel, attending the annual Westerners dinner in New York in 1960 and then speaking to classes for two days at Cornell University in Ithaca, New York. He traveled to Lincoln, Nebraska, to address the annual meeting of the Nebraska State Historical Society on "My Memories of Black Elk." He spoke in Red Cloud, Nebraska, at the dedication of a museum to Willa Cather.

He began supplying material to Lucile F. Aly, who had undertaken to write an admiring biography, the first of Neihardt since Julius House's book in 1920. Aly had first become acquainted with Neihardt in 1956 while she worked on her doctoral dissertation at Missouri, a study of Neihardt as a speaker and reader of his own poetry. "I knew almost at once that I would want to undertake a biography later."[20] Aly, who lived in Eugene, Oregon, in addition to interviewing Neihardt several times, often sent him written questions, which he would answer in long letters that sought to explain his philosophy and approach to poetry. Later, once she began to write, she sent him sections of her manuscript that he would comment on and correct. In May 1967 Neihardt traveled to Aly's home in Oregon to work with her on the biography. At times he grew concerned that the book was not going well. "I wonder if I have been too hopeful all these years."[21] Eventually, though, Neihardt liked what Aly had crafted. When he finally saw a complete manuscript in early 1970, he was happy. "Golly! What a book you've done," he wrote to her.[22] In 1977 her book *John G. Neihardt: A Critical Biography* was published by

Rodopi in Amsterdam as the seventh volume in the Melville Studies in American Culture.[23]

Several libraries—chief among them the Library of Congress—began to express interest in Neihardt's personal library of five thousand books as well as his correspondence and manuscripts. "I'm deeply interested in the disposition of my belongings, such as they are, for I feel the time is right for my thinking about my going hence."[24] In the end Neihardt chose to house his papers and his library at the University of Missouri, and in the spring of 1961 a dinner was held in Columbia to mark the gift. Aly spoke, telling those who gathered that "Mr. Neihardt is one of the rare men who has really lived his philosophy."[25]

Neihardt had always been interested in paranormal phenomena, seeing it as just one more way to try to connect with "the otherness of things." In 1907 the *Smart Set* had published his short story "Beyond the Spectrum" about a man who lives with a Chinese houseboy and a white cat with whom he seems to be able to communicate on a deep level. The man is immersed in the study of an alternate reality, an arena "beyond the spectrum" of light that allows for normal seeing and hearing. Throughout his life Neihardt had visited mediums, never taking them completely seriously but always interested in what they had to say. He once prepared a hand-written list of questions before such a visit, a list that sought insight into his and his children's employment possibilities and the outlook for his work, both before and after his death. He frequently reviewed books on paranormal activities, arguing that people did not take such experiences seriously enough, often treating any discussion of spiritism flippantly. When author Upton Sinclair wrote and in 1929 self-published *Mental Radio*, a book about psychic phenomena, Neihardt praised him for doing it.[26] He was a fan of the work of F.W.H. Myers, a poet, classicist, and founder of the Society of Psychical Research, and often mentioned Myers's most noted work, *Human Personality*, in reviews. Essentially, Neihardt believed that psychic phenomena simply represented another avenue for humanity's "ancient religious yearning." "Psychical research," he wrote, "is a distinctly modern attempt to arrive at some livable conception of man's relation to some larger and more significant pattern of existence than that which the five senses reveal to us."[27]

In the 1960s Neihardt decided to try some research himself, and he invited students to Skyrim to take part in paranormal experiments. The next year he formed a group, the Society for Research on Rapport and Telekinesis, or SORRAT; as the name makes clear, the idea was specifically to experiment with psychokinesis—essentially moving objects without touching them or levitating or transporting. He and a select group of students sat around a wooden table in his living room, their hands lightly touching the tabletop. Records were kept, and photographs were taken, but little public mention was made of the experiments until years later when one of the student-participants, John Thomas Richards, published an account of their attempts, *SORRAT: A History of the Neihardt Psychokinesis Experiments, 1961–1981.*[28] Neihardt enjoyed the investigation and was unembarrassed about the work, once even giving an impromptu lecture on extrasensory perception in the University of Missouri student union. "The ballroom where I spoke was filled," he wrote to a friend, "and the audience was very responsive."[29] But it is also clear that like his visits to mediums over the years, his study was less a passion than an entertaining hobby. "It may seem to you that I am more interested in this than I really am," he wrote to that same friend only a few weeks later. "I am very much interested while we are doing it, and I think it is important, but it doesn't fill my world by any means."[30]

Of all the students Neihardt had during his teaching years at Missouri, none meant more to him than Stanley Smith. Smith had been among Neihardt's first students, taking his Epic America class the first year it was offered, and he became a frequent visitor at Neihardt's farm. The two maintained their friendship after Smith's graduation through regular correspondence and occasionally traveling through the western United States together, visiting Neihardt's grandparents' homestead on the Upper Solomon River in northwestern Kansas one time and following the Oregon Trail another. "Our sustenance consisted of beer, Swiss cheese, and Neihardt's memories," Smith wrote. The two planned a third trip, a return visit for Neihardt to Fort Benton, Montana, where he had started his *River and I* trip in 1908, but Neihardt was injured in a car accident in South Dakota and had to be hospitalized for several days.[31]

Almost ten years after graduating and now the editor of the weekly *Wauneta Breeze* in southwestern Nebraska, in February 1961 Smith read that Nebraska was creating a state Hall of Fame, and the first designee was to be George Norris, who had served as a U.S. representative and senator. To signify the honor, a bronze bust of Norris was to be permanently placed in the State Capitol. Smith agreed that Norris deserved such an honor, but although the rules required people to have been dead for at least thirty-five years before they could be considered for the Hall of Fame, Smith saw no reason why a bust of Neihardt could not be added to the Capitol. "I intend to rally as many people as possible behind this noble cause," he wrote in a *Breeze* editorial. Neihardt was a "special breed of man," Smith argued. "His early life reads like a novel: Student, teacher, newspaper reporter and editor, tramp, farm-hand, hod carrier, clerk, office boy, marble-polisher, Indian agent, and stenographer."[32] Though Neihardt had no connection to Wauneta—other than that his former student ran the newspaper there—he became regular front-page news in the *Breeze*. In March Smith published a story announcing that Nebraska Governor Frank Morrison liked the idea of adding Neihardt's bust, though he believed the Hall of Fame Commission would have to make the final decision. Neihardt's biographer Lucile Aly wrote to the newspaper offering her support, as did Mari Sandoz, another Nebraska author. In the end Smith found no fight, and in June the state legislature approved a resolution that called for placing Neihardt's bust in the Capitol. A fund drive was organized to pay for the casting of a bust that Mona Neihardt had sculpted, and that December it was unveiled in a celebration at the Capitol.

Some 250 people, including daughters Hilda and Alice and five grandchildren, gathered to hear speeches that focused on Neihardt's then forty-year reign as Nebraska's poet laureate, on his time as a student in Wayne, Nebraska, and on Mona's roles as wife and artist. Music was provided by the orchestra from a Lincoln junior high school named for

Neihardt's uncle, Charles Culler, who had become a well-known local educator. At one point Neihardt stood next to the bust. At eighty he was fuller of face and now sported glasses, but his trademark thick head of hair had not changed, parted slightly to the left of center and flowing back, full about his ears. When Neihardt spoke that day, he stood on a box of law books in order to see over the podium. "Surely I have a rare advantage here today," he said, waving his hand toward the bust, "for I know the secrets of this image with its sphinxlike reticence. I know what shouts of triumph, what bitter cries, what singing words are sleeping on its lips. I know what visions are implicit in its seeming vacant gaze. And much of what I know has made me grateful beyond joyous laughter to express, and more, has made me humble beyond tears.[33] The *Omaha World-Herald* pointed out to readers of its front page the next morning that Nebraska's poet laureate had left the state forty years earlier—then quoted Neihardt's rejoinder: "Much of the best of me has never moved away."[34]

Neihardt was deeply touched by the event. And it was just the beginning. From then on, the 1960s were a time of celebration for Neihardt. In 1961 the television department of the University of Nebraska, which would become the Nebraska ETV Network, produced a series of three television programs that brought him and his work to a wider audience. In 1965 residents of Bancroft, Nebraska, organized a fund-raising dinner to restore Neihardt's former study, the one-room shack where he had done most of his writing in Bancroft, and to build a Sioux prayer garden. He traveled to Bancroft to speak at the banquet, and he took the opportunity to visit familiar spots and old friends.

That same year the Nebraska State Historical Society installed a roadside marker outside Bancroft to call attention to Neihardt's early life there and to two members of the La Flesche family who had meant so much to Neihardt, Susan and Susette. Neihardt was thrilled. "I can remember times in Bancroft when it would have been a godsend to know that someday such a thing would be. It seems trivial, in a way," he said, "but how it would have helped me to live and to go on trying."[35]

Now in his mid-eighties, Neihardt finally decided to retire from his teaching job. A few years earlier the University of Missouri had chosen his Epic America class as one of the first courses to be videotaped and offered as a televised course in nearly fifty half-hour lectures, so Neihardt's leaving did not mean an end to his class. Missouri continued to offer it for years.[36]

With Neihardt free of the classroom, the Nebraska Centennial Commission and the Nebraska State Historical Society organized "a triumphal march" across Nebraska for Neihardt—he presented forty-seven programs over five weeks. This victory lap, which organizers called the Second Laureate Tour of Nebraska, took Neihardt around the state, starting in late September 1965 with two speeches at Midland College in Fremont, one in the morning and the other that evening. Neihardt and the manager of the tour—his friend and former student Stanley Smith—then drove the back roads of the state, from the Missouri River to Colorado and back again. "[H]e talked to westerners at Bayard, to easterners at Omaha, to southerners at Red Cloud," Smith said. Eventually Neihardt ended up in Lincoln, where he read "The Death of Crazy Horse" to an audience in the University of Nebraska student union. "Neihardt traveled about Nebraska reading, talking, and remembering," Smith said.[37]

In 1967 Nebraska celebrated its centennial, and the Lincoln Journal suggested in an April editorial that residents should also celebrate Neihardt, who was only fourteen years younger than the state itself. A year later he won the University of Missouri's Thomas Jefferson Award, which honors a member of the university community who best exemplifies Jefferson's principles. One journalist summed up Neihardt's life that year by writing, "Life hasn't always been filled with the soft kiss of the wind for Neihardt. . . . But the last few years have brought that kiss of honor to this 87-year-old pioneer."[38]

On one of Neihardt's many trips to Lincoln, this time to speak to the Legislative Ladies, a group of wives of Nebraska's state senators, one of the women asked a Lincoln City Council member's wife if she knew a place where Neihardt might stay while he was in town. She suggested the home of her parents, J. D. and Myrtle Young.[39] The Youngs had first met Neihardt in the summer of 1923, when he joined Julius House and the Neihardt Club of Wayne, Nebraska, at the forks of the Grand River, twenty miles outside the town of Lemmon in northwestern South Dakota. The group, about a dozen people in total, gathered there because it was a key spot in the saga of Hugh Glass, and the club wanted to build a small memorial with a plaque to memorialize Glass's ordeal of one hundred years earlier. J.D. was one of House's former students, and Young and his bride of two months, Myrtle, drove their Ford Model T some two hundred miles from their new home in Murdo, South Dakota, to be a part of the 1923 gathering on the Grand River.

Neihardt and the Youngs became reacquainted, and in the fall of 1967 the Youngs loaded Neihardt into their Rambler and drove again to South Dakota, where they visited Otto Weinkauf, now ninety-two years old, a farmer who had provided the cement mixer and the labor to build the Glass monument. Neihardt recited poetry at Spearfish State College, not far from where he had spent the summer of 1907 with his mother, and he and the Youngs stopped to visit the cabin where he and his mother had stayed. "That was a magical summer, 60 years ago," Neihardt wrote to Smith. "I had just returned from New York where my *Bundle of Myrrh* was making a big splash, and the world was my oyster."[40] They stopped to visit sculptor Korczak Ziolkowski, then less than twenty years into his project of carving Neihardt's hero Crazy Horse out of Thunderhead Mountain north of Custer, South Dakota.

In January 1968, after having spent several weeks with the Youngs at different times in 1967, Neihardt moved in with them, a change that was difficult for his family in Columbia. "It was sad for us," granddaughter Coralie said many years later, "but a renaissance for him."[41] With all the celebrations Neihardt was experiencing in Nebraska, and all the traveling back and forth he was being required to do, the move made sense. Although he never mentioned returning to Nebraska while he lived in Missouri, now that he was back he thought differently about the state, telling a reporter, "I have never ceased during all my years in Missouri to think it was time just visiting and that Nebraska was still home."[42]

The move to the Youngs' home made sense in another way as well. In

November 1966 Neihardt had begun writing his autobiography, the first writing he had done since finishing *When the Tree Flowered* fifteen years earlier. "I had been happy and content in just being," he told a reporter. "Then I began hearing this story in my heart."[43] Neihardt knew from the beginning that it would not be a standard autobiography. "I don't like the word," he said. "I call it a chain of recollections."[44] It was not a chronological record of his life but rather an accumulation of moments he considered important, the "bright spots." "The plan," he wrote to a friend, "is clear to me."[45] He resurrected a title he had considered for *When the Tree Flowered*, planning to call his new book *The Old Man Remembers*. By now Neihardt's eyesight was poor enough that he scribbled on a yellow legal pad and Myrtle Young rewrote the prose in a neat, simple style about four times larger so that he could read what he had composed as he went along. Neihardt had his own room at the Youngs' home, he had his dog with him, and he could work—and nap—as he saw fit. "[H]ere I have ideal conditions for writing."[46] By early 1969 he estimated he had written forty thousand words. "It's really a pleasure to do the job. At present in my 'autobiography' I am only fourteen years old, but I am getting older fast, and soon there will be adult doings."[47] On Good Friday 1970 he finished what he considered the "youth section" of his story—"ending with the burning of *The Divine Enchantment*."[48]

16 A BOOK AND AN AUTHOR REBORN

In 1932 a disappointed John Neihardt had accepted the failure of *Black Elk Speaks* to reach any real audience. Though reviewers had praised it, the book had died swiftly, and for a while he regretted that he had not bought up remaindered copies. He scavenged the book for what he could use, having his campers reenact Black Elk's horse dance at his YMCA job in Chicago and pulling out a section and republishing it as the short story "High Horse's Courting" in *Indians at Work*. Though he often complained about not being able to find copies of his collected lyrics or, later, his *Cycle of the West*, he inquired only once about the possibility of publishing a new edition of *Black Elk Speaks*. As far as Neihardt was concerned, the book, as good as he thought it was, was dead.

But if *Black Elk Speaks* had disappeared from Neihardt's life, Nicholas Black Elk himself certainly had not. Since Neihardt had first met him late in the summer of 1930, Black Elk had continued to have a presence in Neihardt's life. Neihardt felt uniquely connected to Black Elk. The elderly Lakota had opened Neihardt's eyes wider to the injustices America's indigenous peoples had suffered and had strengthened his own commitment to his poetic values and his exploration of the mystical otherness he longed for. Over the years Neihardt corresponded with Black Elk and his son Ben, and he visited Pine Ridge several times. Neihardt regularly presented programs about Black Elk. In February 1967 he spoke about Black Elk during the National Conference on Manpower Programs for Indians, sponsored by the U.S. Department of Labor in Kansas City. In April that year he spoke at Warren Methodist Church in Lincoln on "The Gospel According to Black Elk," telling his listeners: "We're a troubled race." Once teaching at Missouri, Neihardt routinely included Black Elk and his vision as parts of the lectures.[1]

Neihardt's work with Black Elk had served as well as an entry point for others. In 1947 a young scholar of religion with a special interest in Native American traditions, John Epes Brown, had written to Neihardt for information about Black Elk. When Neihardt told Brown that Black Elk was still alive, Brown went for a visit and, that fall, spent five months with Black Elk and his family, during what became a year-long study of spiritual leaders among Plains Indians. His time with Black Elk resulted in Brown's book *The Sacred Pipe: Black Elk's Account of the Seven Rites of the Oglala Sioux.* "[H]e asked me to write up—as he should dictate—a history of the sacred pipe," Brown told Neihardt, "which really amounted to a description of the seven major Siouian rites (as originally performed) with a commentary, which only a man of [Black Elk's] understanding could give, and which for almost the first time makes clear the profundity which lies behind the Siouian religion. I think that really your book was the first to bring this out."[2]

Brown was upset that copies of *Black Elk Speaks,* in which he believed Neihardt had "given to us the essence of the man," were difficult to find. In 1948 Brown tried to get William Morrow & Company, the original publishers, to print a new edition. "[B]ut it seems that the Americans are not intelligent enough to realize its importance."[3] During several trips to Europe, however, Brown promoted *Black Elk Speaks* to friends there, which eventually led to translations into French, Italian, and German.[4]

The German-language version was likely helped, in part, by the Swiss psychotherapist Carl Jung, who had been impressed with *Black Elk Speaks* when he came across it during a lecture tour of America. An American woman who had moved to Switzerland to work with Jung, Carol Sawyer Baumann, had begun writing to Black Elk in 1942, working on a manuscript that considered his vision from a psychological viewpoint. In the summer of 1950 she had traveled to Pine Ridge to visit Black Elk and found him "as thin as a skeleton, bed-ridden, ailing, and completely blind." She told Neihardt she stayed only a few minutes on each of her visits. Ben Black Elk translated for Baumann, as he had for Neihardt. "When I spoke of his vision," Baumann wrote, "he said: 'I hope you can see it clear. I see it clearer all the time. I can't see you, but I can see the other world clearer than daylight. Soon I will be free to go there, and then my son will be free of caring for me, and my old body will go back to Grandmother Earth.'"[5] On August 19, 1950, just three weeks after Baumann left, Black Elk died.

Among the most fervent fans of *Black Elk Speaks* was Mari Sandoz, another writer originally from Nebraska whose work focused mostly on the Great Plains. Neihardt and Sandoz, who now lived in New York, had known each other for years, having first met in the 1930s while she was living in Lincoln, and they had long admired each other. In 1942 Sandoz had written the biography *Crazy Horse: The Strange Man of the Oglalas*, and Neihardt had praised the book in a review in the *New York Times Book Review*. He especially liked the fact that she had interviewed "the old 'long-hairs' themselves, who had lived their part in the great man's saga," and had not relied only on the records of the white conquerors.[6] As part of her research on Crazy Horse, Sandoz had attempted to interview Black Elk shortly before Neihardt had first met with him, but Black Elk had refused to talk with her, a rebuff that had never dampened her enthusiasm for *Black Elk Speaks*.[7]

When the director of the University of Nebraska Press, the academic publisher of the state's university, began looking in 1960 for books to reissue as part of a new paperback line, Sandoz called his attention to *Black Elk Speaks*. Bruce Nicoll had been administrative assistant to the university's chancellor before becoming the press director in 1957, and although he took the job without having any previous experience in publishing, he immediately began to strengthen the press. While it continued to publish scholarly works, Nicoll also inaugurated several new book series, chief among them Bison Books. He planned that Bison

Books would be quality paperbacks—mostly reissues of what he considered the "classics of frontier life in the trans-Missouri West"—and they would be sold not only in bookstores but also in nontraditional outlets like drugstores, motels, grocery stores, and tourist stops.[8]

Nicoll was interested in making Sandoz's *Crazy Horse* one of the first Bison Books, and he asked Sandoz to suggest other titles. Her first suggestions, in February 1960, included Eugene Ware's *The Indian War of 1864*, Edgar Beecher Bronson's *Reminiscences of a Ranchman*, and George A. Armes's *Ups and Downs of an Army Officer*.[9] That June, however, after a friend had paid twelve dollars in a used bookstore for a battered copy of *Black Elk Speaks*, Sandoz wrote to Nicoll again. "I feel a little shame-faced about making any more suggestions to you," she wrote, but she thought Neihardt's book was worthy of being reissued. "It is one of the three best and practically only first-hand accounts of American Indians with any flavor of the old days left." The other two were Thomas Bailey Marquis's *A Warrior Who Fought Custer* and Frank Linderman's *American: The Life Story of a Great Indian: Plenty-coups, Chief of the Crows*. "The most poetic and in many ways the most valuable is this one that Neihardt took down with a poet's hand," she told Nicoll. "Neihardt had sense enough to let Black Elk speak for himself."[10] Nicoll quickly read *Black Elk Speaks* and in the fall of 1961 made it one of the first ten Bison Books, the only one of Sandoz's suggestions to make the list.[11]

The timing of the new edition could not have been better. *Black Elk Speaks*, thirty years out of print and virtually forgotten, stormed across college campuses. Young people were just beginning to turn against what they viewed as "the establishment"—the dominant older generations—their parents and grandparents—who ruled business, education, religion, the military, essentially all sections of American culture, with what now seemed to young people as unthinking conformity. An abyss had developed between the young and their elders—"generation gap" entered the cultural lexicon—and many young people began seeking alternatives to the lives they had been expected to lead. Over the next ten years college-aged Americans embraced fights for civil rights, for women's equality, for black power and red power, and against a surging military effort in far-off Vietnam. The growing counterculture also espoused rebellions of a more recreational nature—free love, powerful music, and drugs— creating a rich mixture of seriousness and fun that promoted a youthful vision of a different world.

The counterculture engulfed campuses across the country, and a selection of books in philosophy, social and political theory, anthropology, and religion as well as powerful new fiction became required reading. Though *Black Elk Speaks* was one of the oldest of the 1960s guidebooks, it was almost always treated as a newly published book. It became one of the required texts, first as a Bison Book and later in several other editions, and Neihardt, nearing ninety, was on his way, as one magazine put it, "to becoming one of the authentic legendary folk heroes of our time."[12] Sales of *Black Elk Speaks* launched a Neihardt resurgence, bringing new readers not only to this but also to his other books, many of which were soon reissued as Bison Books as well. "There certainly has been a groundswell of interest in my work," Neihardt told a newspaper reporter at the time. "It's a little hard to explain but I'm certainly happy about it."[13] For the first time in his long career, in addition to features in newspapers and magazines, academic journals began publishing articles about Neihardt. *Western American Literature*, the journal of the Western Literature Association, carried articles like "Ethic and Metaphysic: A Study of John G. Neihardt" and "*Black Elk Speaks*: And So Does John Neihardt," which called the book "an underground classic fast coming above ground."[14] The *Quarterly Journal of Speech* looked at the "Resurgence of Neihardt."[15]

The Youngs' home became a staging site in Neihardt's resurgent popularity. At times the dining room table was stacked with newly printed copies of his books, and he would spend hours autographing them. At other times he would sit in the living room surrounded by large groups of young people, college students mostly, who would come by to listen to him recite and talk and to take his photograph. After a decade and a half of teaching college students, Neihardt was comfortable around young people. He liked them, and he seemed to understand them—even their mode of dress and drug use, their rejection of the military and other standards of American society and business. Just as he had always called the Indian elders he knew "the old long-hairs," he dubbed the college students "the new long-hairs."[16] He wholeheartedly supported their spiritual search, especially when it came to their embrace of *Black Elk Speaks*. "You know, Black Elk wanted me to take his message out to the world," Neihardt told an interviewer at the time. "We were just 40 years too soon."[17]

In January 1971 John Neihardt, never more widely known than he was at that moment, turned ninety. Not surprisingly, his age was beginning to show. He had had cataract surgery, and he now wore thick eyeglasses. He sometimes had trouble hearing clearly and often wore a hearing aid. He was wobbly on his feet and took to using a cane. Still, when a reporter from Kansas City came to Lincoln for a visit, she was surprised at what good shape he was in. "Neihardt stands erect, his hair not yet entirely white, his eyes shining as if his years were an enhancement to him not a burden," she wrote. "His voice is steady, soothing, lingering over vowels and rolling across elegant phrases, bringing back vivid memories and dwelling on his hopes for the future."[18]

This was the John Neihardt whom Dick Cavett met when he came to Nebraska later that month. Cavett, a Nebraska native, was then the host of a late-night television program, the *Dick Cavett Show*, produced in New York and featuring Cavett's interviews with actors and entertainers, well-known men and women like Katharine Hepburn, Groucho Marx, and Judy Garland. Cavett was widely praised for his intelligence and wit, his boyishness and modest manner. "He comes on like a Charlie Brown who spent some time in graduate school," one television reviewer wrote. "He seems, unashamedly, to have read books."[19]

Cavett's friends and family back in Nebraska often suggested people they thought would make good guests on his program, some small-town man or woman they found funnier than the last comedian Cavett had interviewed or a local singer whose voice they enjoyed more than that of a famous entertainer he had featured. So he was wary when his father and stepmother urged him to interview an elderly man whom they had seen on one of the university television programs and who had later kept guests enthralled in their living room with his conversation and poetry recitations. After hearing the same suggestion from others, however, he decided to take a chance. At the end of January Cavett flew to Nebraska with an ABC television crew. He met Neihardt and his daughter Hilda at the Youngs' home in Lincoln one afternoon, visited for nearly five hours, and then taped several hours of questions and answers the next morning at the studios of Omaha station KETV. The interview, edited into a ninety-minute program, was first broadcast in April 1971, the fiftieth anniversary of Neihardt's selection as the state's poet laureate.

A haunting harmonica played as the opening title appeared on the screen—"A Conversation With Dr. John G. Neihardt." Neihardt wore a dark suit for the program, a white handkerchief folded into the jacket's breast pocket, a white shirt, and bolo tie topped by a circular medallion sporting a six-pointed star. On his right wrist he wore a beaded bracelet, and he occasionally fumbled with a walking stick that leaned against his chair. The set was simple, brownish orange and bright blue, and Neihardt and Cavett sat nearly facing, with only a small six-sided table between them to hold Cavett's few notecards, a glass of water for each, and a paperback copy of *Black Elk Speaks*.

Seventy years earlier, when he had visited the Omaha Indians, and again thirty years after that, when he had spent time with Black Elk, Neihardt was the young amanuensis to the elderly long-hairs, humbly listening to their moving stories of lives he could scarcely imagine. Now he was on the other side. Cavett, the thirty-five-year-old curious and well-read listener, was the awestruck young interviewer, probing gently at a ninety-year-old long-hair who had experienced a life no longer possible. Cavett was struck that Neihardt had talked with participants from both sides of the Battle of the Little Bighorn and that he had known an officer—Maj. H. R. Lemly—who had been present when Crazy Horse was killed in western Nebraska. At one point Cavett told Neihardt that listening to the stories gave him goosebumps. "I find it incredible."

Neihardt occasionally had trouble hearing the soft-spoken Cavett. When, before a scheduled commercial break, Cavett suggested a topic he wanted to cover when the show resumed, Neihardt misunderstood and immediately took off on the story. Cavett let him go. Cavett asked Neihardt whether he missed being young, and Neihardt said he sometimes thought of old times, with their "little tug at your heart," but that "forward is the direction." "I wouldn't want to go back," he said. "You can't go back. No reason why you should want to. I'm sure that what's coming is going to be mighty interesting." When Cavett asked about Crazy Horse, Neihardt offered some background and then, looking directly at Cavett, launched into a recitation from memory of the final section of "The Death of Crazy Horse"—more than a thousand words—that closes *The Song of the Indian Wars*. Two or three times he stumbled, and he occasionally offered an aside for explanation, but the recitation was powerful. When he finished, like an actor after a draining scene, Neihardt sat, unmoving. When Cavett offered, "That was wonderful," all Neihardt could muster in response was a quiet "Uh-huh."

Cavett told his viewers that in a way, he had *two* guests on the show, Neihardt *and* Black Elk, for Black Elk had become such a part of Neihardt's life. Black Elk, Neihardt told Cavett, "taught me and is still teaching me." As Neihardt explained Black Elk's sacred hoop of the universe, with its four directions and red and black roads, Cavett tilted forward in his chair, leaning in toward Neihardt. When Cavett told Neihardt he could not get over the fact that he was ninety years old, Neihardt quickly responded, "I can't get over it either."

Neihardt's appearance on Cavett's program, which caught him at the peak of his popularity and then pushed him even higher, drew mail the likes of which Cavett had never seen. "John is a born performer," Cavett later wrote, "and to hear such vivid and moving recollections . . . was a unique experience."[20] The *Lincoln Star* reported that in the week after the program was first broadcast, some sixteen thousand copies of *Black Elk Speaks* were sold.[21] The only negative response came from some American Indians who in the 1970s were struggling to get the country's attention. Vine Deloria Jr., an author, theologian, and historian who had served as executive director of the National Congress of American Indians, was critical. "As we work harder to tell our story to America," Deloria wrote in the *Los Angeles Times*, "Dick Cavett interviews John

Neihardt, an aging Nebraska poet, who tells the nation that he knows all about the Sioux."[22] A little more than ten years later Deloria, the nephew of Ella Deloria, who had praised *Black Elk Speaks* when it was first published, would edit a book of tributes to Neihardt.[23]

The next summer, in June 1972, the Cavett program was rebroadcast, and that fall Neihardt's memoir of his younger years, now titled *All Is But a Beginning: Youth Remembered, 1881–1901*, was published. He dedicated the book to his ten grandchildren and eight great-grandchildren. Cavett, now firmly a fan of Neihardt and his work, played a role in getting *Beginning* published. Cavett's own autobiography was being edited by noted editor Julian P. Muller at Harcourt Brace Jovanovich in New York, and Cavett took Neihardt's manuscript there. Harcourt Brace Jovanovich agreed to publish it, and Muller ended up editing it as well, at one point meeting Neihardt in Columbia, Missouri, to confer on revisions. "Neihardt was then quite elderly, a congenial man, but the weight of years told on him," Muller remembered.[24] The book's eighty-two chapters were generally short, some only two paragraphs, and as Neihardt had planned, it was a string of episodes from his early life. Though it recounted events from the late nineteenth century, the book had a contemporary feel. Gone were all the archaic allusions that had marked so much of his earlier work. Here, with nothing left to prove, Neihardt vividly and simply rendered the high points of his childhood with grace and good humor. "When a man of my years begins remembering," he wrote, "Time ceases to seem the orderly progression it is commonly supposed to be and becomes a reservoir of contemporaneous voices and echoes. *Thens* neighbor familiarly with *nows*, their changeless pictures waiting in a motionless forever."[25]

He began the book poetically—"There was no one yet, and it was nowhere. It was not even now, for time had not begun." He told the story in roughly chronological order.[26] Though it is clear that he loved and appreciated his mother, he spends more time on his father, a man who was "always a mystery to me."[27] He wrote of his first "grand passion," a pretty little playmate by the name of Etta Stadden in Springfield, Illinois, when he was only four years old, and of his first true boyhood friend,

Dick Scammon, whom he met in Kansas City. "I had never known a boy like him," Neihardt wrote. "Sometimes he talked like a grownup or like something out of a book, and he was very polite."[28] Teachers played an important role, from the tall, slim "goddess" Lulu Lobb in Kansas City to James M. Pile and Ulysses S. Conn, the "great-hearted, great-spirited men" under whom he studied at Nebraska Normal in Wayne.

All Is But a Beginning is more than just a smattering of heart-tugging memories. As he had often done in his early stories on the Omaha and in his novel *When the Tree Flowered*, Neihardt included descriptions of a way of life that had disappeared by the time he wrote the book, drawing attention not only to the progress experienced in rural America but also to the elements of community now lost. He went into significant detail about the days on his grandparents' farm outside Wayne that were devoted to threshing—separating the edible part of a grain from the inedible part. Once a labor-intensive production involving a team of men in the field and a team of women in the kitchen, and often a team of horses for power, threshing, by the 1970s, had been eliminated, replaced by modern methods and equipment. Neihardt made clear that something was lost in the "improvement." The term *threshing*, he wrote, "had developed rich overtones and had come to signify something like a movable feast, dedicated to the principle that hard work could be a lot of fun when a number of friendly people did it together. . . . That was before the combine came in and substituted a single man with an oilcan and a monkey wrench for a whole crew of merry men!"[29]

Neihardt addressed the book, in its early pages, to "my family and friends, and for anybody else who may love me at least a little."[30] And in an epilogue he added another group he hoped would read it: "the young of the much discussed present generation." Though a "generation gap" might separate many young people from their elders, "Happily there is no 'gap' between us," Neihardt wrote, "for it will be noted that my somewhat garrulous rememberings alternate freely between tears and laughter, and I am therefore not unacquainted with the hardships and hilarities incidental to growing up in a world notoriously out of joint."[31] He believed that young people, the college students who were reading his

Black Elk Speaks in such large numbers as part of their own searches for spiritual meaning, were caught up in "the greatest social revolution the world has ever known." In Neihardt's view, young people had a right to be upset with the way their elders were running things. "It is no wonder that our youngsters would reject the mad world they have inherited."[32]

But he cautioned, by recounting a visionary daydream he had had, that they should not believe there was nothing good in the world. There were, by his reckoning, at least four things that were undeniably good. "First: Surely love is good," he wrote, "love given rather than love received." Second on Neihardt's list was the satisfaction of the instinct of workmanship. "Just do your best at any cost," he advised. Third was the "exaltation of expanded awareness in moments of spiritual insight," the results of his never-ending search for "otherness," and fourth was simply "deep sleep."[33] What connected the four, Neihardt believed, was that all involved the loss of self into something larger.

Reviewers were generally charmed by *All Is But a Beginning*. One critic, citing the book's "mystical quality," applauded it as "a lovely new dimension in autobiography."[34] Unlike many other autobiographies, yet another reviewer wrote, Neihardt's book contained "much of broad historical and literary value," such as its exploration of nineteenth-century "frontier society" and its focus on a pursuit of knowledge and its insights into midwestern attitudes toward urbanization and foreign relations. This reviewer, a Great Plains historian, found *Beginning* to be not only a worthwhile historical source on nineteenth-century American life but also "essential to the understanding of Neihardt as a writer."[35]

By the time *All Is But a Beginning* was published, Neihardt had completed nearly half of a second volume.

Neihardt had been living with the Youngs for more than four years, and it had become home for him. As he worked on the second volume of his memoir, he also answered mail—from former students, from friends from his long life, and from new fans and other well-wishers. People stopped in to see him, and they noticed that though his mind remained sharp, his body was giving out. Katie Kelly, a former student and now a writer, dropped in on him in 1972. "His face was a soft maze of wrinkles like a much-folded parchment map of the back roads of the prairie," she wrote later. "His step was somewhat uncertain, his hearing bolstered by a hearing aid. Two severe cataract operations had left him almost sightless and his once-bright eyes had to twinkle out through thick corrective lenses. But the mind was still as brisk as the step was not; the spirit was far-seeing as the eyes were dim."[36]

A couple of days before Neihardt's ninety-second birthday on January 8, 1973, Gene Blackledge, a reporter for the Associated Press, visited him and found him working on the second volume of his memoir—Neihardt still held to a schedule of writing in the mornings and receiving visitors in the afternoon. "His tiny hands gripped a felt-tip pen as he conveyed the memories . . . onto a yellow legal-sized pad," Blackledge wrote. The second volume, like the first, was made up of linked episodes from Neihardt's past, and occasionally the narrative jumped back and forth in time. Blackledge found that a conversation with Neihardt carried with it the same potential for movement from "the distant past to the future, and from one experience to another without much apparent form." Blackledge found that if he paid close attention, however, "the transitions were logical."

Neihardt seemed to want to talk about death that day. "Rumors of the flesh and whisperings of the spirit have alerted me to the fact that I am getting somewhat nearer to the great change," Neihardt told Blackledge, "and I do not regret the fact." Blackledge was recording the interview, but Neihardt, in a process reminiscent of his own interviews with Black Elk, insisted that Blackledge read back to him what he had said so that he could verify it as correct. "I have a warm feeling for this world," Neihardt told him, "but I believe in a continuing life, and I am sure that death will be an astonishing adventure, not to be feared at all." The two went over that quote several times, Neihardt wanting to ensure that Blackledge was getting it down just right. For Blackledge's final question, he asked Neihardt how much longer he thought he would be around. Neihardt, who in his early years had always thought he would die young, now went in the other direction. "I promised several people I would live to 104 and I hope to keep that promise."[37]

At one point during the interview Neihardt had grown tired and excused himself to take a short nap. Blackledge waited around, and when Neihardt reappeared, he said he had had an interesting dream and was disappointed that he had awakened before seeing the end of it. In the dream Neihardt's only son, Sigurd, who had accompanied him on his first visit to Black Elk, traveled with him for years, and was now in poor health at his home in Phoenix, was, in Neihardt's words, "fighting his way out." He made it sound to Blackledge as though Sigurd was in a pretty tough fight. Later, after Blackledge had returned to his office, Myrtle Young called him to say Neihardt had just received word from Arizona that Sigurd had died that day.[38]

In early 1973 another interviewer came calling. William McIntyre traveled to Columbia, Missouri, where he met Neihardt at Hilda's home for several weeks of recording Neihardt as he recited his poetry and answered questions. The recordings, which resulted that fall in a three-record spoken-word boxed set, produced by McIntyre and Nik Venet for United Artists Records, served as a coda to more than ninety years of living—and nearly eighty years of poetry. McIntyre drew Neihardt out, getting him to tell stories about his poems and other writings. The sessions were often taxing for Neihardt, and during the tapings he occasionally stumbled, sometimes searching to understand what was going on around him. He needed his cane, which he called "his stick," to get around, and he occasionally had a tough time hearing and became easily confused, wheezing and able to see only if he had the right pair of glasses and a well-positioned lamp. Sometimes, he told McIntyre, it was like "looking through a dirty window." The records begin with him telling McIntyre, "When you look back over your life, it seems fast. It seems that things developed awful fast and you got old quick. Although, when you look at it carefully, it seems a long time, too. It seems both."[39] After that he alternates between telling stories about his past and reciting a selection of his poetry. When he simply talks, his breathing is pronounced, loud, and he sounds very much the ninety-two-year-old man that he is, often punctuating his discussions with a charming old-man chuckle. When he begins to recite, however, the years disappear, his voice becomes strong, and he once again stretches out the vowels, performing the poems the way he had for more than sixty years.

As 1973 wore on, Neihardt's health deteriorated. In June stabbing pains in his ribs and back sent him in for X-rays, which revealed a collapsed vertebra. A brace helped. He also had difficulty breathing at times and suffered a kidney infection. "He was really just wearing out," remembered Florence Boring, who acted as a secretary for Neihardt in his later years.[40] When a journalist from the *Omaha World-Herald* photographed Neihardt and his dog in Lincoln that August, Neihardt kidded him. "Shoot fast, you may never get another chance."[41]

That fall Neihardt continued to work on the second volume of his memoirs. Friends and family had encouraged him for some time to write about Mona: their unlikely courtship and their nearly fifty years of married life. But he had always wanted to save that telling for later, working on every other story first, almost as if once again, Mona was holding him back until precisely the right time. "I think when he finally laid aside other episodes he had planned to write and began on the one that lay closest to his heart, we should have been forewarned," Boring recorded. "I think the trouble was it lay too near his heart."[42] In mid-October he asked to be taken back to Columbia. His family thought he would be more comfortable at Hilda's home outside town than at his own home at Skyrim. There Hilda and Alice along with granddaughters Gail, Coralie, and Lynn cared for him. Enid and her husband, Ollie, visited, as did the other grandchildren. On Friday, November 2, Boring and J. D. and Myrtle Young came from Lincoln, and the next day Neihardt slept fitfully throughout the beautiful autumn day. Myrtle was reading to him from an unpublished section of his memoir, a favorite part of his about Grant Marsh, the veteran steamboat pilot who had become his friend during his Missouri River trip in 1908, when she called out to the others. "I think something is happening," Boring remembered her saying.

Daughters Hilda and Alice, grandchildren Robin and Coralie, the Youngs, and Boring surrounded Neihardt's bed, and moments later Enid and Ollie joined them. "Looking directly at me, my father did not speak, but he tapped the middle finger of his right hand several times on his chest," Hilda Neihardt wrote years later. "Then, with something like a *whoosh* we felt his great spirit leave."[43] Though they coaxed him to keep trying, his breathing stopped. Efforts to revive him, both by family members and by an emergency crew that soon arrived, failed. At roughly 3:30 in the afternoon on Saturday, November 3, 1973, the life that had begun in a small room in a house outside Sharpsburg, Illinois, ended in a house outside Columbia, Missouri. Late in his life Neihardt had once scoffed when a reporter expressed concern about a trip the poet was about to take. "You think something might happen to me?" Neihardt asked him. "Death cannot rob me of my life. I've already lived it. Oh, how I've lived it. Oh, how I have lived. I do not fear it. I look forward to it as my last great adventure."[44]

EPILOGUE

No Regrets

On November 29, 1973, on what would have been John and Mona Neihardt's sixty-fifth wedding anniversary, Hilda and Alice mixed their parents' ashes together and scattered them from a small twin-engine airplane as they flew over a broad bend in the Missouri River, the waterway that had meant so much to Neihardt and his work. Fulfilling their parents' wish, the two daughters carried with them a copy of "When I Have Gone Weird Ways," Neihardt's poem first published in 1909 in which he lays out his wishes for what he wants to happen after his death. Though overwhelmed by the emotion of their undertaking, Hilda and Alice tried to recite the poem, which opens with the lines

"When I have finished with this episode,
Left the hard up-hill road,
And gone weird ways to seek another load,
O Friend, regret me not, nor weep for me—
Child of Infinity!"

It was fitting that Neihardt urged those who loved him to have no regrets, for he himself had had so few. Throughout his long writing career, Neihardt had routinely updated his friends and family on how his writing was going. He never made any of his self-imposed deadlines, usually missing them by months if not years. Whatever project he was working on, it always seemed to be going well, better than expected, better than the last one. He would usually broadcast the terms of his latest contract and the amount of his advance, but once the book was published, after a brief initial reaction to the criticism, both professional and personal, he moved on. He had never regretted not achieving great fame or fortune, for neither had been his goal. What he had always wanted was for his work to endure, and for most of his career he had thought his most lasting work would be his *Cycle of the West*. For nearly four decades he had believed the *Cycle* would endure long after he was gone, that readers eventually would flock to it and he would be thought of in the same way he thought of Tennyson. His heroes would lead readers across the pages of his poetry, and he would preserve their exploits and, more important, their values for all time. When it did not happen, he was devastated. But then, quietly but quickly, he moved on. He simply taught his students, making a textbook of his beloved *Cycle*, turning a new generation on to Jed Smith and Hugh Glass, Crazy Horse, and Red Cloud.

Editors in New York and California had regularly published his short stories, but Neihardt had never dreamed of being a great short story writer, never listed short story writers among his idols or influences. His early lyrics had gained him a place in the vanguard of modern poetry, but he had given up writing them before he was thirty years old and then turned against most of the modern tendencies. Of a group of men who acted as confidants, brothers, even father figures to Neihardt—Robert Davis, Volney Streamer, Louis Ledoux, George Sterling, Julius House, Stanley Smith—none came close to matching the influence of Nicholas Black Elk. (It is too easy to point out that Black Elk, when selecting a white man's first name, chose the same name as that of Neihardt's father.) Yet the book that grew from their unique relationship, *Black Elk Speaks*, for all of its power and longevity, was a byproduct of research done for what Neihardt saw as his life's work, the *Cycle of the West*.

For of all of Neihardt's work that was published in his lifetime—three novels, two collections of short stories, five volumes of lyrics, five book-length narrative poems, four volumes of nonfiction, one of poetic drama, and thousands of newspaper reviews and articles—this one book, *Black Elk Speaks*, first published more than eighty years ago and regularly reissued in new editions, accounts today for virtually all of his renown. Neihardt lived long enough to know that *Black Elk Speaks* was likely to be his legacy, and he never expressed anything but joy about the late success of the book and the opportunity it gave him to speak of Black Elk.

More than a hundred years ago, in the opening decade of the twentieth century, Gerald Stanley Lee, a clergyman and essayist, prophesied that Neihardt's work might last a long time because people could never quite make up their minds about him. "People have been known to keep an author living generation after generation," he wrote, "so as to have one more last word about him."[1] Neihardt knew enough about writers and poets and history and life to know that people do not get to choose their own destiny. He would express no regret that today, more than forty years after his death, he is remembered.

ACKNOWLEDGMENTS

Many people helped me as I researched the life of John Neihardt, starting with his daughter Hilda Neihardt. Her enthusiastic response to my first letter twenty years ago was followed by books, audiotapes, and videotapes as well as personal interviews in two states.

My thanks also go to librarians and historical society staff in New York, West Virginia, Illinois, Iowa, Nebraska, South Dakota, and Missouri, especially Laura Jolley at the State Historical Society of Missouri. John Wunder, then of the University of Nebraska–Lincoln history department, was a great help in focusing my thinking when I wrote about a brief section of Neihardt's early life as my master's thesis. Lew Serviss, a former colleague at *New York Newsday* and the *New York Times*, deserves a hat tip for critiquing an early portion of the book. Stan Smith offered encouragement at the beginning, along with advice and photos. Bridget Barry at University of Nebraska Press helped me finish the project, graciously providing quality editing, advice—and a few trims, and Sally Antrobus fine-tuned it all with her expert copyediting.

I owe special thanks to the Richard S. Brownlee Fund at the State Historical Society of Missouri for supplying early research funding.

It would have been difficult to keep at this as long as I did without the continual encouragement of friends and family. My thanks to all of you who read early chapters and never failed to ask how the project was going.

Few writers live with award-winning editors, but I do. My wife, Nancy, helped me make copies at the New York Public Library at the beginning, and she thoroughly edited the manuscript at the end. Though any errors of fact or phrasing are my own, it's safe to say there would have been more of both without her.

NOTES

ABBREVIATIONS

Davis
Robert H. Davis Papers, Manuscripts and Archives Division, New York Public Library, Astor, Lenox, and Tilden Foundations, New York

Flaming Rainbow
Unedited interview recordings, John G. Neihardt Center, Bancroft NE, or album boxed set (identified accordingly)

Journal
Minneapolis Journal

Journal-Post
Kansas City Journal-Post

Macmillan
Macmillan Company Papers, Manuscripts and Archives Division, New York Public Library, Astor, Lenox, and Tilden Foundations, New York

Monroe
Harriet Monroe Papers, Special Collections Research Center, University of Chicago

Neihardt/Bancroft
John G. Neihardt Papers, John G. Neihardt Center, Bancroft NE

Neihardt/WHMC
John G. Neihardt Papers, Western Historical Manuscripts Collection, State Historical Society of Missouri, Columbia

Neihardt/NSHS
John G. Neihardt Papers, Nebraska State Historical Society, Lincoln

npn
no page number

Post-Dispatch	*St. Louis Post-Dispatch*
Robinson	Doane Robinson Papers, South Dakota State Historical Society, Pierre
Smith/WHMC	Stanley C. Smith Papers, Western Historical Manuscripts Collection, State Historical Society of Missouri, Columbia
Sterling, Huntington	George Sterling Papers, Huntington Library, San Marino CA
Sterling, New York	George Sterling Papers, Berg Collection of English and American Literature, New York Public Library, Astor, Lenox and Tilden Foundations, New York

PROLOGUE

1. Neihardt, *Beginning*, 4.
2. Details of the circumstances of Neihardt's birth are recounted, in part, in earlier biographies and in numerous newspaper and magazine articles. In the end, however, all accounts are based on what he remembers being told. The best retelling is his own, in *All Is But a Beginning*, starting on p. 4.
3. The spelling of Neihardt in the family history is inconsistent. Neihardt's father and other ancestors did not use the *d*; Neihardt and his mother eventually did.

1. A HEART-BREAKING FAREWELL

1. Neihardt, *Cycle*, introduction, viii.
2. Except where otherwise noted, the genealogical information on John G. Neihardt's family comes from Dennis Allen Kastens's *Neuhart Chronicle*.
3. Neihardt, *Beginning*, 7.
4. *Bancroft Blade*, February 24, 1905. Short articles in the *Bancroft Blade* often carried no headline or byline, and the *Blade* was often published without page numbers; other newspaper citations lacking a headline, author, or page number reflect limited detail available.
5. Alice M. Neihardt's application for a "Declaration for Widow's Pension," John G. Neihardt Papers, John G. Neihardt Center, Bancroft NE (hereafter cited as Neihardt/Bancroft).
6. Neihardt, *Beginning*, 10.
7. Neihardt, *Beginning*, 10.
8. Neihardt, *Beginning*, 10.
9. Campbell, *200 Years*, 142.
10. Neihardt, *Beginning*, 8.

11. Neihardt, *Beginning*, 11.
12. Lewis, *Mammoth Book of the West*, 222.
13. Neihardt, *Song of Three Friends*, 94.
14. Neihardt, *Beginning*, 14.
15. Neihardt, *Beginning*, 13.
16. Neihardt, *Beginning*, 14.
17. Neihardt, *Beginning*, 14.
18. Neihardt, *Beginning*, 19.
19. *Neihardt: A Journey Home*, 60-minute videocassette, executive producer Ron Hull, Lincoln NE: Great Plains National Television, 1975.
20. Neihardt, *Beginning*, 23.
21. Neihardt, *Beginning*, 23.
22. Neihardt, *Beginning*, 24.
23. Haskell and Fowler, *City of the Future*, 69.
24. Neihardt, *Beginning*, 24.
25. Neihardt, *Beginning*, 28.
26. Neihardt, *Beginning*, 41.
27. Neihardt, *Beginning*, 41.
28. Neihardt, *Beginning*, 7.
29. Neihardt, *Beginning*, 45.
30. Neihardt, *Beginning*, 32.
31. Greene, *Samuel Johnson*, 133–39.
32. Neihardt, *Beginning*, 32.
33. Neihardt, *Beginning*, 25.
34. Neihardt, *River*, 61–62.
35. Neihardt, *River*, 68.
36. Neihardt, *River*, 107.
37. Neihardt, *River*, 2–3.
38. Neihardt, *River*, 3.
39. Neihardt, *River*, 7
40. Neihardt, *River*, 62.
41. Sworn testimony given by Lulu McDonald in Minneapolis MN, October 16, 1930, during a deposition by a field representative of the Bureau of Pensions in the case of Alice Neihardt's request for a widow's pension. Neihardt/Bancroft.
42. Neihardt, *Beginning*, 42.
43. Neihardt, *Beginning*, 61–62.
44. Nicholas N. Neihart, untitled poem, dated 1887, John G. Neihardt Papers,

Western Historical Manuscripts Collection, State Historical Society of Missouri, Columbia MO (hereafter cited as Neihardt/WHMC).

45. Neihardt, *Beginning*, 61–62.
46. Neihardt, *Beginning*, 5.
47. Neihardt, *Patterns*, 79–80.
48. Neihardt, *Beginning*, 43.
49. Alice Neihardt to John G. Neihardt, 1930s, Neihardt/WHMC.
50. Neihardt, *Beginning*, 43.

2. A VOICE ECHOING IN THE DISTANCE

1. Nyberg, *History of Wayne County*, 8.
2. *Lincoln (NE) State Journal*, June 5, 1887.
3. Commager, *American Mind*, 35.
4. Neihardt to McCluskey, August 31, 1966, John G. Neihardt Papers, Nebraska State Historical Society, Lincoln NE (hereafter cited as Neihardt/NSHS).
5. Neihardt, *Beginning*, 48.
6. John G. Neihardt, quoted in *Voice of the Plains: John G. Neihardt*, 60-minute videocassette, Lincoln NE: Nebraska ETV Network, 1983.
7. Peg McMahon, "Youth Hears the Old Poet's Songs," *Kansas City Star Magazine*, March 7, 1971, 8.
8. Neihardt, quoted in *Voice of the Plains*.
9. Neihardt, quoted in *Voice of the Plains*.
10. Johnson, *Rasselas*, 512.
11. Neihardt, *Beginning*, 56.
12. Neihardt, *Beginning*, 36.
13. Neihardt to Donna Guse, undated, Neihardt/WHMC.
14. Alice M. Neihardt, quoted in *Omaha World-Herald*, December 9, 1922.
15. Neihardt, *Beginning*, 55.
16. John G. Neihardt, "How It Feels to Be a Poet Laureate," *Omaha Daily News Magazine*, November 13, 1921, 7.
17. Clair Goodwin, "Poet Has Deep Feeling About His Life's Work," *Joplin (MO) News-Herald*, October 16, 1967, 1B.
18. Neihardt, *Beginning*, 58.
19. Tennyson, *Idylls*, 252.
20. Mona Neihardt, "Letter to Biographer," October 1938, Neihardt/WHMC.
21. John G. Neihardt, "Remarks at Bancroft," *Nebraska History* 46 (September 1965): 254.
22. Neihardt, "How It Feels," 7.

23. Neihardt, "The Larger Environment," *Journal Post*, April 25, 1926, 6-D.

24. Neihardt to Lucile F. Aly, February 6, 1958, Neihardt/Bancroft.

25. Neihardt to Chaffee, February 5, 1958, Neihardt/Bancroft.

26. Neihardt to Chaffee, February 21, 1958, Neihardt/Bancroft.

27. John G. Neihardt, "The Harpist," *Wayne* (NE) *Democrat*, December 6, 1895, 1.

28. Neihardt, *Beginning*, 60–61.

29. Neihardt's daughter Hilda had copies of the unedited interviews recorded for *Flaming Rainbow: Reflections and Recollections of an Epic Poet* (Los Angeles CA: United Artists Records, 1973). They are now part of the Neihardt Collection at the Neihardt Center, Bancroft NE; most citations in these notes are from the unedited interviews (hereafter cited as *Flaming Rainbow* interviews) and a few are from the finished album set (cited as *Flaming Rainbow* album).

30. Neihardt, *Beginning*, 59.

31. Neihardt, *Beginning*, 82.

32. Neihardt, *Beginning*, 97.

33. John G. Neihardt, quoted in Stanley C. Smith and Robert Houston, "Nebraska Poet Laureate Popular Teacher at 80," *Omaha World-Herald*, May 21, 1961, 3.

34. Neihardt, *Beginning*, 101.

35. Unheadlined item, *Wayne Democrat*, January 31, 1896, no page number (hereafter npn).

36. Neihardt, *Beginning*, 107.

37. John G. Neihardt, quoted in "'Must Study Past' Dr. Neihardt Feels," *Columbia* (MO) *Missourian*, April 26, 1959, 8B.

38. Morgan to McCluskey, July 18, 1974, Neihardt/NSHS.

39. "Boyhood of Neihardt and 'The Poet's Town,'" *Omaha Bee*, March 18, 1923, 8-A.

40. Neihardt, *Beginning*, 65.

41. W. A. Brandenburg, president of Nebraska State Teacher's College, Wayne, remarks at Neihardt bust dedication, December 7, 1961, Neihardt/WHMC.

42. Neihardt, *Beginning*, 63.

43. Neihardt, *Beginning*, 64.

44. Neihardt, *Beginning*, 69.

45. *Flaming Rainbow* album.

46. Neihardt, *Beginning*, 68.

47. *Flaming Rainbow* interviews.

48. Neihardt, *Beginning*, 70–75.

49. Helen Pile Newton to Neihardt, July 12, 1962, Neihardt/WHMC.

50. Goldie to Neihardt, November 8, 1896, Neihardt/WHMC.

51. *Flaming Rainbow* interviews.

52. John G. Neihardt, "Literature and the Unlettered," *Post-Dispatch*, December 4, 1926, 6.

53. Quote from Neihardt, "The Poet's Town," *Stranger*, 29.

54. *Flaming Rainbow* interviews.

55. Neihardt, "The Poet's Town," *Stranger*, 29.

56. Myrtle Young, interview with John G. Neihardt, cassette recording made February 1972, Kay Young private collection, Lincoln NE. Transcript in possession of the author.

57. Torwesten, "Introduction," *Vedanta*, 7.

58. Neihardt, *Beginning*, 69.

59. *Flaming Rainbow* interviews.

60. Neihardt, *Beginning*, 114.

61. Grant, "Poetic Development of John G. Neihardt," 5.

62. Neihardt, *Divine Enchantment*, 9.

63. Neihardt, *Divine Enchantment*, 10.

64. Neihardt, *Divine Enchantment*, 18.

65. Aly, *Neihardt*, 24–25.

66. Neihardt to Stanley C. Smith, August 7, 1964, Neihardt/WHMC.

67. Howard Owen Erickson, "Neihardt Burned Own Manuscripts for Years," *Omaha World-Herald*, February 21, 1926, magazine section, 1.

68. Neihardt, *Beginning*, 106.

69. Taine, *English Literature*.

70. Taine, *English Literature*, 535.

71. Childs to Aly, July 29, 1957, Neihardt/Bancroft.

72. Neihardt, *Beginning*, 105.

73. John G. Neihardt, "A Notable Accomplishment," *Journal*, November 17, 1912, Women's Section, 5.

74. Neihardt, *Beginning*, 117.

75. Neihardt, *Beginning*, 130.

76. Neihardt, *Beginning*, 131.

77. Neihardt, *Beginning*, 129.

78. Neihardt, *Beginning*, 145.

79. Neihardt to Aly, February 6, 1958, Neihardt/Bancroft.

80. Olson and Naugle, *History of Nebraska*, 257.

81. Neihardt to Smith, March 10, 1961, Neihardt/WHMC.

82. Neihardt/WHMC.

83. Neihardt, *Beginning*, 120.

84. Neihardt, *Beginning*, 115.
85. Neihardt, *Beginning*, 119.
86. Neihardt, *Beginning*, 158.
87. Neihardt, *Beginning*, 163.
88. Neihardt to Macmillan, May 3, 1899, Macmillan Company Papers, Manuscripts and Archives Division, New York Public Library, Astor, Lenox, and Tilden Foundations, New York (hereafter cited as Macmillan).
89. Erickson, "Neihardt Burned Own Manuscripts," 1.
90. *Albany* (NY) *Times-Union*, June 15, 1900; *Pittsburgh* (PA) *Times*, June 30, 1900.
91. Neihart to Neihardt, July 10, 1898, Neihardt/WHMC.
92. Neihart to Neihardt, October 25, 1898, Neihardt/WHMC.
93. Neihart to Neihardt, February 9, 1899, Neihardt/WHMC.
94. Neihart to Neihardt, June 20, 1900, Neihardt/WHMC.
95. H. David Brumble, "John G. Neihardt," *American National Biography* (Oxford: Oxford University Press, 1999), 271.

3. A BIG-CITY ADVENTURE

1. Heritage Book Committee, *History of Bancroft*, 2.
2. *Flaming Rainbow* interviews.
3. John G. Neihardt, quoted in House, *Neihardt*, 16.
4. Neihardt, *Patterns*, 20.
5. "The *Companion's* Seventy-Fifth Birthday," *Youth's Companion*, April 18, 1901, 205.
6. Willa Cather's poem "The Night Express," which drew on her Nebraska roots, was published in the *Youth's Companion* on June 26, 1902.
7. "Nebraska Poet Wrote His First Poem on Back of His Hoe Blade," *Omaha World-Herald*, circa January 1917, npn.
8. John G. Neihardt, "The Song of the Hoe," *Youth's Companion*, September 27, 1900, 472.
9. "Nebraska Poet Wrote His First Poem," *Omaha World-Herald*.
10. John G. Neihardt, "Skating Song," *Youth's Companion*, January 31, 1901, 56.
11. *Flaming Rainbow* interviews.
12. Neihardt, "Song of the Turbine Wheel," *Man-Song*, 42–43.
13. Neihardt, *Patterns*, 4.
14. Neihardt to Macmillan, October 20, 1900, Macmillan.
15. Neihardt to Macmillan, February 8, 1901, and February 11, 1901, Macmillan.
16. Neihardt, *Patterns*, 12.
17. *Bancroft Blade*, September 27, 1901, 3.

18. John G. Neihardt, "Rainy Evening in the City," *Omaha Daily News*, September 29, 1901, 4.

19. John G. Neihardt, "How It Feels to Be a Poet Laureate," *Omaha Daily News Magazine*, November 13, 1921, 7.

20. Neihardt, *Patterns*, 10.

21. Neihardt, "Lonesome in Town," *Man-Song*, 40.

22. Neihardt, *Patterns*, 19.

23. John G. Neihardt, "To William McKinley," *Omaha Daily News*, September 15, 1901, 4.

24. Neihardt, *Patterns*, 13.

25. Neihardt, "Czolgosz," *Man-Song*, 34.

26. Neihardt, *Patterns*, 18.

27. Neihardt, *Patterns*, 21–24.

4. A SENSE OF ALIENATION

1. La Flesche to A. B. Meacham, December 20, 1878, in Dorsey, *Cegiha Language*, 681.

2. La Flesche to La Flesche, September 1878, in Dorsey, *Cegiha Language*, 488.

3. Green, *Iron Eye's Family*, 65.

4. Neihardt, "The American Indian," *Post-Dispatch*, December 24, 1926, 11.

5. Note among Neihardt's personal papers, Neihardt/WHMC.

6. Neihardt to Macmillan, April 29, 1902, Macmillan.

7. Neihardt, "When the Snows Drift," *End of the Dream*, 1.

8. Neihardt, "Little Wolf," renamed "The Beating of the War Drums," *End of the Dream*, 42.

9. Neihardt, "The Look in the Face, *Lonesome Trail*, 31–33.

10. Neihardt, "The Epic-Minded Scot," *Ancient Memory*, 152.

11. Neihardt, "The Beating of the War Drums," *End of the Dream*, 41.

12. Neihardt, "The Ancient Memory," *Ancient Memory*, 13.

13. Neihardt, "The Singer of the Ache," *Lonesome Trail*, 116.

14. Neihardt, "The Singer of the Ache," *Lonesome Trail*, 110.

15. Neihardt, "The Spirit of Crow Butte," *End of the Dream*, 33.

16. Neihardt, "The Spirit of Crow Butte," *End of the Dream*, 35.

17. Neihardt to Davis, November 14, 1905, Robert H. Davis Papers, Manuscripts and Archives Division, New York Public Library, Astor, Lenox, and Tilden Foundations, New York (hereafter cited as Davis).

18. Neihardt, "The Last Thunder Song," *Lonesome Trail*, 278.

19. "Tales of the Northwest," *New York Times Book Review*, June 1, 1907, 350.

20. Neihardt, "Feather for Feather," *Lonesome Trail*, 45.

21. Neihardt, "Dreams Are Wiser Than Men," *Lonesome Trail*, 204.

22. Neihardt, "The Smile of God, *Lonesome Trail*, 221.

23. Neihardt, "The Fading of Shadow Flower," *Lonesome Trail*, 75.

24. Neihardt, "The Spirit of Crow Butte," *End of the Dream*, 36.

25. Neihardt, "The Singer of the Ache," *Lonesome Trail*, 110.

26. Neihardt to Davis, April 26, 1906, Davis.

27. Neihardt, "The Alien," *Lonesome Trail*, 11.

28. Neihardt, "Dreams Are Wiser Than Men," *Lonesome Trail*, 209.

29. Neihardt to Davis, July 12, 1906, Davis.

30. Neihardt, "The Revolt of a Sheep," *Lonesome Trail*, 173.

31. Neihardt, "The Beating of the War Drums," *End of the Dream*, 39.

32. Neihardt to Davis, July 12, 1906, Davis.

33. Neihardt, "A Simply Told Story of Francis of Assisi's Great Life," *Journal Post*, July 11, 1926, 4-D.

34. *Bancroft Blade*, March 14, 1902, npn.

35. *Bancroft Blade*, April 10, 1903, npn.

36. John G. Neihardt, quoted in Grant, "Poetic Development of John G. Neihardt," 44.

37. Neihardt, "A Political Coup at Little Omaha," *Lonesome Trail*, 255.

38. Neihardt, "Political Coup," *Lonesome Trail*, 257.

39. Neihardt, "Political Coup," *Lonesome Trail*, 258.

40. Neihardt, "Political Coup," *Lonesome Trail*, 270.

41. *Bancroft Blade*, March 6, 1903, npn.

42. *Bancroft Blade*, March 20, 1903, npn.

43. Hickey, *Nebraska Moments*, 265.

44. *Flaming Rainbow* interviews.

45. Neihardt, *Patterns*, 42.

46. An excellent telling of Standing Bear's plight and the work of Tibbles and Bright Eyes on his behalf can be found in Joe Starita's *"I Am a Man."*

47. Neihardt, *Patterns*, 43.

48. Neihardt, unpublished letter left inside Neihardt's copy of *Buckskin and Blanket Days* by Thomas Henry Tibbles in Neihardt's private library, University of Missouri.

49. Neihardt, introduction to Tibbles, *Ponca Chiefs*, npn.

5. A POWERFUL ENDORSEMENT

1. *Bancroft Blade*, August 21, 1903, npn.

2. "Republican Caucus," *Bancroft Blade*, October 2, 1903, 1.
3. *Bancroft Blade*, September 4, 1903, npn.
4. "Sinclair Sells Out," *Bancroft Blade*, September 18, 1903, npn.
5. "To the Public," *Bancroft Blade*, September 18, 1903, npn.
6. *Bancroft Blade*, September 25, 1903.
7. "Editorial," *Bancroft Blade*, October 9, 1903, npn.
8. "Editorial," *Bancroft Blade*, January 22, 1904, npn; "Editorial," *Bancroft Blade*, January 15, 1904, npn.
9. "Editorial," *Bancroft Blade*, October 23, 1903, npn.
10. "Editorial," *Bancroft Blade*, November 27, 1903, npn.
11. "Nebraska Reveres the Memory of Two Pioneers," *Omaha World-Herald*, August 4, 1904, 1, 5.
12. Song of Solomon 1:13.
13. Neihardt, "I Would Sing as the Wind," *Bundle* (1903), npn.
14. Neihardt, "Lines in Late March," *Bundle* (1907), npn.
15. Neihardt, "The Last Altar," *Bundle* (1907), 58.
16. Neihardt, "A Witless Musician," *Bundle* (1903), npn.
17. Doris Minney, "Nebraska's Poet Laureate," *Omaha World-Herald*, magazine section, June 1, 1951, 13.
18. "Notice," *Bancroft Blade*, January 20, 1905, 1.
19. "Concerning Gossip," *Bancroft Blade*, January 27, 1905, 1.
20. *Wausa Gazette*, reprinted in *Bancroft Blade*, February 10, 1905, 1.
21. "To Our Readers," *Bancroft Blade*, February 3, 1905, npn.
22. Neihardt, "To My Cat," *Man-Song*, 44; "It May Be," *Bundle* (1907), 14.
23. *Bancroft Blade*, October 27, 1905, npn.
24. Neihardt, "The End of the Dream," *Lonesome Trail*, 152.
25. Neihardt to Davis, April 18, 1906, Davis.
26. Davis to Neihardt, April 23, 1906, Davis.
27. Davis to Neihardt, November 17, 1905, Davis.
28. Neihardt to Davis, December 2, 1905, Davis.
29. Davis to Neihardt, July 17, 1906, Davis.
30. Davis to Neihardt, November 24, 1924, Neihardt/WHMC.
31. Neihardt to Davis, January 4, 1906, Davis.
32. Neihardt to Davis, November 9, 1906, Davis.
33. Davis to Neihardt, April 19, 1907, Davis.
34. Davis to Neihardt, May 15, 1907, Davis.
35. Davis to Neihardt, November 17, 1905, Davis.
36. Neihardt to Louis V. Ledoux, August 19, 1907, Neihardt/NSHS.

37. Neihardt, "To Volney Streamer," *Man-Song*, 46–47.
38. Neihardt to Davis, July 12, 1906, Davis.
39. *Flaming Rainbow* interviews.
40. Neihardt, "These Modern Goings On," *Journal-Post*, June 6, 1926, 4-D.
41. Neihardt to Ledoux, November 6, 1907, Neihardt/NSHS.
42. Neihardt to Ledoux, April 1, 1909, Neihardt/NSHS.
43. Ledoux, undated note, Neihardt/NSHS.
44. Neihardt to Davis, April 20, 1907, Davis.
45. Neihardt, *Bundle* (1907), 16, 52.
46. *New York Times Saturday Review*, May 11, 1907.
47. Neihardt, "Nemesis and the Four Deuces," *Washington Post*, April 28, 1907, MS9.
48. Amy C. Rich, "Books of the Day," *Arena*, August 1907, 222; "Tales of the Northwest," *New York Times Book Review*, June 1, 1907, 350.
49. Neihardt, *Patterns*, 39–40.
50. Susan La Flesche Picotte, quoted in "Editor's Note," *Munsey's Magazine*, June 1906, 489.
51. Susan La Flesche Picotte, "An Indian's View of *The Lonesome Trail*," letter to *New York Times Saturday Review*, June 15, 1907, 397.
52. *Bancroft Blade*, June 1, 1906, npn.
53. *Bancroft Blade*, April 19, 1907, npn.
54. Neihardt to Davis, July 7, 1907, Davis.
55. Neihardt to Ledoux, August 14, 1907, Neihardt/NSHS.
56. Neihardt to Davis, April 20, 1907, Davis.
57. Neihardt to Ledoux, August 14, 1907, Neihardt/NSHS.
58. Davis to Neihardt, January 14, 1908, Davis.
59. Frothingham to Hoffman, February 20, 1908, Neihardt/WHMC.
60. Whitney to Neihardt, March 23, 1908, Neihardt/WHMC.
61. Agnes C. Laut, "Neihardt's Poems Show New Spirit," *New York Times Review of Books*, February 15, 1908, 83.
62. "Three Young Poets," *Outlook* 89 (May 30, 1908): 260.
63. Gerald Stanley Lee, "Deciding About a New Author," *Putnam's and the Reader* 4, no, 4 (July 1908): 474.
64. Neihardt to Smith, n.d., Neihardt/WHMC.
65. Neihardt to Ledoux, May 1, 1908, Neihardt/NSHS.

6. A PARTNER IN ART AND MARRIAGE

1. "Financier Martinsen's Death," *New York Times*, December 24, 1892, npn.

2. F. Edwin Elwell, "Mart," *Arena*, October 1905, 352.

3. Elwell, "Mart," 352.

4. Neihardt, *Black Elk and Flaming Rainbow*, 5.

5. Betty Mitchell, "Mrs. Neihardt Finds Models for Her Sculpting at SkyRim Home," *Columbia Missourian*, April 4, 1951, 6.

6. Grunfeld, *Rodin*, 49.

7. Mitchell, "Mrs. Neihardt Finds Models," 6.

8. Neihardt to Mary Holm, April 6, 1939, Neihardt/Bancroft.

9. Neihardt to Ledoux, May 13, 1908, Neihardt/NSHS.

10. Neihardt to Ledoux, May 29, 1908, Neihardt/NSHS.

11. Neihardt to Ledoux, June 5, 1908, Neihardt/NSHS.

12. Neihardt to Ledoux, June 25, 1908, Neihardt/NSHS.

13. Mott, *American Magazines*, 637.

14. Neihardt to Ledoux, March 1, 1908, Neihardt/NSHS.

15. Neihardt, *River*, 20.

16. Neihardt to Ledoux, n.d., 1908, Neihardt/NSHS.

17. *Flaming Rainbow* interviews.

18. Neihardt, *River*, 103.

19. Neihardt, *River*, 104.

20. Neihardt, *River*, 250.

21. Neihardt, *River*, 315.

22. Neihardt to Robinson, September 5, 1908, Doane Robinson Papers, South Dakota State Historical Society, Pierre (hereafter cited as Robinson).

23. Neihardt to Ledoux, September 25, 1908, Neihardt/NSHS.

24. Neihardt to Robinson, September 5, 1908, Robinson.

25. Neihardt, *River*, 325.

26. Neihardt, *River*, 325.

27. Neihardt, *River*, 48.

28. "The River and the Poet," *New York Times Book Review*, May 14, 1911, 297.

29. "Notes," *Nation*, December 8, 1910, 556.

30. Richard Burton, "Bellman's Bookshelf," *Bellman*, June 3, 1911, 690.

31. *Dial*, December 16, 1910, 525.

32. Neihart to Jonas Neihart, January 21, 1910, Neihardt/WHMC.

33. Neihardt to Ledoux, August 5, 1908, Neihardt/NSHS.

34. Neihardt to Ledoux, September 25, 1908, Neihardt/NSHS.

35. Neihardt to Ledoux, October 5, 1908, Neihardt/NSHS.

36. Martinsen to Ledoux, October 13, 1908, Neihardt/NSHS.

37. Neihardt, *Patterns*, 94.

38. "Marriage of an Author and Artist," *Omaha World-Herald*, November 30, 1908, 8.

39. Neihardt, *Broidered Garment*, 215.

40. Neihardt, *Patterns*, 98.

41. Davis to Neihardt, December 19, 1908, Davis.

42. Neihardt to Ledoux, December 13, 1908, Neihardt/NSHS.

43. Neihardt to Ledoux, December 30, 1908, Neihardt/NSHS.

44. Neihardt to Robinson, December 21, 1908, Robinson.

45. Neihardt to Robinson, December 9, 1909, Robinson.

46. Neihardt to Ledoux, August 6, 1909, Neihardt/NSHS.

47. Neihardt to Ledoux, June 25, 1908, Neihardt/NSHS.

48. Neihardt to Ledoux, August 6, 1909, Neihardt/NSHS.

49. Neihardt, "A Vision of Woman," *Man-Song*, 6.

50. Neihardt's daughter Hilda had copies of the unedited interviews recorded for *Flaming Rainbow: Reflections and Recollections of an Epic Poet* (United Artists Records, Los Angeles CA, 1973). They are now part of the Neihardt Collection at the Neihardt Center, Bancroft NE.

51. Harriet Monroe, "Modern American Poetry," *Poetry Review*, October 1912, 472.

52. Neihardt to Ledoux, May 1, 1909, Neihardt/NSHS.

53. Neihardt to Ledoux, May 1, 1909, Neihardt/NSHS.

54. Neihardt, "Love-Cry," *Man-Song*, 15–17.

55. Neihardt, "Outward," *Man-Song*, 29–30.

56. John G. Neihardt, "How It Feels to Be a Poet Laureate," *Omaha Daily News Magazine*, November 13, 1921, 7.

57. Neihardt, "Battle Cry," *Man-Song*, 27–28.

58. Cowan, *Clarence Darrow*, 333–34.

59. Secretary to Samuel Gompers to Neihardt, August 26, 1918, Neihardt/WHMC.

60. "Julian Accused of Plagiarism," *Los Angeles Times*, October 2, 1924, A8.

61. Bliss Carman, "Some New Poems by J. G. Neihardt," *New York Times Saturday Review of Books*, November 20, 1909, 724.

62. Jim Tully, "The Epic Poet of the Pioneer West," *Literary Digest International Book Review*, October 1924, 783.

63. London, *Jack London*, 378.

64. H. L. Mencken, "George Bernard Shaw as a Hero," *Smart Set*, January 1910, 155.

65. "Qwertyuiop," *Saturday Review of Literature*, January 29, 1927, 545.

66. Pattee, *New American Literature*, 290.

67. Neihardt, *Dawn-Builder*, 177.

68. Neihardt, *Dawn-Builder*, 213–14.

69. Neihardt, *Dawn-Builder*, 217–18.

70. William Morton Payne, "Recent Fiction," *Dial*, April 1, 1911, 269.

71. "Life's Lure," *New York Times Review of Books*, November 8, 1914, 488.

72. Neihardt, "A Whitman's First Edition," *St. Louis Post-Dispatch*, March 16, 1927, 21.

73. Neihardt to Ledoux, October 3, 1920, Neihardt/NSHS.

7. A FATAL ROW

1. Neihardt, "Literature of the Trail," *New York Times*, March 12, 1911, 142.

2. Neihardt, "Literature of the Trail," 142.

3. Neihardt, "Literature of the Trail," 142.

4. Neihardt, "The Soul of the Indian," *New York Times*, April 23, 1911, 247.

5. Neihardt, *Broidered Garment*, 228, 236.

6. Neihardt to Ledoux, October 6, 1911, Neihardt/NSHS.

7. John G. Neihardt "Remarks at Bancroft, August 1, 1965," *Nebraska History*, September 1965, 256.

8. Neihardt, "In the Night," *Stranger*, 10.

9. William Morton Payne, "Recent Poetry," *Dial*, August 16, 1912, 103.

10. Neihardt, "The Weavers," *Stranger*, 1.

11. Joyce Kilmer, "Neihardt's New Poems," *New York Times Review of Books*, March 10, 1912, 137.

12. Streamer to Neihardt, July 21, 1911, Neihardt/WHMC.

13. Neihardt to Ledoux, October 25, 1911, Neihardt/NSHS.

14. Kilmer, "Neihardt's New Poems," 137.

15. Payne, "Recent Poetry," 103.

16. Neihardt to Stanley C. Smith, December 2, 1955, Neihardt/WHMC.

17. Neihardt, "The Poet's Town," *Stranger*, 29–37.

18. House to Neihardt, February 26, 1936, Neihardt/WHMC.

19. Neihardt, *Patterns*, 5.

20. Neihardt, "Money," *Stranger*, 63.

21. Neihardt, "Cry of the People," *Stranger*, 67.

22. Markham, *Poetry*, 596.

23. Neihardt to Sinclair, January 10, 1915, Upton Sinclair Letters, Lilly Library, Indiana University, Bloomington; Neihardt to Latham, November 3, 1942, Macmillan.

24. Neihardt, "Prefatory Note," *Lyric*, vi.

25. Neihardt, "The Ghostly Brother," *Stranger*, 49–51.

26. House, *Neihardt*, 29–32.

27. *Flaming Rainbow* interviews.

28. Andrew Sinclair, introduction to London's *Martin Eden*, 17.

29. Neihardt, "The Poetry of George Sterling," *Journal*, September 29, 1912, women's section, 7.

30. Sterling to Neihardt, July 21, 1912, George Sterling Papers, Berg Collection of English and American Literature, New York Public Library, Astor, Lenox, and Tilden Foundations, New York (hereafter cited as Sterling/New York).

31. Neihardt, "The Renascence of Poetry in America," *Journal*, September 15, 1912, 7.

32. Neihardt, "The Renascence of Poetry in America," 7.

33. Neihardt, "The Renascence of Poetry in America," 7.

34. Cahill, *Monroe*, 13–14.

35. Malcolm Bradbury, "American Risorgimento: The United States and the Coming of the New Arts," in Cunliffe, *Penguin History of Literature*, 11.

36. Myrtle Young, interview with John G. Neihardt, February 1972.

37. Neihardt to Monroe, August 10, 1912, Harriet Monroe Papers, Special Collections Research Center, University of Chicago (hereafter cited as Monroe).

38. Monroe to Neihardt, August 15, 1912, Monroe.

39. Harriet Monroe, "Modern American Poetry," *Poetry Review*, October 1912, 472.

40. Neihardt to Monroe, September 4, 1912, Monroe.

41. Monroe to Neihardt, September 14, 1912, Monroe.

42. Monroe to Neihardt, September 23, 1912, Monroe.

43. Monroe to Neihardt, September 23, 1912, Monroe.

44. Neihardt to Monroe, October 3, 1912, Monroe.

45. Neihardt to Monroe, October 17, 1912, Monroe.

46. Neihardt, "What Is Minor Poetry?" *Journal*, November 17, 1912, woman's section, 5.

47. Morris, *Sigurd the Volsung*.

48. Sterling to Neihardt, January 10, 1913, Sterling/New York.

49. Sterling to Neihardt, January 28, 1913, Sterling/New York.

50. Neihardt to Monroe, January 11, 1913, Monroe.

51. Neihardt, "The Inevitability of Form in Art," *Journal*, February 23, 1913, woman's section, 5.

52. Neihardt, "Inevitability of Form," *Journal*, 5.

53. Neihardt, "Gossamer-Spinning," *Journal*, February 16, 1913, woman's section, 5.

54. Monroe to Neihardt, June 24, 1913, Monroe.

55. Monroe to Neihardt, June 24, 1913, Monroe.
56. Sterling to Neihardt, July 30, 1913, Sterling/New York.
57. Neihardt to Monroe, June 18, 1913, Monroe.
58. Monroe to Neihardt, June 24, 1913, Monroe.
59. Neihardt, "A New Demand for New Poetry," *Journal*, April 13, 1913, section 2, 4.
60. Neihardt to Ledoux, August 22, 1913, Neihardt/NSHS.
61. Monroe to Pound, March 13, 1913, quoted in Williams, *Harriet Monroe*, 55.
62. Monroe to Pound, March 13, 1913, quoted in Williams, *Harriet Monroe*, 55.
63. Neihardt to Seymour, September 11, 1922, John G. Neihardt Papers, Special Collections and Archives, Knox College, Galesburg IL.

8. AN UNTOUCHED EPIC

1. Lee, "John G. Neihardt," 15.
2. Myrtle Young, interview with John G. Neihardt, February 1972.
3. Neihardt to Ledoux, August 22, 1913, Neihardt/NSHS.
4. Sterling to Neihardt, September 7, 1913, Sterling/New York.
5. Myrtle Young, interview with John G. Neihardt, February 1972.
6. Neihardt to Sterling, December 6, 1913, George Sterling Papers, Huntington Library, San Marino CA (hereafter cited as Sterling/Huntington).
7. Neihardt to Sterling, February 24, 1914, Sterling/Huntington.
8. Neihardt to Sterling, January 10, 1915, Sterling/Huntington.
9. Neihardt to Ledoux, August 22, 1913, Neihardt/NSHS.
10. Neihardt to Elmer E. Holm, November 22, 1938, Neihardt/NSHS.
11. Neihardt to Sterling, February 24, 1914, Sterling/Huntington.
12. Neihardt to Aly, October 16, 1957, Neihardt/Bancroft.
13. Sterling to Neihardt, April 22, 1914, Sterling/New York.
14. Neihardt to Sterling, April 29, 1914, Sterling/Huntington.
15. Neihardt to Sterling, November 25, 1914, Sterling/Huntington.
16. Neihardt, "The Red Roan Mare," *Indian Tales*, 179.
17. Neihardt, "The Red Roan Mare," *Indian Tales*, 184.
18. Charles J. Finger, "Twilight Magic," *New York Herald Tribune*, Books Section, June 5, 1927.
19. William Rose Benét, "A Homer of the West," *Saturday Review of Literature*, August 13, 1927, 39.
20. Neihardt, "The Farmer's Thanksgiving," *Quest*, 165.
21. Neihardt, "Katharsis," *Quest*, 163.
22. *Flaming Rainbow* interviews.

23. Neihardt to Ledoux, January 28, 1915, Neihardt/NSHS.
24. Neihardt to Lulu and Donald McDonald, July 19, 1915, Neihardt/Bancroft.
25. Neihardt, "To Sigurd, Scarcely Three," *Song of Hugh Glass*, v.
26. Neihardt, "Introduction," *Song of Hugh Glass*, xii.
27. Neihardt, "Note," *Song of Hugh Glass*, vii.
28. Neihardt, "Introduction," *Song of Hugh Glass*, xviii.
29. Neihardt, "Tagore Again," *Journal*, December 23, 1913, 13.
30. *Flaming Rainbow* interviews.
31. Neihardt, *Song of Hugh Glass*, 1–2.
32. Neihardt to Robinson, March 30, 1914, Robinson.
33. Roger L. Sergel, "The Song of Hugh Glass," *Midland: A Magazine of the Middle West*, January 1916, 25.
34. Jim Tully, "The Epic Poet of the Pioneer West," *Literary Digest International Book Review*, October 1924, 784.
35. "A Year's Harvest in American Poetry," *New York Times Book Review*, November 28, 1915, 464–465.
36. Harriet Monroe, review of *Song of Hugh Glass*, *Poetry: A Magazine of Verse* 7 (1916): 266.
37. M.A., "The Heroic Couplet," *New Republic*, April 12, 1919, 356, 359.
38. Sterling to Neihardt, December 22, 1915, Sterling/New York.
39. Robinson to Neihardt, December 4, 1915, Robinson.
40. Neihardt to McDonald, November 1, 1916, Neihardt/Bancroft.
41. Frank Luther Mott, "John G. Neihardt and His Work," *Midland: A Magazine of the Middle West*, November 1922, 324.
42. Neihardt to Ledoux, November 22, 1915, Neihardt/NSHS.
43. Neihardt to Sterling, December 28, 1915, Sterling/Huntington.
44. Myrtle Young, interview with John G. Neihardt, February 1972.
45. Chittenden, *American Fur Trade*, 710–11.
46. Neihardt to Sterling, July 17, 1916, Sterling/Huntington.
47. Neihardt to Ledoux, February 17, 1916, Neihardt/NSHS.
48. Neihardt to McDonalds, November 1, 1916, Neihardt/Bancroft.
49. Neihardt to Ledoux, December 8, 1916, Neihardt/NSHS.
50. "'Fired' by News, Now He's Famous," *Omaha Daily News*, January 27, 1917, 1.
51. "Vigorous Originality," *Omaha World-Herald*, January 24, 1917, 4.
52. "There Is a Great Demand at the Library for the Poems of John G. Neihardt," *Omaha Daily News*, January 28, 1917, 1.
53. Neihardt to Mott, June 6, 1917, Frank Luther Mott Papers, Western Historical Manuscripts Collection, State Historical Society of Missouri, Columbia.

54. Neihardt, "A Spiritual Niece of Keats," *Journal*, March 14, 1916, 15; Masters quote from Neihardt, "The Year's Poetry," *Journal*, February 1, 1916, 19.
55. Untermeyer, preface to *Modern Poetry*, 39.
56. Morris, *Young Idea*.
57. Harriet Monroe, in Morris, *Young Idea*, 59–60.
58. John G. Neihardt, in Morris, *Young Idea*, 189–91.
59. Morris, *Young Idea*, 206–8.
60. "The Young Idea," *New York Times Book Review*, May 20, 1917, 198.
61. Neihardt to George Brett, May 9, 1913, Macmillan.
62. "The New Movement in American Poetry," *New York Times Review of Books*, January 7, 1917, 1.
63. "Stops of Various Quills," *Dial*, February 22, 1917, 139.
64. O.W. Firkins, "A Tryst With the Poets," *Nation*, June 14, 1917, 709.
65. Harriet Monroe, "Other Books of Verse," *Poetry: A Magazine of Verse* 9 (1917): 325.
66. Neihardt to Sterling, March 13, 1917, Sterling/Huntington.
67. Sterling to Neihardt, April 6, 1917, Sterling/New York.
68. Neihardt to Sterling, June 18, 1917, Sterling/Huntington.

9. A MOVE AND A TRIBUTE
1. Neihardt to Mona Neihardt, March 4, 1918, Neihardt/WHMC.
2. Neihardt to Mona Neihardt, February 23, 1918, Neihardt/WHMC.
3. Neihardt to Alice M. Neihardt, March 8, 1918, Neihardt/WHMC.
4. Neihardt to Mona Neihardt, March 2, 1918, Neihardt/WHMC.
5. Neihardt, *Song of Three Friends*, 78.
6. Neihardt to Robinson, January 26, 1916, Robinson.
7. Neihardt, *Song of Three Friends*, 96.
8. William Stanley Braithwaite, "The Song of Three Friends: A Poet of the Pioneer Days of the West," *Boston Evening Transcript*, March 12, 1919, Part 2, 6.
9. M.A., "The Heroic Couplet," *New Republic*, April 12, 1919, 356, 359.
10. "Recent Books of Poetry," *Nation*, June 7, 1919, 918.
11. Towne to Neihardt, June 12, 1919, Neihardt/WHMC.
12. "An American Saga," *New York Times Book Review*, August 10, 1919, 410.
13. Harriet Monroe, "A Laurelled Poem," *Poetry: A Magazine of Verse* 17 (1920): 94.
14. Sterling to Neihardt, April 9, 1919, Sterling/New York.
15. Neihardt to Sterling, April 14, 1919, Sterling/Huntington.
16. Boodin to Neihardt, December 14, 1919, Neihardt/WHMC.
17. Neihardt to Sterling, December 17, 1918, Sterling/Huntington.

18. Neihardt, *Splendid Wayfaring*, 2.
19. Neihardt to Robinson, April 4, 1914, Robinson.
20. Robinson, *South Dakota*.
21. Smith to Robinson, November 11, 1909, Robinson.
22. Glass to father of John Gardner, June 1823, South Dakota State Historical Society. Though the letter is signed "Yr Obt Svt, Hugh Glass," it is likely that Glass dictated the letter to someone else, for by all accounts he was illiterate.
23. Neihardt, *Splendid Wayfaring*, 8.
24. Robinson to Taft, December 28, 1923, Robinson.
25. Robinson to Taft, Jan. 26, 1924, Robinson.
26. Myrtle Young, interview with John G. Neihardt, February 1972.
27. Neihardt to Putnam, August 1935, Neihardt/WHMC.
28. Hazard, *Frontier in American Literature*, 127–28.
29. Neihardt to McDonald, August 1920, Neihardt/Bancroft.
30. Neihardt to Sterling, January 17, 1920, Sterling/Huntington.
31. Neihardt to Ledoux, August 6, 1909, Neihardt/NSHS.
32. Neihardt to Robinson, October 9, 1920, Robinson.
33. Neihardt to Sterling, January 23, 1921, Sterling/Huntington.
34. Neihardt to Mildred Piper, December 29, 1920, Neihardt/Bancroft.
35. Neihardt to Piper, November 28, 1920, Neihardt/Bancroft.
36. Neihardt to Sterling, January 23, 1921, Sterling/Huntington.
37. Lucius A. Sherman, quoted in Neihardt, *Laureate Address*, 10.
38. Neihardt, *Laureate Address*, 15.
39. Neihardt, *Laureate Address*, 17.
40. Neihardt, *Laureate Address*, 19–20.
41. Neihardt, *Laureate Address*, 23.
42. Neihardt, *Laureate Address*, 27.
43. Neihardt, *Laureate Address*, 42–45.
44. Sterling to Neihardt, July 17, 1921, Sterling/New York.
45. "Keep Neihardt in Nebraska," editorial, *Omaha Bee*, February 28, 1923, 6.
46. "From a Nebraskan at Carleton," *Omaha Bee*, April 7, 1923, 4.
47. *Flaming Rainbow* interviews.
48. *Flaming Rainbow* interviews.
49. "A New Easter Song," *Omaha Bee*, March 28, 1923, 1.
50. Christ to Neihardt, September 7, 1957, Neihardt/WHMC.
51. Schott to Neihardt, September 13, 1963, Neihardt/WHMC.
52. "States and Colleges Make Rival Claims for Neihardt," *Omaha Bee*, April 1, 1923, 1.

53. Clipping, dated May 1923 and identified only as being from the *Journal*, John G. Neihardt Collection, Archives and Special Collections, University of Nebraska–Lincoln Libraries, Lincoln.

54. Neihardt to Avery, September 23, 1923, Samuel Avery Papers, Archives and Special Collections, University of Nebraska–Lincoln Libraries, Lincoln.

10. A STORY THAT NEEDS NO EMBELLISHMENT

1. Neihardt to Mona Neihardt, March 13, 1918, Neihardt/WHMC.
2. Neihardt to Robinson, October 1, 1918, Robinson.
3. Neihardt to Robinson, November 4, 1918, Robinson.
4. Lemly to Neihardt, February 20, 1920, Neihardt/WHMC.
5. Neihardt to Seymour, December 5, 1923, George Steele Seymour Collection, Special Collections and Archives, Knox College, Galesburg IL.
6. Frederica de Laguna, "Poet to Speak at Ebell," *Los Angeles Times*, December 16, 1923, III-40.
7. Neihardt to Alice M. Neihardt, January 12, 1924, Neihardt/Bancroft.
8. Neihardt to Sterling, September 5, 1924, Sterling/Huntington.
9. H. R. Lemly, "Major H. R. Lemly's Story," in Brininstool, *Crazy Horse*, 57.
10. Neihardt, *Song of the Indian Wars*, 227.
11. Lemly, "Lemly's Story," 59.
12. Neihardt, *Song of the Indian Wars*, 229.
13. Neihardt, *Song of the Indian Wars*, 99–100.
14. "Neihardt Wins Loud Praise From Students," *Omaha World-Herald*, January 17, 1925, npn.
15. E.P.F., review of *Song of the Indian Wars*, *Midland: A Magazine of the Middle West*, September 15, 1925, 309.
16. Arthur Guiterman, "Truly American Poetry," *Outlook*, October 21, 1925, 286.
17. Berenice Van Slyke, "Neihardt's Epic," *Poetry: A Magazine of Verse* 27 (1926): 328.
18. Lemly to Neihardt, January 29, 1925, Neihardt/WHMC.
19. Neihardt to Seymour, February 27, 1925, George Steele Seymour Collection, Special Collections and Archives, Knox College, Galesburg IL.
20. Neihardt, "To Alice, Three Years Old," *Song of the Indian Wars*, 5.
21. Neihardt to Mott, November 13, 1924, Frank Luther Mott Papers, Western Historical Manuscripts Collection, State Historical Society of Missouri, Columbia.
22. Neihardt to Davis, November 18, 1924, Davis.
23. Neihardt to Sterling, November 20, 1924, Sterling/Huntington.
24. Neihardt, *Poetic Values*, 136.

25. Neihardt to House, January 2, 1925, Neihardt/Bancroft.

26. Neihardt to House, November 14, 1925, Neihardt/Bancroft.

27. Neihardt to House, January 20, 1925, Neihardt/Bancroft.

28. Neihardt, "Lovable Tales," *Post-Dispatch*, July 21, 1927, 21.

29. Jim Tully, "The Epic Poet of the Pioneer West," *Literary Digest International Book Review*, October 1924, 784.

30. P.K., "Has America Found an Epic Voice?" *Christian Science Monitor*, March 31, 1925, 9.

31. Howard Owen Erickson, "Neihardt Burned Own Manuscripts for Years," *Omaha World-Herald*, magazine section, 1, 3.

32. Neihardt to House, August 1925, Neihardt/Bancroft.

33. "Dedicate Neihardt Monument in Wayne," *Omaha World-Herald*, August 20, 1925, npn.

34. Neihardt to House, August 26, 1925, Neihardt/Bancroft.

35. Neihardt to Alice M. Neihardt and Grace Neihardt, undated but likely late 1924 or early 1925, Neihardt/WHMC.

36. Neihardt to Aly, October 7, 1957, Neihardt/Bancroft.

37. Neihardt, *Poetic Values*.

38. Neihardt to House, August 10, 1925, Neihardt/Bancroft.

39. Neihardt, *Black Elk and Flaming Rainbow*, 19.

40. Neihardt to N. Chatterji, September 1957, Neihardt/Bancroft.

41. Neihardt to Aly, February 16, 1958, Neihardt/Bancroft.

42. Neihardt, "Note," *Poetic Values*, v.

43. Neihardt, *Poetic Values*, 8.

44. Neihardt, *Poetic Values*, 143.

45. "Poetry Reduced to Principles," *New York Times Book Review*, January 31, 1926, 6.

46. Edmund Wilson, review of *Poetic Values*, *New Republic*, November 17, 1926, 384.

47. "Briefer Mention," *Dial* 81 (1926): 83.

48. William Rose Benét, "Poets in Collected Editions," *Yale Review* 17 (1927): 371.

49. Neihardt, "The Mood of the Moment," Neihardt/WHMC.

50. Neihardt to Alice M. Neihardt, 1926, Neihardt/WHMC.

51. "Omahan Tells How Poet Implanted Desire in Him for Reading Good Books," *Omaha World-Herald*, magazine section, 3.

52. Neihardt, "A Nosegay of Posies," *Journal*, December 1, 1912, woman's section, 5; "Four Hundred Pages of It," *Journal*, January 18, 1921, 13.

53. Neihardt, "The Child's Reading," *Journal*, December 9, 1913, 15; "Emerson, the Poet," *Journal*, February 14, 1915, city section, 2; "Another Jack London Book," *Journal*, March 9, 1913, woman's section, 5.

54. Neihardt, "Three Representative Poets," *Journal*, March 17, 1914, 15; "Edwin Arlington Robinson," *Journal*, November 3, 1912, woman's section, 5.; "The Splendor of the Passing Thing," *Journal*, January 12, 1913, woman's section, 5; "Sara Teasdale," *Journal*, January 19, 1913, woman's section, 5; "The New Poets," *Journal*, November 30, 1915, 17.

55. Neihardt, "The Renascence of Poetry in America," *Journal*, September 15, 1912, 7.

56. Neihardt, "Isn't Something Wrong?" *Journal*, March 16, 1913, woman's section, 5.

57. Neihardt, "Romance of Ancient Athens," *Journal*, February 23, 1913, woman's section, 5.

58. Neihardt, *Poetic Values*, 7.

59. Neihardt, "Vandals in the Temple," *Journal*, October 28, 1913, 16.

60. Neihardt, "The Making of Poetry," *Journal*, October 20, 1912, woman's section, 7.

61. Neihardt, "Poetry and the Public," *Journal*, September 29, 1912, section 2, 4.

62. Neihardt, "Vandals in the Temple," *Journal*, October 28, 1913, 16.

63. Neihardt, "Past and Future of the Family," *Journal*, October 27, 1912, woman's section, 5.

64. Neihardt, "The Political Essays of John Jay Chapman," *Journal*, September 15, 1912, woman's section, 7.

65. Neihardt, "A Book of Bosh," *Journal*, June 22, 1913, section 2, 4.

66. Neihardt, "The Uses of Poetry," *Journal*, November 16, 1913, section 2, 4.

67. Neihardt, "The Renascence of Poetry in America," *Journal*, September 15, 1912, 7.

68. Neihardt, "The Uses of Poetry," *Journal*, November 16, 1913, section 2, 4.

69. Neihardt, "Poetry and the Public," *Journal*, September 29, 1912, section 2, 4.

70. Neihardt, "Signs of the Poetic Renascence," *Journal*, November 25, 1913, 9.

71. "John Neihardt to Write Book Surveys for Journal-Post," *Journal-Post*, February 28, 1926, 5-D.

72. Neihardt, "The New Reading Public," *Journal-Post*, March 7, 1926, 7-D.

73. Neihardt, "Is the Truth Bitter?" *Journal-Post*, March 21, 1926, 6-D.

II. AN OFFER DECLINED AND ANOTHER MOVE

1. Macy, *American Literature*, 5.

2. Neihardt, "Philistine Criticism," *Journal*, March 2, 1913, woman's section, 5.

3. Neihardt, "Best Men Have Thought," *Journal-Post*, April 4, 1926, 6-D.

4. Macy to Neihardt, May 11, 1926, Neihardt/WHMC.
5. Latham to Neihardt, May 19, 1926, Neihardt/WHMC.
6. Neihardt, "The New Reading Public," *Journal-Post*, March 7, 1926, 7-D.
7. Neihardt, "Education and Literature," *Journal-Post*, May 2, 1926, 6-D.
8. Neihardt, "Half Century Ago Custer and His Command Were Slain at Battle of Little Big Horn," *Journal-Post*, June 20, 1926, 4-D.
9. Neihardt, "Half Century Ago."
10. Neihardt, "These Modern Goings On," *Journal-Post*, June 6, 1926, 4-D.
11. Thomas Hinkle, "A Word of Praise," *Kansas City Journal-Post*, May 2, 1926, 6-D.
12. Neihardt to House, July 31, 1926, Neihardt/Bancroft; Sherman to Neihardt, June 19, 1926, Neihardt/WHMC.
13. Neihardt to House, November 16, 1926, Neihardt/Bancroft.
14. Sterling to Neihardt, May 18, 1926, Sterling/New York.
15. Neihardt to House, November 22, 1926, Neihardt/Bancroft.
16. Neihardt, "The Passing of a Great Poet," *Post-Dispatch*, November 27, 1926, 13.
17. Neihardt, "The Renascence of Poetry in America," *Journal*, September 15, 1912, 7.
18. Neihardt, "The Lyric Deed," *Post-Dispatch*, June 19, 1927, 2B.
19. Neihardt to House, June 21, 1927, Neihardt/Bancroft.
20. Neihardt to House, May 27, 1927, Neihardt/Bancroft.
21. "'Understanding America' Goal for Unique Travel Group," *Christian Science Monitor*, February 15, 1928, 3.
22. Neihardt to House, March 8, 1928, Neihardt/Bancroft.
23. Neihardt to House, May 8, 1928, Neihardt/Bancroft.
24. Neihardt to House, September 21, 1928, Neihardt/Bancroft.
25. Neihardt to Alice Neihardt, November 13, 1928, Neihardt/WHMC.
26. Neihardt to Alice Neihardt, December 28, 1928, Neihardt/WHMC.
27. Neihardt to Alice Neihardt, December 28, 1928, Neihardt/WHMC.
28. Neihardt to House, January 16, 1929, Neihardt/Bancroft.
29. Neihardt, *Song of Hugh Glass*, 24.
30. Neihardt to House, February 5, 1929, Neihardt/Bancroft.
31. Neihardt to House, February 15, 1929, Neihardt/Bancroft.
32. Neihardt to House, February 15, 1929, Neihardt/Bancroft.
33. Neihardt to House, April 10, 1929, Neihardt/Bancroft.
34. Neihardt to House, April, 1929, Neihardt/Bancroft.
35. Neihardt to Brett, April 13, 1929, Macmillan.
36. Macmillan to Neihardt, April 15, 1929, Macmillan.
37. "Another Poet in Congress," *New York Times*, December 20, 1929, 28.

38. Neihardt to House, March 20, 1920, Neihardt/Bancroft.
39. Neihardt to House, October 2, 1929, Neihardt/Bancroft.

12. A PILGRIMAGE TO PINE RIDGE

1. Mooney, *Ghost-Dance*, 771–72.
2. Mooney, *Ghost-Dance*, 654.
3. Mooney, *Ghost-Dance*, 869.
4. Neihardt to House, February 14, 1925, Neihardt/Bancroft.
5. Neihardt to House, October 12, 1925, Neihardt/Bancroft.
6. Neihardt to House, November 18, 1925, Neihardt/Bancroft.
7. Neihardt to House, January 31, 1926, Neihardt/Bancroft.
8. Neihardt to House, October 2, 1929, Neihardt/Bancroft.
9. "500 Lines in Five Years," *Omaha World-Herald*, July 16, 1930, npn.
10. Neihardt, "Light on Our Generation," *Post-Dispatch*, January 4, 1927, 15.
11. Neihardt, "Napoleon at St. Helena," *Post-Dispatch*, September 10, 1927, 5.
12. Neihardt to House, June 20, 1930, Neihardt/Bancroft.
13. Neihardt to House, June 20, 1920, Neihardt/Bancroft.
14. Neihardt, preface, *Black Elk Speaks*, vii.
15. Neihardt, preface, *Black Elk Speaks*, viii.
16. "Discovering and Preserving the 'Great Vision' of an Indian Seer and Poet," *St. Louis Post-Dispatch Sunday Magazine*, March 6, 1932, 4.
17. Neihardt, preface, *Black Elk Speaks*, viii.
18. Neihardt to House, October 27, 1930, Neihardt/Bancroft.
19. Neihardt to Nicholas Black Elk, November 6, 1930, Neihardt/NSHS.
20. Neihardt to House, November 27, 1930, Neihardt/Bancroft.
21. Neihardt to House, January 5, 1931, Neihardt/Bancroft.
22. Neihardt to House, November 27, 1930, Neihardt/Bancroft.
23. Neihardt to House, December 17, 1930; January 10, 1931.
24. Neihardt to House, February 7, 1931, Neihardt/Bancroft.
25. Neihardt to House, March 3, 1931, Neihardt/Bancroft.
26. Neihardt to House, July 27, 1931, Neihardt/Bancroft.
27. Neihardt to House, February 9, 1931, Neihardt/Bancroft.
28. Neihardt to House, November 6, 1930, Neihardt/Bancroft.
29. Neihardt to House, March 3, 1931, Neihardt/Bancroft.
30. Neihardt to House, uncertain date, likely early 1931, Neihardt/Bancroft.
31. Wilbur to Neihardt, May 1, 1931, Neihardt/WHMC.
32. McDowell to Courtright, May 8, 1931, Neihardt/WHMC.
33. Enid Neihardt, "My Diary," Neihardt/WHMC.

34. Neihardt, *Black Elk and Flaming Rainbow*, 31.
35. Enid Neihardt, "My Diary," Neihardt/WHMC.
36. Dorothy Cook, "J. G. Neihardt Made a Member of the Sioux Tribe," *Sunday State Journal* (Lincoln NE), June 7, 1931, C-2.
37. Neihardt to House, April 30, 1931, Neihardt/Bancroft.
38. Neihardt, *Black Elk and Flaming Rainbow*, 38.
39. Neihardt, *Black Elk and Flaming Rainbow*, 37.
40. Neihardt and Utecht, *Black Elk Lives*, 132.
41. Enid Neihardt's typewritten transcript of her stenographic notes is the source for all that was said during the Neihardt–Black Elk interviews, unless otherwise noted, Neihardt/WHMC.
42. Cook, "J. G. Neihardt Made a Member of the Sioux Tribe."
43. Neihardt to House, June 3, 1931, Neihardt/Bancroft.
44. Neihardt to House, June 3, 1931, Neihardt/Bancroft.
45. Neihardt to Cullers, June 21, 1931, Neihardt/WHMC.

13. A WISE AND GOOD BOOK

1. Mead, *Indian Tribe.*
2. Linderman, *Plenty-coups* and *Pretty-shield.*
3. Sandoz, *Crazy Horse.*
4. Neihardt to Wilbur, June 1931, Neihardt/Bancroft.
5. Neihardt, "Merejkowski's Thesis," *Post-Dispatch*, July 3, 1931, 7A.
6. Neihardt to House, June 3, 1931, Neihardt/Bancroft.
7. Neihardt to Nicholas Black Elk, approximately June 8, 1931, Neihardt/Bancroft.
8. Neihardt to Nicholas Black Elk, June 27, 1931, Neihardt/Bancroft.
9. Neihardt to L. V. Jacks, August 8, 1931, Neihardt/WHMC.
10. DeMallie, in his book *The Sixth Grandfather*, and years later in his annotated edition of *Black Elk Speaks*, makes clear where Neihardt followed the notes and where he added or deleted information. It was his conclusion, as he states in the introduction to *Sixth Grandfather*, that Neihardt completed the task as "an extraordinarily faithful spokesman for Black Elk."
11. Neihardt to Morrow, June 21, 1931, Neihardt/WHMC.
12. Neihardt to House, March 26, 1932, Neihardt/Bancroft.
13. Neihardt, *Black Elk Speaks*, 21.
14. Neihardt, *Black Elk Speaks*, 276.
15. Grant, "Poetic Development of John G. Neihardt," 178.
16. Neihardt to House, September 25, 1931, Neihardt/Bancroft.
17. Neihardt to House, January 14, 1932, Neihardt/Bancroft.

18. Neihardt to House, October 31, 1931, Neihardt/Bancroft.

19. Neihardt to House, January 14, 1932, Neihardt/Bancroft.

20. Walter R. Brooks, "The New Books," *Outlook*, March 1932, 194.

21. "Indians' Last Struggle Told by Tribal Chief," *Chicago Tribune*, February 18, 1932, 13.

22. John Chamberlain, "A Sioux Indian Tells a Tragic Story," *New York Times Book Review*, March 6, 1932, 4.

23. Phillip H. Jewett, "Black Elk, Sioux of Three Score Ten, Speaks of His Life," *Philadelphia Inquirer*, March 12, 1932, npn.

24. Charles Clayton, "*Black Elk Speaks*, a Vivid Indian Saga by John G. Neihardt," *St. Louis Globe Democrat*, April 2, 1932, npn.

25. "Black Elk Tells His Story," *Los Angeles Times*, April 17, 1932, npn.

26. Marquis Childs, "Morituri," *New Republic*, June 22, 1932, 161.

27. Neihardt to House, March 12, 1932, Neihardt/Bancroft.

28. Deloria to Neihardt, March 18, 1932, Neihardt/WHMC.

29. Deloria to Neihardt, May 11, 1932, Neihardt/WHMC.

30. Brooks Atkinson, "Crusader's Paradise in 'Rendezvous' With Which Arthur Hopkins Opens His Season," *New York Times*, October 13, 1932, 22.

31. Neihardt to House, January 16, 1932, Neihardt/Bancroft.

32. Neihardt to House, September 11, 1932, Neihardt/Bancroft.

33. Neihardt to House, September 11, 1932, Neihardt/Bancroft.

34. Neihardt to Conn, February 10, 1932, Neihardt/Bancroft.

35. Neihardt to Conn, February 10, 1932, Neihardt/Bancroft.

36. "Classical Program—Dr. Neihardt and Son Delight Students and Faculty With Music and Poetry," *Mount*, November 1939, 329.

37. Neihardt to House, December 17, 1932, Neihardt/Bancroft.

38. Neihardt to House, August 15, 1934, Neihardt/Bancroft.

39. Neihardt to House, October 2, 1929, Neihardt/Bancroft.

40. Neihardt to House, September 11, 1932, Neihardt/Bancroft.

41. George Currie, "Passed in Review," *Brooklyn Daily Eagle*, April 2, 1935, 20.

42. Neihardt, *Song of the Messiah*, 1.

43. Neihardt, *Messiah*, 4.

44. Neihardt, *Messiah*, 6.

45. Neihardt, *Messiah*, 10.

46. Neihardt, *Messiah*, 11.

47. Neihardt, *Messiah*, 14.

48. Neihardt, *Messiah*, 51.

49. Neihardt, *Messiah*, 52–55.

50. Neihardt, *Messiah*, 108–9.
51. John Holmes, "An Epic in American Poetry," *Boston Evening Transcript*, January 4, 1936, 4.
52. Marquis W. Childs, "Books in Brief," *New Republic*, February 12, 1936, 27.
53. Robinson to Neihardt, March 3, 1938, Neihardt/WHMC.

14. A TIME OF CRISIS

1. House, *John G. Neihardt*, 132.
2. Neihardt to Roger Toll, August 27, 1935, Neihardt/WHMC.
3. Neihardt, "Is Evolution the Enemy of Religion?" *Journal-Post*, May 9, 1926, 4-D.
4. Neihardt to Smith, June 12, 1964, Stanley C. Smith Papers, Western Historical Manuscripts Collection, State Historical Society of Missouri, Columbia (hereafter cited as Smith/WHMC).
5. Neihardt to Long, August 13, 1935, Neihardt/WHMC.
6. Haley, *Jeff Milton*.
7. Latham to Neihardt, August 7, 1935, Neihardt/WHMC.
8. Neihardt to Long, August 13, 1935, Neihardt/WHMC.
9. Neihardt to Charles Kelly, October 7, 1935, Neihardt/WHMC.
10. Neihardt to Long, August 13, 1935, Neihardt/WHMC.
11. Latham to Neihardt, December 18, 1935, Neihardt/WHMC.
12. Neihardt to Sterling, February 1, 1918, Sterling/Huntington.
13. Neihardt to Mona Neihardt, November 28, 1921, Neihardt/WHMC.
14. Neihardt, "An Excellent Biography," *Post-Dispatch*, April 25, 1928, 21.
15. Myrtle Young, interview with John G. Neihardt, February 1972.
16. Latham to Neihardt, August 7, 1935, Neihardt/WHMC.
17. Neihardt to Duncan Vinsonhaler, September 4, 1937, Neihardt/WHMC.
18. Neihardt to Mona Neihardt, March 1939, Neihardt/WHMC.
19. Neihardt to Fink, September 25, 1940, Neihardt/Bancroft.
20. Neihardt, *Song of Jed Smith*, 2.
21. Ncihardt, *Jed Smith*, 9.
22. Neihardt, *Jed Smith*, 10.
23. Neihardt, *Jed Smith*, 10.
24. Neihardt, *Jed Smith*, 11, 77.
25. Neihardt, *Jed Smith*, 15.
26. Neihardt, *Jed Smith*, 17.
27. Neihardt, *Jed Smith*, 40.
28. Neihardt's encounter with Leona Boyles was first chronicled in Sally McCluskey, "She Saw Jed Smith Die," *Frontier Times*, June–July 1975, 16–18, 46–48.

29. Neihardt, *Jed Smith*, 113.
30. Neihardt, *Beginning*, 39.
31. John Selby, "Poet Is Hammering Out Epic at Rate of 3 Lines Per Day," *Omaha World-Herald*, October 2, 1938, 2-c.
32. Neihardt to Horst Franz, August 6, 1939, Neihardt/WHMC.
33. Harry R. Burke, "A Knight in Buckskin and American Poets," *St. Louis Globe-Democrat*, September 27, 1941, 1B.
34. Alvin R. Rolfs, "Stirring Story of Jed Smith Completes the Neihardt Cycle," *St. Louis Post-Dispatch*, November 6, 1941, 2c.
35. Maurice Swan, "The New Books of Poetry," *New York Times Book Review*, December 28, 1941, 5.
36. Coleman Rosenberger, "Two Midwesterners," *Poetry: A Magazine of Verse* 59 (1941): 165.
37. Dillard to Neihardt, September 15, 1941, Neihardt/WHMC.
38. Latham to Neihardt, September 23, 1941, MacMillan.
39. Neihardt to Mrs. John Berg, April 25, 1941, Neihardt/Bancroft.
40. Neihardt to Latham, December 31, 1941, Macmillan.
41. Latham to Neihardt, January 14, 1942, Macmillan.
42. Neihardt to Latham, September 17, 1842, Macmillan.
43. Latham to Neihardt, December 22, 1942, Macmillan.
44. Latham to Neihardt, April 26, 1943, Macmillan.
45. Latham to Neihardt, January 6, 1944, Macmillan.
46. Neihardt to Latham, January 15, 1945, Macmillan.
47. Neihardt to Mona Neihardt, December, 1939, Neihardt/WHMC.
48. Frank Luther Mott, "John G. Neihardt and His Work," *The Midland: A Magazine of the Middle West*, November 1922, 321.
49. "The Parable of the Sack," *Indian Tales*, 139.
50. Mona Neihardt to Finks, September 8, 1940, Neihardt/Bancroft.
51. Mona Neihardt to Enid Fink, October 15, 1940, Neihardt/Bancroft.
52. Mona Neihardt to Finks, December 1940, Neihardt/Bancroft.
53. Neihardt to Mona Neihardt, November 1940, Neihardt/WHMC.
54. Neihardt to Sheldon, January 11, 1942, Neihardt/Bancroft.
55. Latham to Neihardt, December 22, 1942, Macmillan.
56. Neihardt to Seymour, April 11, 1943, Neihardt/Bancroft.
57. Neihardt to Aly, January 29, 1958, Neihardt/Bancroft.
58. Neihardt to Aly, January 29, 1958, Neihardt/Bancroft.
59. Neihardt to Aly, January 29, 1958, Neihardt/Bancroft.
60. Neihardt to Finks, March 11, 1945, Neihardt/WHMC.

61. Neihardt to Finks, March 11, 1945, Neihardt/WHMC.

62. Neihardt to Aly, November 2, 1957, Neihardt/Bancroft.

63. Nicholas Black Elk to Neihardt, October 11, 1945, Neihardt/WHMC.

64. Neihardt to Latham, January 13, 1946, Macmillan.

65. Neihardt to Latham, April 24, 1947, Macmillan.

66. Latham to Neihardt, August 10, 1945, Macmillan.

67. Neihardt to Latham, September 5, 1945, Macmillan.

68. Latham to Neihardt, September 12, 1945, Macmillan.

69. "Protest Persecution of Neruda, the Americas' Greatest Poet," *Daily Worker*, April 7, 1948, 13.

70. Neihardt to McCluskey, August 31, 1966, Neihardt/NSHS.

71. Neihardt, "Can Writing Be Taught?" *Journal-Post*, July 11, 1926, 4-D.

72. Neihardt to McCluskey, August 31, 1966, Neihardt/NSHS.

73. "Reprints, New Editions," *New York Herald Tribune Book Review*, June 5, 1949, 13.

74. Harvey Breit, "Repeat Performances," *New York Times Book Review*, June 19, 1949, 20.

75. Hillyer to Neihardt, May 2, 1949, Neihardt/WHMC.

76. Collier to Neihardt, December 8, 1950, Neihardt/WHMC.

77. Neihardt to Smith, September 5, 1970, Smith/WHMC.

78. Neihardt to Latham, July 14, 1949, Macmillan.

79. Neihardt to Smith, September 5, 1970, Smith/WHMC.

80. H. Y. Moffett to Thomas Wright, July 13, 1955, Neihardt/WHMC.

81. Mona Neihardt to Finks, June 17, 1949, Neihardt/WHMC.

82. Harrison Moreland to Anderson, email, September 10, 1997, author's collection.

83. Jerry Fogel to Anderson, September 12, 1997, author's collection.

84. Richard Wood to Anderson, September 17, 1997, author's collection.

85. Darla Parkes to Anderson, September 10, 1997, author's collection.

86. Andrew Coffey to Anderson, October 13, 1997, author's collection.

87. Coffey to Anderson, October 13, 1997, author's collection.

88. Neihardt, "The Twilight of the Sioux," English Topics 101, Program 1, recording of his University of Missouri course, 1962.

89. Fogel to Anderson, September 12, 1997, author's collection.

90. Germond, *Fat Man*, 10.

91. Joseph Kaye, "George Scott Recalls M.U. Days as the Start of His Acting Career," *Kansas City Star*, February 10, 1963, 25-A.

92. Susan Stoltz to Anderson, November 10, 1997, author's collection.

93. Neihardt to Latham, December 15, 1949, Macmillan.

94. Neihardt, *When the Tree Flowered*, 1.
95. Neihardt, *When the Tree Flowered*, 245.
96. Neihardt to Latham, January 27, 1951, Macmillan.
97. William S. Edwards, "The Common Touch," *Feature*, April 1952, 16–17.
98. Neihardt, *When the Tree Flowered*, 42.
99. Neihardt, *When the Tree Flowered*, 248.
100. John Nerber, "A Tale Told by Eagle Voice," *New York Times Book Review*, October 7, 1951, 38.
101. William Lemons, review of *When the Tree Flowered*, *North Dakota History*, April 1952, 151.
102. Whittaker to Neihardt, November 7, 1952, Neihardt/WHMC.
103. Neihardt to Upton Sinclair, February 5, 1957, Neihardt/Bancroft.
104. Gracie Taylor to Neihardt, July 14, 1955, Neihardt/WHMC.
105. Parkes to Anderson, September 10, 1997, author's collection.

15. THE LOSS OF A COMRADE

1. Interview by author with Hilda Neihardt, March 20, 2000, Phoenix, Arizona.
2. Mona Neihardt to Holm, October 1838, Neihardt/NSHS.
3. Interview with Hilda Neihardt, March 20, 2000, Phoenix, Arizona.
4. Neihardt to Aly, May 3, 1958, Neihardt/Bancroft.
5. Neihardt to Aly, April 30, 1958, Aly.
6. Mona Neihardt to Holm, April 6, 1939, Neihardt/NSHS.
7. Neihardt to Cullers, March 12, 1955, Neihardt/WHMC.
8. Neihardt to Chaffee, February 5, 1958, Neihardt/Bancroft.
9. "Neihardt Will Speak at Alumni Rally at Wayne," *Columbia* (MO) *Daily Tribune*, June 23, 1954, 6.
10. Neihardt to Cullers, March 12, 1955, Neihardt/WHMC.
11. Neihardt to Chaffee, February 5, 1958, Neihardt/Bancroft.
12. "2 Women Injured Slightly in 3-Car Crash Downtown," *Columbia Missourian*, April 3, 1958, 1.
13. Interview with Hilda Neihardt, March 20, 2000, Phoenix, Arizona.
14. Neihardt to Aly, April 23, 1958, Aly.
15. Neihardt to Aly, April 30, 1958, Aly.
16. Neihardt to Aly, August 1, 1959, Aly.
17. Neihardt to Aly, August 1, 1959, Aly.
18. Max Baird, "Benton and Neihardt Meet for First Time in 20 years," *Columbia Daily Tribune*, May 2, 1959, 3.
19. Michener to Neihardt, January 12, 1962, Neihardt/WHMC.

20. Aly, quoted in Stan Smith, "Breezes: Hot 'n Cold," *Wauneta* (NE) *Breeze*, March 23, 1961, 4.

21. Neihardt to Smith, July 1, 1967, Smith/WHMC.

22. Neihardt to Aly, March 28, 1970, Neihardt/Bancroft.

23. Aly, *Neihardt*.

24. Neihardt to Aly, February 13, 1960, Aly.

25. "Mrs. Lucile Aly pays tribute to Poet John G. Neihardt," *Wauneta* (NE) *Breeze*, May 4, 1961, 1.

26. Neihardt, "Sinclair's Latest Conviction," *Post-Dispatch*, June 4, 1929, 25.

27. Neihardt, "Spiritualistic Doctrine," *Post-Dispatch*, December 12, 1927, 17. On Myers see Neihardt, "The Indian's Lost World," *Post-Dispatch*, May 8, 1930, 30; "Intimate View of T. E. Lawrence," *Post-Dispatch*, March 20, 1928, 15.

28. Richards, *SORRAT*.

29. Neihardt to Smith, December 13, 1966, Smith/WHMC.

30. Neihardt to Smith, January 10, 1967, Smith/WHMC.

31. Stanley C. Smith, "Aeschylus Wanders Back: Neihardt Comes Home," unpublished master's thesis, Kearney State College, 29, Smith/WHMC.

32. Stanley C. Smith, "Breezes: Hot 'n Cold," *Wauneta* (NE) *Breeze*, February 16, 1961, 1.

33. Tom Allan, "Neihardt Well Acquainted With Unveiled Bronze Bust," *Omaha World-Herald*, December 8, 1961, 1.

34. Allan, "Neihardt Well Acquainted," 1.

35. Neihardt to Smith, October 17, 1963, Smith/WHMC.

36. "M.U. to Start Telecast Class," *Columbia Missourian*, August 30, 1958, 10.

37. Smith, "Aeschylus Wanders Back: Neihardt Comes Home," unpublished master's thesis, Kearney State College, 50, Smith/WHMC.

38. Ronald G. Bliss, "John G. Neihardt: Like a Prairie Wind," *Omaha World-Herald Magazine of the Midlands*, November 24, 1968, 10–11.

39. Ruth Thone, "Capital Chatter: Poet, Guardian Angels a Tale of Friendship," *Omaha World-Herald*, July 26, 1970, 16 E.

40. Neihardt to Smith, November 9, 1967, Smith/WHMC.

41. Interview by author with Coralie Hughes, May 17, 2012, Coatesville, Indiana.

42. Tom Allan, "Poet Laureate 'Home' to Write Autobiography," *Omaha World-Herald*, March 10, 1968, 2-B.

43. Allan, "Poet Laureate 'Home,'" 2-B.

44. Neihardt to Wright, February 23, 1968, Neihardt/WHMC.

45. Neihardt to Smith, November 20, 1966, Smith/WHMC.

46. Neihardt to Smith, March 23, 1968, Smith/WHMC.

47. Neihardt to J. B. Rhine, February 22, 1969, Neihardt/WHMC.

48. Neihardt to Aly, March 28, 1970, Neihardt/Bancroft.

16. A BOOK AND AN AUTHOR REBORN

1. "Poet Neihardt Explores Sioux Indian Themes," *Lincoln Star*, April 3, 1967, 7.

2. Brown to Neihardt, December 3, 1948, Macmillan.

3. Brown to Neihardt, December 3, 1948, Macmillan.

4. Brown, preface to seventh printing, *Sacred Pipe*, xi.

5. Carol Baumann, "Meeting Black Elk and Attending a Yuwipi Rite," APC (Analytical Psychology Club of New York Bulletin) 2 (1950–51): 35.

6. Neihardt, "Crazy Horse, Who Led the Sioux at Custer's Last Fight," *Times*, December 20, 1942, 4.

7. Stauffer, *Mari Sandoz*, 81.

8. "Paperbound Texts May Aid High School Teaching," *Daily Nebraskan*, July 18, 1961, 3; Knoll, *Prairie University*, 124.

9. Sandoz to Nicoll, February 6, 1960, Sandoz.

10. Sandoz to Nicoll, June 12, 1960, Sandoz.

11. Nicoll to Sandoz, June 21, 1960, Sandoz.

12. Jerry Gallagher, review of *All Is But a Beginning*, *Best Sellers*, November 1, 1972, 357.

13. Clarissa Start, "At 90, a New Flush of Fame," *St. Louis Post-Dispatch*, Everyday Magazine, October 5, 1971, 1D.

14. W.E. Black, "Ethic and Metaphysic: A Study of John G. Neihardt," *Western American Literature* 2, no. 3 (fall 1967): 205–12; Sally McCluskey, "*Black Elk Speaks*: And So Does John Neihardt," *Western American Literature* 6, no. 4 (winter 1972): 231–42.

15. Frank Luther Mott, "Resurgence of Neihardt," *Quarterly Journal of Speech* 48, no. 2 (April 1962): 198–201.

16. Mira M. Vest, "He Walked the Earth Gently," *Lutheran Journal* 46, no. 3 (autumn 1979): 6.

17. Katie Kelly, "Our Legacy for the Future," *Omaha World-Herald Magazine of the Midlands*, January 2, 1977, 3–4.

18. Peg McMahon, "Youth Hears the Old Poet's Songs," *Kansas City Star Magazine*, March 7, 1971, 6.

19. John Leonard, "A Late-Night Talker Who Knows How to Listen," *Life*, February 13, 1970, 10.

20. Dick Cavett, introduction to Neihardt, *Beginning*, xiv.

21. Wayne Kreuscher, "Poet Laureate J. G. Neihardt, 91, May Be Reaching Peak Popularity," *Lincoln Star*, August 19, 1971, 3.

22. Vine Deloria Jr., "Bury Our Hopes at Wounded Knee," *Los Angeles Times*, April 1, 1973, 11.

23. Deloria, *Sender of Words*.

24. Muller to Anderson, March 4, 2002, author's collection.

25. Neihardt, *Beginning*, 9.

26. Neihardt, *Beginning*, 3.

27. Neihardt, *Beginning*, 5.

28. Neihardt, *Beginning*, 31.

29. Neihardt, *Beginning*, 87–88.

30. Neihardt, *Beginning*, 3.

31. Neihardt, *Beginning*, 170.

32. Neihardt, *Beginning*, 170.

33. Neihardt, *Beginning*, 172.

34. Thorpe Menn, "Life in Kansas City Obviously Affected Two Kinds of Writing," *Kansas City Star*, October 1, 1972, 2D.

35. John Wunder, review of *All Is But a Beginning*, *Pacific Northwest Quarterly*, April 1974, 88.

36. Katie Kelly, "Our Legacy for the Future," *Omaha World-Herald Magazine of the Midlands*, January 2, 1977, 3–4.

37. Gene Blackledge, copy of his original manuscript of an article he wrote in 1978, author's collection.

38. Blackledge, copy of manuscript.

39. *Flaming Rainbow* album.

40. Florence Boring, unpublished manuscript, November 22, 1973, Neihardt/Bancroft.

41. "Indians, Nebraska Lost Old Friend," *Omaha World-Herald*, December 16, 1979, 6-G.

42. Florence Boring, unpublished manuscript, November 22, 1973, Neihardt/Bancroft.

43. Neihardt, *Black Elk and Flaming Rainbow*, 115.

44. Tom Allan, "Poet Neihardt Has Last Great Venture," *Omaha World-Herald*, November 4, 1973, 1.

EPILOGUE

1. Gerald Stanley Lee, "Singing as the Storm," *Mount Tom*, March 4, 1909, 70.

BIBLIOGRAPHY

ARCHIVES AND MANUSCRIPT MATERIALS

Samuel Avery Papers, Archives and Special Collections, University of Nebraska–Lincoln Libraries, Lincoln NE.

Robert H. Davis Papers, Manuscripts and Archives Division, New York Public Library, Astor, Lenox, and Tilden Foundations, New York.

Macmillan Company Papers, Manuscript and Archives Division, New York Public Library, Astor, Lenox, and Tilden Foundations, New York.

Harriet Monroe Papers, Special Collections Research Center, University of Chicago, Chicago.

Frank Luther Mott Papers, Western Historical Manuscripts Collection, State Historical Society of Missouri, Columbia MO.

John G. Neihardt Papers, John G. Neihardt Center, Bancroft NE.

John G. Neihardt Papers, Special Collections and Archives, Knox College, Galesburg IL.

John G. Neihardt Papers, Nebraska State Historical Society, Lincoln NE.

John G. Neihardt Collection, Archives and Special Collections, University of Nebraska–Lincoln Libraries, Lincoln NE.

John G. Neihardt Papers, Western Historical Manuscripts Collection, State Historical Society of Missouri, Columbia MO.

Doane Robinson Papers, South Dakota State Historical Society, Pierre SD.

Mari Sandoz Collection, Archives and Special Collections, University of Nebraska Lincoln Libraries, Lincoln NE.

George Steele Seymour Collection, Special Collections and Archives, Knox College, Galesburg IL.

Upton Sinclair Letters, Lilly Library, Indiana University, Bloomington IN.

Stanley C. Smith Papers, Western Historical Manuscripts Collection, State Historical Society of Missouri, Columbia MO.

George Sterling Papers, Huntington Library, San Marino CA.

George Sterling Papers, Berg Collection of English and American Literature, New York Public Library, Astor, Lenox, and Tilden Foundations, New York.

George Edward Woodberry Papers, Houghton Library, Harvard University, Cambridge MA.

PUBLISHED WORKS

Aly, Lucile F. *John G. Neihardt: A Critical Biography.* Amsterdam: Rodopi, 1977.

Brininstool, E. A., ed. *Crazy Horse: The Invincible Ogalalla Sioux Chief.* Los Angeles: Wetzel, 1949.

Brown, John Epes. *The Sacred Pipe: Black Elk's Account of the Seven Rites of the Oglala Sioux.* Norman: University of Oklahoma Press, 1989.

Cahill, Daniel J. *Harriet Monroe.* New York: Twayne, 1973.

Campbell, Bruce Alexander. *200 Years: An Illustrated Bicentennial History of Sangamon County.* Springfield IL: Phillips Brothers, 1976.

Chittenden, Hiram Martin. *The American Fur Trade of the Far West.* New York: Francis P. Harper, 1902.

Commager, Henry Steele. *The American Mind: An Interpretation of American Thought and Character since the 1880s.* New Haven: Yale University Press, 1950.

Cowan, Geoffrey. *The People v. Clarence Darrow: The Bribery Trial of America's Greatest Lawyer.* New York: Times Books, 1993.

Cunliffe, Marcus, ed. *The Penguin History of Literature: American Literature since 1900.* New York: Penguin, 1993.

Deloria, Vine Jr., ed. *A Sender of Words: Essays in Memory of John G. Neihardt.* Salt Lake City: Howe Brothers, 1984.

DeMallie, Raymond J. *The Sixth Grandfather: Black Elk's Teachings Given to John G. Neihardt.* Lincoln: University of Nebraska Press, 1984.

Dorsey, James Owen. *The Cegiha Language.* Washington DC: Government Printing Office, 1890.

Germond, Jack W. *Fat Man in a Middle Seat: Forty Years of Covering Politics.* New York: Random House, 1999.

Grant, George Paul. "The Poetic Development of John G. Neihardt." PhD diss., University of Pittsburgh, 1958.

Green, Norma Kidd. *Iron Eye's Family: The Children of Joseph La Flesche*. Lincoln NE: Johnsen Publishing, 1969.

Greene, Donald. *Samuel Johnson*. New York: Twayne Publishers, 1970.

Grunfeld, Frederic V. *Rodin: A Biography*. New York: Henry Holt, 1987.

Haley, J. Evetts. *Jeff Milton: A Good Man With a Gun*. Norman: University of Oklahoma Press, 1948.

Haskell, Henry D. Jr., and Richard B. Fowler. *City of the Future: A Narrative History of Kansas City, 1850–1950*. Kansas City: Frank Glenn, 1950.

Hazard, Lucy Lockwood. *The Frontier in American Literature*. Thomas Y. Crowell, 1927.

Heritage Book Committee, ed. *History of Bancroft, Nebraska: 1884–1984*. Dallas: National ShareGraphics, 1984.

Hickey, Donald R. *Nebraska Moments: Glimpses of Nebraska's Past*. Lincoln: University of Nebraska Press, 1992.

House, Julius T. *John G. Neihardt: Man and Poet*. Wayne NE: F. H. Jones, 1920.

Johnson, Samuel. *Rasselas, Poems and Selected Prose*, edited by Bertrand H. Bronson. New York: Holt, Rinehart and Winston, 1966.

Kastens, Dennis Allen. *Neuhart Chronicle*. St. Louis: Concordia Theological Seminary, 1984.

Knoll, Robert E. *Prairie University: A History of the University of Nebraska*. Lincoln: University of Nebraska Press, 1995.

Lee, Fred L. "John G. Neihardt: The Man and His Western Writings, The Bancroft Years, 1900–1921." *Trail Guide* 17, nos. 3–4 (September–December 1973): 1–35.

Lewis, Jon E. *The Mammoth Book of the West: The Making of the American West*. New York: Carroll and Graf, 1996.

Linderman, Frank. *Plenty-coups: Chief of the Crow*. Lincoln: University of Nebraska Press, 1962.

———. *Pretty-shield*. Alexandria VA: Time-Life, 1932.

London, Charmian. *The Book of Jack London*. New York: Century, 1921.

London, Jack. *Martin Eden*. New York: Penguin, 1984.

Macy, John. *The Spirit of American Literature*. New York: Doubleday, Page, 1913.

Markham, Edwin. *The Book of Poetry, Vol. I*. New York: Wm. H. Wise, 1927.

Mead, Margaret. *The Changing Culture of an Indian Tribe*. New York: Capricorn, 1966.

Mooney, James. *The Ghost-Dance Religion and the Sioux Outbreak of 1890*. Lincoln: University of Nebraska Press, 1991.

Morris, Lloyd. *The Young Idea: An Anthology of Opinion Concerning the Spirit and Aims of Contemporary American Literature*. New York: Duffield, 1917.

Morris, William. *The Song of Sigurd the Volsung and the Fall of the Niblungs*. Boston: Roberts Brothers, 1877.

Mott, Frank Luther. *A History of American Magazines*, vol. V: *1905–1930*. Cambridge MA: Harvard University Press, 1968.

Neihardt, Hilda. *Black Elk and Flaming Rainbow: Personal Memories of the Lakota Holy Man and John Neihardt*. Lincoln: University of Nebraska Press, 1995.

Neihardt, Hilda Martinsen. *The Broidered Garment: The Love Story of Mona Martinsen and John G. Neihardt*. Lincoln: University of Nebraska Press, 2006.

Neihardt, Hilda, and Lori Utecht, eds. *Black Elk Lives: Conversations with the Black Elk Family*. Lincoln: University of Nebraska Press, 2000.

Neihardt, John G. *All Is But a Beginning: Youth Remembered, 1881–1901*. New York: Harcourt Brace Jovanovich, 1972.

———. *The Ancient Memory and Other Stories*. Lincoln: University of Nebraska Press, 1991.

———. *Black Elk Speaks: Being the Life Story of a Holy Man of the Ogalala Sioux*. New York: William Morrow, 1932.

———. *A Bundle of Myrrh*. Bancroft NE: Bancroft Blade, 1903.

———. *A Bundle of Myrrh*. New York: Outing Publishing, 1907.

———. *Collected Poems of John G. Neihardt*. New York: Macmillan, 1926.

———. *A Cycle of the West*. New York: Macmillan, 1949.

———. *The Dawn-Builder*. New York: Mitchell Kennerley, 1911.

———. *The Divine Enchantment*. New York: James T. White, 1900.

———. *End of the Dream*. Lincoln: University of Nebraska Press, 1991.

———. *Flaming Rainbow: Reflections and Recollections of an Epic Poet*. Unedited interview recordings in John G. Neihardt Center, Bancroft NE, for three-record boxed set of finished albums produced by William McIntyre and Nik Venet. Los Angeles CA: United Artists Records, 1973.

———. *Indian Tales and Others*. New York: Macmillan, 1926.

———. *Laureate Address of John G. Neihardt*. Chicago: Bookfellows, 1921.

———. *Life's Lure*. New York: Mitchell Kennerley, 1914.

———. *The Lonesome Trail*. New York: John Lane, 1907.

———. *Lyric and Dramatic Poems*. New York: Macmillan, 1926 [*Collected Poems*]; repr. Lincoln: University of Nebraska Press, 1991.

———. *Man-Song*. New York: Mitchell Kennerley, 1909.

———. *Patterns and Coincidences*. Columbia: University of Missouri Press, 1978.

———. *Poetic Values: Their Reality and Our Need of Them*. New York: Macmillan, 1925.

———. *The Quest*. New York: Macmillan, 1922.

———. *The River and I*. New York: G. P. Putnam's Sons, 1910.

———. *The Song of Hugh Glass*. New York: Macmillan, 1915.

———. *The Song of the Indian Wars*. New York: Macmillan, 1925.

———. *The Song of Jed Smith*. New York: Macmillan, 1941.

———. *The Song of the Messiah*. New York: Macmillan, 1935.

———. *The Song of Three Friends*. New York: Macmillan, 1919.

———. *The Splendid Wayfaring*. New York: Macmillan, 1920.

———. *The Stranger at the Gate*. New York: Mitchell Kennerley, 1912.

———. *Two Mothers*. New York: Macmillan, 1921.

———. *When the Tree Flowered: An Authentic Tale of the Old Sioux World*. New York: Macmillan, 1951.

Nyberg, Dorothy Huse. *History of Wayne County, Nebraska: Its Pioneers, Settlement, Growth and Development Together with a View of the Territory in 1938*. Wayne NE: Wayne Herald, 1938.

Olson, James C., and Ronald C. Naugle. *History of Nebraska*. Lincoln: University of Nebraska Press, 1997.

Pattee, Fred Lewis. *The New American Literature, 1890–1930*. New York: Cooper Square, 1968.

Richards, John Thomas. SORRAT: *A History of the Neihardt Psychokinesis Experiments, 1961–1981*. Metuchen NJ: Scarecrow, 1982.

Robinson, Doane. *History of South Dakota*. Indianapolis: B. F. Bowen, 1904.

Sandoz, Mari. *Crazy Horse: The Strange Man of the Oglalas*. New York: Hastings House, 1942.

Starita, Joe. *"I Am a Man": Chief Standing Bear's Journey for Justice*. New York: St. Martin's, 2008.

Stauffer, Helen Winter. *Mari Sandoz: Story Catcher of the Plains*. Lincoln: University of Nebraska Press, 1982.

Taine, Hippolyte Adolphe. *History of English Literature*, translated by H. Van Laun. New York: Henry Holt, 1886.

Tennyson, Alfred, Lord. *Idylls of the King*. London: Penguin, 1996.

Tibbles, Thomas H. *The Ponca Chiefs: An Indian's Attempt to Appeal from the Tomahawk to the Courts*. 1879; Bellevue NE: Old Army, 1970.

Torwesten, Hans. "Introduction." *Vedanta: Heart of Hinduism*. New York: Grove Weidenfeld, 1985.

Untermeyer, Louis. *Modern American and British Poetry*. New York: Harcourt, Brace, 1928.

Williams, Ellen. *Harriet Monroe and the Poetry Renaissance: The First Ten Years of Poetry, 1912–22*. Urbana: University of Illinois Press, 1977.

Young, Myrtle. Interview with John G. Neihardt, cassette recording, February 1972. Kay Young private collection, Lincoln NE.

INDEX

holy shirts, 195
horses, mystical, 176, 177, 209, 232
Hott family, 4
"Hot Wind" (Neihardt), 44
House, Julius T., 95, 230; *John G. Neihardt: Man and Poet*, 129–30, 171, 197
"House of Death" (Neihardt). *See* "A Vision of Woman" (Neihardt)
Hughes, Coralie, 223, 230, 245–46
Human Personality (Myers), 225

I Am a Man (Starita), 259n6
Idylls of the King (Tennyson), 18, 94
"If This Be Sin" (Neihardt), 65
Imagism, 101
Indians: accurate portrayals of, 91, 143, 184; as Christ-like, 167, 171; converting to Christianity, 178, 190; depicted as childlike, 45, 47–48; ethics of, 44; forced relocation of, 54; land lost by, 50; monolithic identity of, 47; reception of Neihardt's work by, 68–69, 190–91; religion of, 91–92, 165–67, 168, 184, 185; sympathy for, 63, 69, 156, 184–85, 190; in U.S. Armed Forces, 209; as vanishing people, 48, 91; white Americans' interest in, 183; and white settlers, 43–44, 47, 174
Indians at Work (BIA publication), 209–10, 232
Indian Tales and Others (Neihardt), 155
Indian wars, 137–40, 144; from Indians' viewpoint, 139, 156, 179–80; language used for, 156; U.S. veterans of, 139, 142–43. *See also* Wounded Knee massacre; *specific battles*
"The Inevitability of Form in Art" (Neihardt), 103–4
Ingersoll, Robert G., 13
Inshtamaza. *See* La Flesche, Joseph

"In the Night" (Neihardt), 93
invention, 10
Iron Eye. *See* La Flesche, Joseph
Iron Fireman Manufacturing Company, 208
Iron Hawk, 173, 179
"It May Be" (Neihardt), 61

Jacobs, Will, 77, 78
Jewett, Rutger, 68
John G. Neihardt: A Critical Biography (Aly), 224–25
John G. Neihardt Center, xi
John G. Neihardt: Man and Poet (House), 129–30, 171, 197
Johns, George Sibley, 157
Jones, W. H., 98, 107
Joseph S. Duncan YMCA, 208–9
Julian, C. C., 85
Jung, Carl, 233

Kansas City Journal-Post, 152–53, 156–57
"Katharsis" (Neihardt), 110, 111
Kelly, Katie, 242–43
"the Kid." *See* Marshall, Chester "Chet"
Kilmer, Joyce, 94
Knife, Andrew, 209, 210, 216

La Flesche, Joseph, 43–44
La Flesche, Susan. *See* Picotte, Susan La Flesche
La Flesche, Susette, 54–55, 228
"The Last Stand of the Sioux" (Robinson), 138
"The Last Thunder Song" (Neihardt), 48
Latham, H. S., 155, 189, 204–5, 210–11
Laut, Agnes C., 71
Leaders, Dreamers, and Rebels (Fülöp-Miller), 194

Neihardt, Mona Martinsen, 72–76, 92, 227; advice of, on writing, 97, 107, 134, 192, 198, 199–200, 220–21; burning correspondence with John, 220; death of, 222; engagement of, 80–81; funeral for, 222–23; and John, as empty-nesters, 206–7; and John, Colorado trip of, 207; and John, morning conversations between, 147; John writing about, 245; marriage of, 81–84, 92, 220–21; pregnancies of, 92, 94, 100, 131; sculpting career of, 73, 74–75, 82, 221; sculpting design for *Man-Song*, 84, 92; sculpting John, 92, 207, 227; *Song of the Messiah* dedicated to, 196; violin payed by, 92, 221

Neihardt, Nicholas, 1–2, 52–53; as confectioner, 5; inability of, to support family, 6, 12; items found in wallet of, 13–14; in John's memoirs, 240; John's relationship with, 10–12, 30–31, 112; military career of, 29, 52–53; moving family to Kansas City, 8–9; pride of, in son, 80; verses by, 13

Neihardt, Robin (John's grandson), 245–46

Neihardt, Sigurd Volsung, 170, 222–23; birth of, 103; death of, 244; and father, performing together, 193, 206; marriage of, 206; as pianist, 193, 206; Pine Ridge visited by, 167; reading parents' correspondence, 220; *The Song of Hugh Glass* dedicated to, 111–12

Neihardt family: ancestors of, 3–6; homestead of, 207; spelling of name of, 254n3Pro

Neihart, John, 4

Neruda, Pablo, 211

Neuhart, Conrad, 3–4

Neuhart, Conrad, Jr., 3–4

Neuhart, Eva, 3

"The New Day and the Good Road" (speech), 210

"new poetry," 118–21

"The New Reading Public" (Neihardt), 153

New York travels, 66–68

Nicoll, Bruce, 234–35

"The Night Express" (Cather), 259n6

Nivens family, 7–8

Norris, George, 164, 227

novels, 86–88, 215–16

Nu Zhinga (Little Man), 61–62

"Of Making Many Books" (Neihardt's column), 193

The Old Man Remembers (Neihardt), 230. See also *All Is But a Beginning* (Neihardt)

Omaha, 43–44; Neihardt's stories about, 44–52, 61–62

Omaha Bee, 133–35

Omaha Daily News, 37–38

Order of Bookfellows, 130

Order of the Indian Wars, 144

"Outward" (Neihardt), 84–85

Overland Monthly, 44–45, 53

"The Parable of the Sack" (Neihardt), 72

paranormal phenomena, 71, 98, 130, 162, 202, 225–26

"The Passing of the Lion" (Neihardt), 86

Pattee, Fred Lewis, 86

Petri, Albert, 206

Picotte, Susan La Flesche, 68–69, 228

Pile, James Madison, 20, 241

Pine Ridge, Neihardt's visits to, 165–82, 209, 210, 232; approval for, 167, 171; and the "Great Feast," 175

Poe, Edgar Allen, 150

South Dakota, trips to, 70, 193
Speyer, Leonora, 162
The Spirit of American Literature
  (Macy), 154
"The Spirit of Crow Butte" (Neihardt),
  47
spiritualism, 98, 221–22, 225
spirituality. *See* religion
The Splendid Wayfaring (Neihardt),
  126–29, 199
Spoon River Anthology (Masters), 117
Spotted Eagle (Big Foot, Sitanka), 166,
  195–96
spring, 59, 164
Squire, 200
Standing Bear (Black Elk's friend), 169–
  70, 179; on Black Elk's illness, 179;
  Hilda's recollections of, 173; illustrat-
  ing book, 170; on white settlers, 174
Standing Bear (Ponca chief), 54–55,
  261n46
Starita, Joe: *I Am a Man*, 259n6
Sterling, George, 99–100, 113–14, 120–21,
  133; critiquing Neihardt, 109; death
  of, 158; dispute of, with Harriet Mon-
  roe, 103; Neihardt reviewing, 150, 158;
  Neihardt visiting, 122; in *The Poet's
  Pack*, 130; praising Neihardt, 125–26
St. Louis Post-Dispatch, 157, 159–60, 161,
  164, 186; lay-offs at, 192, 193, 206;
  "Of Making Many Books" column
  in, 193
The Story of the World's Literature
  (Macy), 154–55
The Stranger at the Gate (Neihardt), 92–
  98; reception of, 93, 94
Straws in the Wind (Neihardt), 161, 171
Streamer, Volney, 65–66; Enid Volnia
  named for, 94

students, Neihardt's relationships with,
  214, 215, 218–19, 226–27

Tae-Nuga-Zhinga (Little Bull Buffalo),
  62, 68
Taft, Lorado, 128
Taine, Hippolyte Adolphe: *History of
  English Literature*, 26
Talbot, Frank, 115–16; as Frank Talbeau,
  72, 116, 124. *See also The Song of the
  Three Friends* (Neihardt)
Teasdale, Sara, 150
technology, 159
"The Temple of the Great-Outdoors"
  (Neihardt), 88
Tennyson, Alfred, Lord, 17, 18, 94; *Idylls
  of the King*, 18, 94
"The Tentiad," 22–23
threshing, 241
Tibbles, Thomas Henry, 53–55, 261n46;
  The Ponca Chiefs, 55
"To a Cat" (Neihardt), 61
"To William McKinley" (Neihardt), 40
Towne, Charles Hanson, 125
traditionalism, 103–5, 109, 113, 117–21,
  132–33, 212
tree metaphor, 181, 186, 188
Truman, Harry, 223
truth and facts, relationship between,
  87–88
Tully, Jim, 86, 113, 145
Tvietmoe, Olaf, 85
Twilight of the Gods (Neihardt), 36
Tyler, George C., 87

University of Missouri, 212, 213–15; Nei-
  hardt's library given to, 225; Thomas
  Jefferson Award, 229
University of Nebraska, 133, 157;

CPSIA information can be obtained at www.ICGtesting.com
Printed in the USA
LVOW11*2100120916

504271LV00006B/54/P

9 780803 290259